The Anti-American Generation

*trans*action/**Society** Book Series

The Anti-American Generation

Edited by

EDGAR Z. FRIEDENBERG

ta

Transaction Books
New Brunswick, New Jersey
Distributed by E. P. Dutton & Co., Inc.

Transaction Books
Rutgers University
New Brunswick, New Jersey 08903

Library of Congress Catalog Card Number: 78-33310
ISBN: 0-87855-069-0 (cloth); 0-87855-566-8 (paper)

Printed in the United States of America.

Contents

PREFACE

For the past decade, *trans*action, and now **Society**, has dedicated itself to the task of reporting the strains and conflicts within the American system. But the magazine has done more than this. It has pioneered in social programs for changing the social order, offered the kind of analysis that has permanently restructured the terms of the "dialogue" between peoples and publics, and offered the sort of prognosis that makes for real alterations in economic and political policies directly affecting our lives.

The work done in the magazine has crossed disciplinary boundaries. This represents much more than simple cross-disciplinary "team efforts." It embodies rather a recognition that the social world cannot be easily carved into neat academic disciplines; that, indeed, the study of the experience of blacks in American ghettos, or the manifold uses and abuses of agencies of law enforcement, or the sorts of overseas policies that lead to the celebration of some dictatorships and the condemnation of others, can best be examined from many viewpoints and from the vantage points of many disciplines.

The editors of **Society** magazine are now making available in permanent form the most important work done in the magazine, supplemented in some cases by additional materials edited to reflect the tone and style developed over the years by *trans*action. Like the magazine, this series of books demonstrates the superiority of starting with real world problems and searching out practical solutions, over the zealous guardianship of professional boundaries. Indeed, it is precisely this approach that has elicited enthusiastic support from leading American social scientists, many of whom are represented among the editors of these volumes.

The subject matter of these books concerns social changes and social policies that have aroused the long-standing needs and present-day anxieties of us all. These changes are in organizational lifestyles, concepts of human ability and intelligence, changing patterns of norms and morals, the relationship of social conditions to physical and biological environments, and in the status of social science with respect to national policy making. The editors feel that many of these articles have withstood the test of time, and match in durable interest the best of available social science literature. This collection of essays, then, attempts to address itself to immediate issues without violating the basic insights derived from the classical literature in the various fields of social science.

As the political crises of the sixties have given way to the economic crunch of the seventies, the social scientists involved as editors and authors of this series have gone beyond observation of critical areas, and have entered into the vital and difficult tasks of explanation and interpretation. They have defined issues in a way that makes solutions possible. They have provided answers as well as asked the right questions. These books, based as they are upon the best materials from *trans*action/**Society** magazine, are dedicated to highlighting social problems alone, and beyond that, to establishing guidelines for social solutions based on the social sciences.

The remarkable success of the book series to date is indicative of the need for such "fastbacks" in college course work and, no less, in the everyday needs of busy people who have not surrendered the need to know, nor the lively sense required to satisfy such knowledge needs. It is also plain that what superficially appeared as a random selection of articles on the basis of subject alone, in fact, represented a careful concern for materials that are addressed to issues at the shank and marrow of society. It is the distillation of the best of these, systematically arranged, that appears in these volumes.

THE EDITORS
*trans*action/**Society**

Introduction

The title assigned this volume by the editors of *trans*-action seems to me misleading, though, as the middle-class middle-aged say, I can live with it. It is hard to be sure just what my age and class mates mean by the phrase "to live with"; but we use it, in any case, to refer only to persons and conditions we don't feel very strongly about. There are a lot of those. Most young people never use it at all.

Though it is indeed true that the United States, with its folkways, mores, and foreign policy constitutes a set that a great many young people do feel strongly—and negatively —about, and that this certainly helps distinguish them from my generation, I don't think the distinction is a matter of being anti-American. The middle-class, middle-aged, are not pro-American. One of the curious distinctions of our time and place is that *no* significant social group seems to be affirmatively pro-American. Who defends the war in Vietnam as public policy, or the satisfactions offered by the media as aspects of a truly good and bounteous life? Even

1

the working class, though conventionally patriotic, intends its flags and diurnal auto-headlights as symbols of resentment and hatred, not of affirmation and well-being. If you want to see an ordinary American leap with joy, it would be best, perhaps, to go wait on the moon. The astronauts seem genuinely joyful in their patriotism, are certainly ordinary; and, anyway, the leaping is easier. Closer to home, it's a lot harder to make it.

What tends to distinguish the generations is not so much their feeling about America as their feeling about feeling and what people should do about their feelings. This is brought out in several of the articles included in this book. In our society, people over 30 are likely to look upon their feelings as a problem rather than a resource or reliable guide. We try to compensate for them, so as to remain unbiased; to control ourselves and our impulses so that they will not lead us into temptation or *liaisons dangereuses*, or even into behavior that, granted other people's expectations of persons in our role, would be embarrassing or disruptive. When this process becomes unbearably depriving we seek therapeutic help in strengthening the rational component of our psyche, which we have learned to think of as compartmentalized, to keep us from doing what we know we aren't supposed to do. If this fails, we seek further help, as needed, to keep us from feeling guilty about having done it, since we know that guilt makes us inefficient and may lead to various somatic disorders, reduced efficiency and possibly lowered life-expectancy, none of which should happen to a rational man. The more sophisticated middle-aged may also seek therapeutic help in becoming able to love, and, in the language of our generation, to relate meaningfully to others, since these are among the most important duties of a responsible member of the middle-class, and closely linked, as we say, to self-esteem.

The young, by contrast, are more likely to look upon

their feelings as a guide to what is good, and certainly to what is good for them, and to view the demands of society and the expectations of others—if these are based on role rather than the way each perceives the other as a person— as the problem; and often as a problem that cannot and should not be approached by rational means, since what is defined as rationality in our society is in itself a supremely alienating form of self-abuse. It would surely be repetitious here to restate the by now over-familiar insistence of the young on spontaneity and authenticity as the wellsprings of responsible moral action. Nevertheless there are certain aspects even of this familiar dialectic that still seem— indeed, on the basis of the evidence of the papers in this volume—to require clarification.

First, this generalization, besides being very crude, specifically neglects the effects of social class on the relationship, which distort it considerably, though probably not in a very complex way. Generally speaking, working-class youth will tend to be more uptight and conservative than middle-class. In the working class, there is no anti-American generation; blue-collar youth is likely to be strongly and sometimes violently anti-hippie and, in its own view, apolitical, though working-class hostility may be the prime political fact of our time. Blue-collar youth does not merely support its local police; it *is* the local police. It is also a prime source of conventional challenge to the law and order it will later so grimly support; but this challenge is not ideological. Working-class youth break the law; they don't attack the system, though those aspiring to middle-class status may adopt some "mod" attitudes and manners in the familiar pattern of anticipatory socialization. Walter B. Miller's "White Gangs," which are lower-to working-class in membership are prime examples of this apolitical activism which has not disappeared, and may not even have diminished. It has simply become much less of a threat to the silent majority, which prefers familiar patterns of juvenile delinquency to black militants, to student protest demonstrators whom it calls rioters, and to middle-class youngsters who distribute underground newspapers it regards as obscene and who smoke pot, thereby defining themselves as addicts. The violence of conventional working-class juvenile delinquents may even be encouraged to control the middle-class dissidents—a rather common ploy in high schools which often depend on athletic coaches and their teams of primarily working-class "jocks" to keep the the longhairs literally whipped into line. In English cities, counterinsurgent groups of lower-status native born youth have already institutionalized themselves as "skinheads," closely shaven, whose raison d'etre is the harassment of their long-haired age mates and blacks.

It is of working-class youth, now grown to young manhood, that the American army is largely composed. "The Army," as Paul Goodman said in *Growing Up Absurd,* "is the poor boy's IBM." The Marine Corps, as a matter of policy, is apparently all skinhead, at least in bootcamp; while the tensions and hostilities between white marines—especially non-commissioned officers—and black marines over the Afro hair styles worn by some of the latter at Camp LeJeune suggest that the stress of leaving a young man's hair alone may exceed the Corps' limits of tolerance. Charles Moskos, Jr.'s article "Vietnam: Why Men Fight" is an excellent account of the terrifying ideology that governs the behavior of these young men who so firmly believe they have none; and whose notable lack of patriotic fervor is accompanied by a bovine refusal to consider the war and their roles in it as a part of *any* moral or political context, coupled with a high level of hatred and contempt for those who do.

In their refusal even to admit the relevance of moral judgment to the question of either the continuance of so ghastly a war or their own conduct within it, American soldiers resemble much more closely the attitudes of their elders than those of youth. In this sense, at least, the Army does build men. It might be thought peculiar and, after the events at My Lai positively inconvenient, that a society should have come to define moral insensitivity as a mark of maturity. Yet, this paradox can be explained; and the explanation contributes greatly to an understanding of what "the anti-American generation" is really against, and why a corresponding polarization has developed in every industrialized country of the world, including those, like Canada, that have neither a draft nor direct involvement in the Vietnam war as issues which directly threaten the younger generation.

What is at issue between the dissenting, primarily middle-class youth on the one hand; and their elders and most of the working class regardless of age, is not a difference of opinion about the content of moral behavior, but about the scope of moral judgment. The content issues are obviously phony. It is possible to object sincerely and on moral grounds to the use of drugs that affect the mind—but not for a drinking man. It is possible, as many genuine conservatives have done through the ages, to insist, sincerely, that for the sake of social stability even repressive laws must be enforced. But for those who take this position, it is clearly even more vital that law enforcement officials themselves be held accountable before the law. American law-and-order enthusiasts characteristically take the contrary position; no evidence suffices to convict a policeman for violence against hippies, Black Panthers, war resisters or participants in protest demonstrations; and it is rare for the victim to avoid adding a conviction for resisting arrest or "interfering with government administration" to the physical injuries he has sustained. As Michael E. Brown makes very clear in his article on "The Condemnation and Persecution of Hippies," those who condemn and persecute dissident youth most enthusiastically are in no way committed to respect the legal rights of others as the basis for a just or orderly society.

A rather striking illustration of this proposition is reported in the *Buffalo Evening News* December 6, 1969, in a front page story from Chicago, whose Federal Bench is not distinguished by its tenderness toward young people who took part in protests during the 1968 Democratic National Convention:

A federal jury deliberated less than 30 minutes Friday and found a Chicago policeman innocent of violating a college students' civil rights during last year's Democratic National Convention.

U.S. District Judge James B. Parsons expressed disbelief when the not-guilty verdict was returned in the case of Thomas M. Mayer, 44.

Mayer was charged with threatening and striking Kevin W. Cronin Jr., 20, of Chicago, on August 30, 1968, when he learned the youth had participated in demonstrations.

"Are you certain that's the verdict?" Judge Parsons asked. "I am surprised," he added.

"It is unfortunate under our law that the government doesn't have the right to ask for a new trial. If they did, I'd grant it," Judge Parsons said.

The characteristic of dissenting youth that arouses most hostility in its adversaries is not the specific content of their moral ideology or nature of their impulse-life, but the depth of their conviction that their conduct should be guided by their moral ideology and illuminated by their impulse-life. The dominant ideology of the older generation—and, especially, of the middle-class liberal—is based on a contrary moral view: that it is *wrong* to antagonize people if you can avoid it, or to be arrogant and uncompromising, or to make a divisive display of one's personal views or idiosyncrasies, or to spoil a good team play by acting out on your own. The rationale for this moral position is, of course, derived from the demands of consensus politics in the small group as well as the state. To behave in such a way as to destroy consensus or even to impede its formation is immoral because it is held to be impractical and counter-productive. It disrupts negotiations, and may lose you and your associates their turn next time and their share in the negotiated settlement. Victory, as such, is not anticipated. Only extremists would seek victory in Vietnam; but its destruction ought to be accepted without moral indignation as an unintended but now probably inevitable consequence of the interplay of American social and political interests and ambitions. The Vietnam war is really just a special case of industrial pollution which will have to be dealt with later by appropriate techniques. If we destroy the land of the Vietnamese we can always issue the survivors Diners' Club cards.

The silence of the "silent majority," then, does express a moral position; a genuine and consistent belief in the subordination of impulse and personal conviction to ratio-nal control for the sake of a common purpose and future acceptability and effectiveness. In a contest over the moral-ity of instrumental behavior as compared to expressive behavior, it does seem that the former should win hands down and, presumably, hanging loosely at the sides in an innocent position. It is surely more rational, almost by definition, to behave sensibly rather than to allow oneself to be swayed by emotion. But by definition, though not by current usage, "rational" implies above all a sense of proportion—a ratio in which feeling has its place in the denominator; wisdom does not permit calculation to ap-proach the infinite. And even a trace of linguistics—even the merest smattering of French—suffices to remind that the word "sensible" in English has lost precisely those connotations it retains in French that make it sensible; its root is in feeling, not thought.

What makes this conflict between rational and expressive morality—and hence between the anti-American generation and their elders or straight youth—crucial, dangerous and probably irreconcilable is the fact that our peculiar conception of rationality as a process to which feeling is alien and from which it must be excluded is derived from fundamental aspects of Western industrial society. It is not the result of any misunderstanding that could be cleared up by discussion or education: our educational system, in fact, is designed to indoctrinate students with just this conception of rational authority; which is a major reason that their hatred and distrust have come to center on the schools. And it does not seem to be related to the form of the economy, though capitalist modes still retain certain norms of individualism, largely obsolete in practice but still available as moral resources with which to fight the system, that youth in the more uptight of the communist countries must struggle along without. The most lucid and complete statement of the philosophical and political processes involved in producing this impasse is contained in an essay by the Canadian philosopher, George Grant. Though this is entitled and primarily directed toward "The University Curriculum", (*Technology and Empire* [Toronto, Anansi, 1969] pp. 113-133) Professor Grant's analysis applies to our entire cracked social monolith.

The dynamism of technology has gradually become the dominant purpose in western civilization because the most influential men in that civilization have believed for the last centuries that the mastery of chance was the chief means of improving the race. It is difficult to estimate how much this quest for mastery is still believed to serve the hope of men's perfecting, or how much it is now an autonomous quest. Be that as it may, one finds agreement between corporation executive and union member, farmer and suburbanite, cautious and radical politician, university administrator and civil servant, in that they all effectively subscribe to society's faith in mastery.

The purpose of education is to gain knowledge which issues in the mastery of human and non-human nature. Within the last hundred years, it has become increasingly clear that the technological society requires not only the control of non-human nature, but equally the control of human nature. This is the chief cause of the development of the modern "value-free" social sciences. . . . A society in which there are more and more people living in closer and closer proximity will need enormous numbers of regulators to oil the works through their knowledge of intelligence testing, social structures, Oedipal fixations, deviant behavior, learning theory, etc. . . .

For the social scientists to play their controlling role required that they should come to interpret their sciences as "value-free". . . . Social sciences so defined, are well adapted to serve the purposes of the ruling private and public corporations. . . From the assumption that the scientific method is not concerned with judgments of value, it is but a short step to asserting that reason cannot tell us anything about good and bad, and that, therefore, judgments of value are subjective preferences based on our particular emotional makeup. But the very idea that good and bad are subjective preferences removes one possible brake from the triumphant chariot of technology.

In looking more closely, however, it will be seen that the fact-value distinction is not self-evident, as is often claimed. It assures a particular account of moral judgment, and a particular account of objectivity. To use the language of value about moral judgment is to assume that what man is doing when he is moral is choosing in his freedom to make the world according to his own values which are not derived from knowledge of the cosmos. To confine the language of objectivity to what is open to quantifiable experiment is to limit purpose to our own subjectivity. As these metaphysical roots of the fact-value distinction are not often evident to those who affirm the method, they are generally inculcated in what can be best described as a religious way; that is, as doctrine beyond question.

Class liberalism is the ideological cement for a technological society of our type. Its sermons have to be preached to the young, and the multiversities are the appropriate place. That the clever have to put up with this as a substitute for the cultivation of the intellect is a price they must pay to the interests of the majority who are in need of some public religion. . . . Western men live in a society the public realm of which is dominated by a monolithic certainty about excellence—namely that the pursuit of technological efficiency is the chief purpose for which the community exists. . . . Modern liberalism has been a superb legitimizing instrument for the technological society, because at one and the same time it has been able to criticize out of the popular mind the general idea of human excellence and yet put no barrier in the way of that particular idea of excellence which in fact determines the actions of the most powerful in our society. The mark of education is claimed to be scepticism about the highest human purposes, but in fact there is no scepticism in the public realm about what is important to do.

The fact that in our society the demands of technology are themselves the dominating morality is often obscured by the fact that the modern scientific movement has been intimately associated with the moral striving for equality. . . . The tight circle in which we live is this:

our present forms of existence have sapped the ability to think about standards of excellence and yet at the same time have imposed on us a standard in terms of which the human good is monolithically asserted. . . . It would be presumptuous to end by proposing some particular therapy by which we might escape from the tight circle of the modern fate. The decisions of western men over many centuries have made our world too ineluctably what it is for there to be any facile exit. Those who by some elusive chance have broken with the monolith will return to the problem of human excellence in ways too various to be procrusteanly catalogued. The sheer aridity of the public world will indeed drive many to seek excellence in strange and dangerous kingdoms (as those of drugs and myth and sexuality). In such kingdoms, moderation and courage may be known by the wise to be essential virtues. But when such virtues have been publicly lost they cannot be inculcated by incantation, but only rediscovered in the heat of life where many sparrows fall. Much suffering will be incurred by those who with noble intent follow false trails. Who is to recount how and when and where private anguish and public catastrophe may lead men to renew their vision of excellence.

In the concluding paragraph quoted, Grant is clearly referring to those, among others, who have broken with the monolith to become hippies, and has acutely identified certain of the flaws in the hippie way of life that are most threatening to its viability and its integrity. The total thrust of his argument also sharply contradicts the assumptions of those, among whom Berger may, I think, fairly be counted, who see in the emergence of the hippie subculture largely a rerun of earlier chiliastic countercultural movements. There are resemblances; the hippies do in certain respects resemble the early Christians locked in mortal combat with Rome; at the time, it must have seemed almost as obvious as it does in viewing the condemnation and persecution of hippies that it was *they* the combat was going to be mortal to. History gives us a somewhat different perspective; of the latter centuries of the Roman Empire one may say, elegiacally, if you gotta go, that may be the way to go; while the Christians are more of a problem than ever; and some, like Father Berrigan and Father Groppi, are still pretty early. But the major difference is between the earlier cultures that came to be rejected by their young on moral grounds and our own. Though authoritarian and often even tyrannical, none of these earlier establishments was pervaded by the peculiarly modern and willfully amoral letch for technological domination that Grant ascribes to our own—a state of mind too witless and trashy even to be called hubris. The Romans, by Athenian standards, were technology freaks, to be sure; like us they thought plumbing, turnpikes and military display very valuable. But it is to be doubted that they would have attempted to launch an expedition to the moon; and certainly if they had they would not have dared to identify it with Apollo. It seems unwise. Legend does not hold Apollo, though a moderate god, to be conscientiously opposed to violence; and the Goddess of the moon, Diana, is his sister. And a huntress in her own right.

Grant's argument thus explains, I believe, two very important and unresolved questions about the various social subgroups included in this set of papers as part of "the anti-American generation." It is by no means apparent that they belong together at all. Just as the quality of life that turns them off now poisons the whole world, not just America, though probably more intensely here than elsewhere so far; so, clearly, the subjects of these papers cover a complete range of ages. Yet, they all tend to be lumped together as "youth" and little incongruity is felt.

But, of course, they are youth in precisely the same sense that Negroes—in contrast to blacks—remain "boys." Their position in the counterculture—or, ironically, in the military—excludes them from the kinds of wealth and mastery seeking functions that alone confer adult status in this society. It is frequently argued that the hippies, and youthful protesters generally, are able to reject and attack society only because they are subsidized by it, albeit reluctantly and parsimoniously. They choose, in other words, to remain perpetually dependent juveniles and adolescents and find it easy to remain harsh social critics precisely because they avoid, and are perforce excluded from, the responsible social roles in which they might really learn what society is like and how grown men function in it. Their elders are not their moral inferiors but their superiors inasmuch as they accept the necessity of compromise and impurity in order to function in the world. From this point of view, an Adlai Stevenson becomes indeed a man who sacrificed himself for his principles, rather than one who died tragically without having asserted them.

What Grant's reasoning reveals is not that this argument is true or false, but that it is extremely and, I should say, offensively, ethnocentric. It cannot even be thought to be valid unless one accepts as the sine qua non of maturity the wish to impose one's will on the world and the willingness to sacrifice moral clarity and integrity in what one means to others in order to do so. The sin of a Grayson Kirk or a Teddy Kennedy is not, save in a very narrow sense, spinelessness. It is, rather, a special kind of hubris that holds the salvation of that part of the universe that lies within their hands to depend on their ministrations—an attitude that makes tranquility difficult and resignation, apparently, impossible. But in those cultures whose dominating value has not been technological mastery—and there have been several that were magnificent—wisdom is associated both with maturity and with precisely that capacity for tranquil acceptance of one's changing place in a world one never made which has no use for "know-how." To infer that the anti-American generation generally and hippies particularly call themselves sages but choose to remain infants is one more ploy of a technological society, which has no role for a sage, or guru, except roles defined as childlike, though including, to be sure, the role of the child-star.

The second of these unresolved issues with which Grant's analysis is particularly helpful he refers to only briefly, though explicitly. It has to do with his observation that "the fact that the demands of technology in our society are themselves the dominating morality is often obscured by the fact that the modern scientific movement has been intimately associated with the moral striving for equality." Indeed, it is; indeed, it has; and this fact underlies, I believe, the most difficult dilemma of "the anti-American generation." It involves itself in the most painful contradictions in trying to avoid the implications of its own elitism; and in futilely seeking alliances with the hostile working class. For, of course Sprio T. Agnew is right about this: young militants *are* indeed effete snobs, more privileged than their fellows, not only convinced of their moral superiority but arrogant in daring to raise, in this technology-mad land a moral question at all, and in acting as if some tribal memory—clearly unshared and apparently peculiar to themselves—ought to inform the life of the commonwealth, lending dignity and compassion even to its Federal judges. And of course their way of life *is* inimical to the quest of the silent majority, and, in principle, of the poor as well, for a sense of acceptance and successful participation in the good American life as our society defines it. The poor and the silent majority are in no position to abandon their striving; even less are they in a position to recognize that the goals for which they are striving are, if not worthless, too dear at the price demanded for them in our society. Nor are they mistaken in believing that a school system that people are compelled by law to attend for a decade, and by social pressure to continue in for nearly as long again if they wish to be certified to a social status of relative affluence, and which inculcates the patterns of taste and behavior conducive to the functioning of mass society, is an indispensable part of the opportunity-structure on which most Americans depend for a raison d'etre and a source of self esteem. The flower children are indeed the enemies of mass, industrial society; the revolutions that so often fascinate and beguile them have never brought to power a social-system that would accept them, even when those revolutions succeed in bringing a considerable measure of political power and social amelioration to the previously most disadvantaged classes. "The anti-American generation," like its French and other counterparts, might do well to abandon its heartbreaking efforts to make common cause with a working class that applauds the police who beat the shit out of it, and wear its "effete snob" buttons more proudly. Indeed, the major social contribution of beleaguered hippies and student militants may be to provide us with a salutary reminder that a reexamination of the traditional association between freedom and equality, which, in the democratic myth are supposed to reinforce each other, is long overdue.

I strongly suspect that the feelings of the "the anti-American generation" and the disaffected young nationals of other egalitarian industrial states may largely be attributed to displaced and repressed interclass hostility; their anti-Americanism is, I would suggest, in part a kind of neurosis of liberalism. For the United States, like those of its neighbors with a comparable level of development, has become, in terms of culture, triumphantly and often vindictively an affluent poor-white-trash nation. Its schools, its courts, all its official sources of authority impose as far as they can the moral standards and patterns of life of a resentful and defensive working class, mystified and increasingly angry that higher wages and mass-produced amenities do not bring with them the anticipated increments of status. In fact, they may be worse off than they think; for these do not bring equal stature, either. Construction workers who riot rather than permit programs for the training of blacks to be established in their trade; police who beat hippies and then charge them with resisting arrest, schoolteachers who harass students for their dress and hairstyle, and soldiers who massacre civilians are inferior persons—though they may have become so through the action of circumstances beyond their control—and to be subject throughout life to the social class from which they tend selectively to be drawn is thoroughly obnoxious. Yet, this particular complaint is essentially unavailable to ideologically liberal Americans, and especially, perhaps to the idealists of the anti-American generation. Confronted by as malevolent a social class as has emerged from any society in history, they are unable even to take conscious pride in their difference from it.

While all the papers in this collection seem to me interesting and most of them provocative—otherwise I should not have included them—the fact that it is limited to materials previously published in transaction has perforce left untreated one topic that ought certainly to have been examined rather thoroughly in any definitive work on the anti-American generation. This is the school system itself, which is the mold in which the young are cast—as, it would seem into a bottomless pit. Controversy about the school system has grown so protracted and pervasive, and so many good and searching books have been published about it during *trans*action's span of years, that it would probably be misleading to try to sample the area by including an occasional article here. Instead, I would like to call the reader's attention to such vital and comparatively little known works as David Rogers' *110 Livingston Street,* which is a very thorough and complete study of the social dynamics of urban education as illustrated in the macabre workings of the New York City system; Miriam Wasserman's *The NYC-USA School Fix*, which places an almost equal wealth of case material in an even richer historical context; James Herndon's *The Way It Spozed to Be*, a cool and detailed memoir of an almost all black junior high school in Oakland, California a decade ago, and the canniest of the recent group of perceptive and shocking accounts on school routines as they affect the poor and black; George Dennison's recent moving work *The Lives of Children*, which is in fact a very explicit account of the brief but fruitful life of an unusually intelligently and sensitively conceived "experimental school" in New York; and a new and revealing anthology of excerpts from high school underground papers appropriately called *How Old Will You Be in 1984?* and available as a cheap Avon paperback. The present collection does contain papers that discuss the current college and university scene which is after all, the scene you have to make as a student militant. But those who wish to extend the context geographically and historically will find Stephen Spender's charming and informative book *The Year of the Young Rebels* most helpful; while James S. Kunen's *The Strawberry Statement* seems to me by a fairly wide margin the most sensitive and perceptive account of the Columbia University episodes of the last two years to have been written by a participant in it. (One brief scene in Spender's book also occurs in Grayson Kirk's office, though not in his presence). Richard Zorza's *The Right to Say We* is an even more sensitive and precise account of the comparable conflict at Harvard in 1969.

Irving Louis Horowitz's account of the development of folk-rock in relation to jazz is finally of the greatest value in understanding this beautiful music that has come to serve as the nervous system and even, to a degree, the germ plasm of the anti-American generation, on which it has depended both for communication among its own members and for continuity in its succession. Again, fortunately, a helpful paperback literature is being published. Among the best titles are Ralph J. Gleason's *The Jefferson Airplane and the San Francisco Scene*, a biographical study of this classic group which also provides a social history of the San Francisco rock scene for the past two years or so; Paul Williams book of critical reviews, *Outlaw Blues,* and a very varied book of essays edited by Greil Marcus with contributors who have been closely involved in the rock scene, *Rock and Roll Will Stand.* Since there is, in any case, an element of pathos and absurdity in trying to dig rock by reading about it instead of listening to it, it should be noted that the last two of these works provide excellent discographies; while the periodical *Rolling Stone* is available to keep the reader informed as to recent recordings and developments on the rock scene. Some of *Rolling Stone's* articles, like John Burks, Jerry Hopkins, Paul Nelson and Baron Wolman's long essay "The Groupies and Other Girls" in the February 15, 1969 issue, are social reportage of the highest order.

Finally, for a critical overview of the total culture of the anti-American generation and its intellectual roots, the reader is referred to Theodore Roszak's incomparable *The Making of a Counter-Culture*; for vivid and perceptive vignettes of some of the counter-culture's patterns, to Tom Wolfe's *The Pump-House Gang*; and for a brilliant if somewhat sentimental portrayal of hippie youth Charles Reich's *The Greening of America*.

PART I

Hippies in College

GEOFFREY SIMON/GRAFTON TROUT

Though it isn't generally recognized, hippies living—more or less permanently—in urban hippie colonies such as the Hashbury and the East Village differ very much from their campus confreres. The confusion of the two is not surprising, since the mass media have focused almost exclusively on the city hippies. In addition, much of the hippie style derives from city hippies and rapidly diffuses to the campus scenes.

But while college students with long hair, bare feet and brightly colored beads frequently vacation in the Hashburys of our cities, few wish to settle there. Many return to campuses somewhat disillusioned with the drug abuse (especially of "speed" drugs like methedrine) and with the increasing violence of the "bad scene" of the city. Furthermore, the college hippie wants to "turn on" and "tune in," but not to "drop out," at least not completely.

In our two-year study of the hippie community at a midwestern multiversity, we focused mainly on the process by which college hippies are recruited and socialized. We believe that by finding out how one becomes a hippie, we might contribute something new to the more usual discussions of who becomes a hippie and why. Though personality traits or family experience may predispose a teenager toward becoming a hippie, it is clear that one has to learn how to be hip in association with others. Hippies are made, not born.

A study of hippies, however, cannot be conducted in the usual manner of interviewing and observation. Hippies have little respect for sociology, which they equate with the Establishment and particularly with the university. To them, it is the stereotype classifications of middle-class conformists that keep people from being themselves—from "doing their own thing." They have little enthusiasm for cooperating with social researchers who they believe will simply attempt to fit them into other classifications. Furthermore, the hippies' use of drugs makes access difficult, since the social scientist might seem to be a more sophisticated cover for the "Feds," or local narcotics-squad agents. This particular study was made possible by the younger author's association with the hippie community as an undergraduate and a graduate student. His participant observation was supplemented by some 50 interviews conducted both individually and in groups at parties he gave. While he encountered considerable skepticism regarding the usefulness of the research, the people interviewed were generally cooperative and frank. His inside knowledge of the hippie community and his acceptance in it, minimized the possibility of their attempting to "put him on" or to "blow his mind."

Early in the research, it became clear that campus hippies differ not only from city hippies, but differ among themselves as well. Indeed, many individuals shift from one type of hippie to another as they move through the socialization process within the hippie community. While the campus hippies appear to be similar in dress, coiffure, grooming and in many aspects of their behavior, two categories are readily distinguishable—by their orientation toward political activism and personal hedonism.

One group, known as politicals on many campuses, can be distinguished by their dedication to the achievement of rather well-defined political goals (which may, of course, differ from campus to campus, depending on the current local causes). These are the leaders and followers of the New Student Left. They devote a great deal of time and energy to organizing protest demonstrations and confronting the Establishment—in this case, usually embodied by the university administration. The politicals on the campus we studied used a private cafeteria near the campus as their headquarters. They deprecated the introspective hedonism and political individualism of the second group, known as skuzzies on the campus we studied but called groddies, grotties, grubbies, heads or freaks on other campuses. The skuzzies had taken over the coffee shop in the student union as their headquarters. While they frequently would give verbal and bodily support to the politicals during a crisis, the skuzzies were committed more to "doing their own thing," which did not include the hard, collectively-organized work of political protest and the weekly publication of the local underground newspaper.

The leaders of the skuzzie group are not so easily identified as those of the political group. This is because of the difference in the degree of structuring of the two groups. The political leaders not only are more visible as a result of campus publicity, but also hold official positions, such as chairmanships of steering committees and editorial positions on the underground newspaper. The skuzzies, on the other hand, lack any such formal organization. The skuzzies' leader is distinguished chiefly by his more advanced age and higher class standing, and by his ability to function with a certain degree of social and academic success while continuing to participate in the hippie community. He provides the model of how to turn on without dropping out.

Two further categories are needed to complete the classification of participants in the hippie community. The term teeny-boppers was applied most frequently to the hippie equivalent of the pledge class. These were the incoming freshmen, in the initial stage of developing hippie associations and learning how to be hip. Finally, a group of longstanding and unusually far-out hippies was also encountered in this research. There was no local name applied to this group, so we will call them hippie deviants for purposes of discussion later.

Most of the hippies interviewed were freshmen and sophomores, although the leaders were upperclassmen or (especially among the politicals) graduate students. There was a surprising number of National Merit Scholars and scholarship students. Although most had no preference for an academic major, the most common majors were in social sciences—a curious contradiction, considering their attitude toward the social scientific study of themselves. There was a disproportionate number of Jewish students but only two Negroes. Most of the participants came from middle-to-upper-middle-income families living in urban or suburban areas. Few were the products of broken homes.

While in high school, the potential hippie achieved status primarily through academic success. Few were athletes or student-body officials then. Few identified strongly with their high schools. Upon entering college, the bright and successful high-school upperclassman becomes one of thousands of freshmen, most of whom have nonintellectual orientations. While many students try to shrink the multiversity to human scale by joining clubs and fraternities and sororities, this does not work for the sort of students we have described, since these organizations emphasize just what the potential hippies don't have—social spirit.

Now, many students have awaited college as an opportunity to find other students of similar interests and to begin actively seeking out the likely groups of such students. Among the most visible of these groups today are the hippies, especially the politicals. The politicals are involved in activities that appear to be intellectual and important. Best of all, the politicals are easily accessible. Teenyboppers need no formal introduction. There is no rite of passage, such as smoking pot or tripping with LSD. All they have to do is carry signs, go to committee meetings and drink coffee at the politicals' cafeteria. To the potential hippie, the politicals offer an opportunity to shrink the university, to regain status as an intellectual and to acquire some sort of cause or direction.

The political leaders include self-avowed communists, socialists, Maoists and Trotskyites. But although the political teeny-boppers wear the buttons and carry the signs, the majority do not share the convictions of the leaders. Often they don't even know what these convictions really are.

A key characteristic of the politicals is their selective adherence to the hedonistic hang-loose ethic. Though they often voice approval of the skuzzies' casual acceptance of drugs, they do not share their practices. Since the politicals believe in immediate social reform, any activity not dedicated to this end is considered a dangerous waste of time and is therefore discouraged among their teeny-bopper followers. Status is conferred on the teeny-boppers through political buttons, armbands and committee positions. If anyone shows too much skuzziness, he is drummed out of the ranks with the same dispatch applied to lax wardheelers in any political machine.

Since the politicals do not engage in or encourage what most would call hippie behavior, it may be asked if they are really hippies. The skuzzies don't think so, although the political teeny-boppers believe they are. The politicals' rationale for their deviation from hippie norms is what the skuzzies call paranoia. The following is an example:

Interviewer: "Do you like drugs?"

Political: "Yes, if you mean pot and acid."

Interviewer: "Do you turn on with any of the local heads?"

Political: "Are you out of your mind? I'm currently involved in . . . [an impressive array of New Left activities]. I guess you know I'm being tailed by the Feds and my phone is tapped. They're looking for any excuse to bust me. If I got within smelling distance of any pot they would bust me *so fast*. Not only to break me, but to attach the addict label to my cause."

The skuzzies don't accept this excuse. They have been around long enough to recognize that the politicals are not really hemmed in. Still, the teeny-boppers like the story for the excitement and importance it lends to what they are doing.

But as the teeny-bopper grows older, he is likely to give up on the politicals. The teeny-bopper gradually becomes aware of the meaning of the deviant political philosophies of the political leaders and becomes uncomfortable. Furthermore, and perhaps more important, the teeny-bopper's enthusiasm for constant political effort diminishes. His head is full of tales about what the skuzzies are doing—experimenting with life without the pressure of political activity. He is fascinated by drugs. Hedonism conquers political altruism and activism. He comes to the decision that the politicals are not really so hip. Their chief concern is political evangelism—"dumping"—and not "hanging loose."

It takes only two terms to transform a political teeny-bopper into a skuzzie teeny-bopper. Once in the student union with the skuzzies, he normally fights with his parents, drops out of school (either officially or effectively), and lives off his allowance.

As a political, the teeny-bopper's grades were probably better than average. During his transition from political to skuzzie, his grades usually fall. If he drops out of school and then eventually comes back, they return to better than average.

Still, few teeny-boppers remain in the hippie culture long enough to obtain the seniority needed to become hard-core skuzzies. The two distinguishing characteristics of the hard-core skuzzie are his advanced age and his more conservative adherence to hippie norms. The hard-core skuzzie is older than the teeny-bopper, but not as old as the hard-core political.

The teeny-bopper skuzzies live the free hippie life with great abandon—a life usually far skuzzier than that of the hard-core skuzzies. Like the scene along fraternity row, where the freshman and the sophomore brothers are a bit more pleasure-oriented than the juniors and seniors, the younger skuzzies do most of the sexual and drug experimenting. Just as the younger Greeks drink more, the younger skuzzies smoke more pot. And the older, hard-core skuzzies are also cooler, more individualistic, than their followers in another way: They get better grades.

Thus the hard-core skuzzies do not actively lead their followers. Instead, they serve as models and as living proof that the skuzzie life does not produce useless bums.

The skuzzie life usually lasts about a year and a half. The skuzzie tries to find himself through drugs, drinking, sex and very little work. After that, he usually discovers that it is difficult to find himself and feed himself at the same time. Or, after finding a mate, he may decide that he no longer believes in free sex and communal living. At this point, he may drop out of the skuzzie system and even get a haircut.

The other path out of the skuzzie system leads on to hippie deviance. The deviants should not be confused with the hardest-core skuzzies. The skuzzies hang loose, but not too loose. They justify the hippie way of life on Establishment terms. The deviants consist of promiscuous girls, homosexuals and heavy drug users. Of all the hippie types around the campus, the deviants are the most likely to migrate to the city.

The other campus hippies, no matter how liberal or accepting they are supposed to be, apparently have little use for the drug addict or for completely promiscuous sex of either variety. The hippie deviants mark the outer boundary of hippieness. Nevertheless, the rest of the campus hippies tolerate the deviants. Because they move around a great deal and develop connections with city hippies, the deviants can get drugs more easily than anyone else.

Even as we write about the campus hippies, certain changes seem to be under way. Several years ago, it might have been sufficient to describe the hippies as an emergent deviant subculture generated by people of a certain type sharing a common problem in the new environment of the multiversity. This subculture, having been institutionalized on most large campuses, would presumably then continue to provide a ready-made solution for the problems of the same type of people who originally created that solution.

But something more has happened. The hippies have been publicized and, to an important degree, shaped by the mass media. Knowledge of how to play the game, if not actual participation, begins in high school. With this anticipatory socialization, the freshman may have already taken on some of the hippie values and behavior when he arrives on campus.

Thus, the process of assimilation and socialization has speeded up. This may undermine the role of the politicals as gatekeepers for the hippie subculture, robbing them of the recruits who have carried their posters and sat in their sit-ins for a year or so before freaking out to the life of hedonism and hanging loose. Future generations of hippies may have turned on years before freshman orientation, and therefore may never tune in to political activism.

In addition, the great moral cause of civil rights has been increasingly taken away from the committed white college student, and the student Left is, on many campuses, in disarray. This moral unemployment of the student Left may work against the politicals and in favor of the drug freaks. The hang-loose ethic, the psychedelic experience and the quest for self-knowledge become increasingly attractive as attempts at positive political action become less meaningful and more difficult.

The extent and the impact of the hippie subculture—amplified as it is by new drugs, new music, new sexual morality and a new kind of war—may be, in some respects, unprecedented. We must guard against the easy assumption that, because each student generation develops some sort of deviant subsociety, each of these is basically the same. Changes in American society may provide a more permanent niche for certain aspects of the present, hippie version of campus bohemianism. Whether the eventual standard bearers will be the confirmed drug dropouts, the currently more restrained college skuzzies or the precollege artificial-flower children who flock to New York's turned-on Macdougal Street every weekend from their comfortable homes in the suburbs, the possibility is clear: We may well be in the presence not of just the latest wrinkle in youthful rebellion, but of an emergent social movement.

December 1967

College Live-In

SIM VAN DER RYN

This study of the high-rise dorms at Berkeley was conducted over a four-month period by four undergraduate architecture students and a faculty project leader. It was supported by a grant from the Educational Facilities Laboratories of the Ford Foundation.

The objectives were twofold: to develop methods of environmental analysis that could be used by administrators and planners in clarifying their design objectives; to obtain insights into the conflicts between student activities and a dorm setting.

Five methods were employed in developing date—observation, interview, questionaire, student "diary" or activity log and literature search. Data were collected in three stages. In the first stage, observation, interviews and research were initiated to identify and clarify the specific problems. A more highly structured observation and interview program was coupled with a user questionnaire in the second phase in order to obtain qualitative descriptions of student activities in the dorm. Finally, in stage three, questionnaires and activity logs were used to quantify certain types of behavior and to test the hypotheses formulated during the first stage.

Since 1960, colleges and universities have added to their residential facilities about one million new units costing some $5 billion. Many of these elaborate and expensive new structures have been the object of student protests. Dissatisfied dormitory residents across the country have described their accommodations as sterile, cheerless and inconvenient. Seeking escape from what they call the "animal cage" or the "concrete monster," thousands of students every year have been abandoning their dormitories for off-campus private housing.

The majority of college students, however, are still spending 70 to 80 percent of their time in residence halls that have little relation to their needs and desires. Administrators have been so preoccupied with problems of growth, costs and budgets, that they have seldom bothered to question the basic assumptions of student housing design. Few architects have attempted to understand and interpret the physical implications of changing patterns of student living. Furthermore, there is no feedback; existing facilities have not been systematically evaluated to determine whether they are effectively providing the kind of environment students require.

Our study at Berkeley focused on just such a systematic evaluation of one typical student dormitory. In our concern with evaluating the qualitative aspects of student housing, we tried to go beyond mere quantitative measures of building performance, such as temperature, lighting levels and noise control. We sought an approach to architectural programming that would transcend the calculation of square-footage requirements. We chose, therefore, to focus on the silent partner in the design process—the user affected by design decisions. Our findings show that some of the most cherished assumptions of administrators and designers are inconsistent with the actual preferences and life styles of student residents.

Large universities have traditionally relied on building committees to represent the user's point of view—committees often far removed from the needs and values of the actual users of the building. One subcommittee may be responsible for financing, another for planning, and a third for operating the facility. Because of the resultant "tunnel vision" that dominates the design process, the user has generally been reduced to an abstract ideal; his needs remain obscure to both administrator and architect.

The subject of our study was the high-rise dorm complex in Berkeley. A well-fashioned project, typical of much of the student housing built by large universities in the past 15 years, it was based on plans submitted by the winner of a Berkeley-sponsored design competition.

The Berkeley complex consists of four self-contained, nine-story buildings distributed along the periphery of the site in pinwheel fashion. A continuous covered walkway surrounds the central building, which contains dining commons on the ground level and recreation rooms, courtyards, offices and trunk storage space on the lower level.

The main floor of each dormitory is divided into lobby, main lounge or "living room," library and three multipurpose rooms (now called "date rooms"). Small lounges are located on alternate floors above. Approximately 210 students are housed in the eight upper floors; each floor has 12 double rooms, six on each side of a long, narrow corridor. Each room is approximately 14 feet by 12 feet, and contains a picture window and two fixed closets. A single, common bathroom serves each floor.

Despite long waiting lists for dormitory accommodations in the fall of 1963, many students began to move out of the dorms in the spring of 1964. The Housing Office cited three reasons for the student exodus: withdrawal from the university, acceptance into fraternity and sorority houses, and the location of cheaper living quarters.

By February 1965, the vacancy rate rose to an alarming 10 percent; it had never exceeded 1 percent in a fall semester. The campus and local press interviewed residents to discover the reason for these large-scale departures. The women interviewed said they preferred the amenities of apartment life to the regimentation, restrictions and lack of privacy found in residence halls. They cited as especially bothersome the entire complex of rules concerning served meals, compulsory social dues and house meetings, bed-making and room checks.

Only 48.9 percent of the students who had lived in dorms in the spring of 1965 returned to university residence halls in the fall of that year. By 1967, the percentage had dropped to 37.9. And similar dorms at the University of California's Riverside and UCLA campuses were beginning to have vacancy problems, too. University spokesmen attributed the trend to spring fraternity-sorority rushing. Student newspapers, however, cited "lockout regulations, bad food, irksome rules and noise."

To combat the immediate problem of vacancy rates, the university requested that dormitory residents sign one-year leases, a requirement that led to still further student discontent. At the same time, university officials began to reconsider their plans for building more of the same type of dormitories.

A recent survey by the Chancellor's Advisory Committee on Housing asked 5,000 Berkeley students to list their housing preferences at the university. Dormitory facilities, which house 19.5 percent of the student population, ranked least popular. What are the reasons for such widespread dislike for dormitory living?

Our study uncovered three closely related problems that appear to be at the root of student dissatisfaction with dormitories; all are part of an "institutional syndrome." They are:

☐ Lack of personal choice and responsibility for residents. Because the dorm provides housing and other services for such large numbers of people, its design and operation are highly standardized. Standardization reduces a student's options and constrains his behavior. The mere addition of physical variety will not solve the problem, however. The student must participate as a "variety-making agent." For no matter how pleasing the decor provided by the institution, the occupant who lives with it for many months wants to make his own changes.

☐ Too much of the wrong kinds of space. Such inefficiency is the result of an inaccurate assessment of students' needs by both architect and administrator. Space needs are too often established autocratically and parochially, without consulting the students and without considering the campus and students life as a single fabric of people, activities and buildings. Incorrect assumptions are often made regarding the frequency and number of users involved in an activity, the uses to which the space is put, the amount of space needed for an activity and the suitability of the space to its purpose.

The main lounges in the dorms are a prime example of the kind of faulty space planning that results in the waste of large capital expenditures. Although they are furnished and decorated attractively, they appear mainly as settings created expressly to impress visiting parents. Students commonly refer to these lounges as "furniture showrooms." The lounges seldom fulfill their purpose of bringing people together spontaneously.

☐ Needs of one type of idealized student are catered to at the expense of others. Poor dormitory design is based on the erroneous premise that there is an ideal student with one typical schedule, one set of activities. Because planning based on this premise bypasses the diversified interests of student life, it tends to appeal to a homogeneous group.

A study by Burton Clark and Martin Trow identified four student subcultures on the American college campus— academic, collegiate, nonconformist and vocational. Each tends to operate on different although overlapping orbits and on different life schedules; each has its own values and perceptions.

Since decisions about student housing are usually made

by the business office rather than by academic planners, housing tends to serve administrative rather than educational objectives. Common scheduling is the administrators' only solution to the problem of coordinating efficiently large numbers of people and activities.

From our student-activity diaries and interviews, we learned that residence-hall planning and design at Berkeley have generally been programmed around the collegiate group at the expense of the three others. In fact, dormitory conditions tend to undermine the integrity of the campus community by filtering out students whose presence adds diversity and a sense of intellectual dialogue.

Students spend one-third of their waking hours in their rooms, more time than they spend anywhere else. The design of the individual student room and its immediate surroundings is the key element in dormitory planning. In a large, urban university setting like Berkeley's, the student has a special need for a private haven with which he can identify and over which he exercises control.

Perhaps the greatest single deterrent to adequate privacy is the enforced sharing of less than 200 square feet of space with another person for 35 weeks. The frequent clashes reported between incompatible roommates undoubtedly affect study performance. Over half of the students we interviewed simply told us, "At times I can't stand my roommate." But even when roommates are compatible, they face irritations inherent in sharing private space. One girl said, "You don't have privacy in a dorm when you have a roommate." Another commented, "It's impossible to be by yourself in the dorms; you go to the campus if you want that."

Although many activities can take place in varying degrees of common space, sleep, study and privacy demand personal territory. The most obvious adaptation to double occupancy, then, is simply for one roommate to leave the room. Our data show that both students seldom study in the room at the same time. Thus, the supposed economies of two-to-a-room occupancy are invalidated by the students' use of places outside the dormitory room for study, solitude and relaxation.

Noise is another enemy of privacy. Baily reported that of all the student irritants recorded in his 1968 study, noise was ranked first by 72 percent of the students he interviewed.

Loud noises carry along corridors and through adjacent rooms. Rooms next to lounges, and those across from elevators, laundries or bathrooms are inadequately soundproofed. Even the residents of the quieter rooms at the ends of a hall are disturbed by slamming doors, conversation, radios and hi-fi's. One student observed, "There is a constant low-volume noise which can be very irritating,"

A related source of annoyance is the awareness that one might disturb others. "It would be nicer if the rooms were soundproof. When I practice ballet or play my guitar, there is always someone complaining that they are trying to study."

Inflexibility of room equipment and restrictions governing its use are cited continually as another major source of discomfort. New students moving into the dorm are eager to hang prints and clippings, even to paint the walls. But the university prohibits "tacking, taping, or otherwise marring the wall finish." Although students come and go, explain the housing administrators, the building remains and must be kept up at reasonable expense. Decorating is therefore confined to a 12-inch by 24-inch corkboard, placed behind the door. (Because students have chosen to ignore decorating restrictions, the university holds frequent unannounced inspections.) One girl who had moved from the dorm to an apartment exulted, "We've got space . . . I can hang things up on the walls if I want to, and rearrang the furniture . . . everything!"

Students resent built-in furniture and fixed elements because they limit the possible rearrangements of personal space. To escape from the uniformity of decor, they have devised a number of arrangements of movable furniture—arrangements which, of necessity, fall into identical patterns. On the average, roommates rearrange their furniture as often as once every 10 weeks.

In double-occupancy units, the desire to create personal territory appears stronger than the desire to share space with a roommate. Roommates try to escape each other's field of vision; they seek spatial isolation while sleeping. Ninety-four percent of the sample group we surveyed reported using arrangements in which each roommate's furniture was completely to one side of a hypothetical line that splits the room into halves. We also found that students want to study without being observed by their roommates; in the majority of rooms, each occupant arranged his desk so as to exclude the other from view.

The housing officer at the Santa Barbara campus of University of California suggests that the reason why students there favor the old Las Casitas housing over accommodations of better quality is that they can do whatever they want in decorating their rooms. This freedom to personalize the environment accounts as well for the popularity of the rather cramped trailer units used at Santa Cruz for temporary housing. And at the Davis campus, juniors and seniors wait in line to sign up for rooms in the old temporary barracks, which afford the same flexibility in decorating.

The editor of *The Daily Californian*, in an editorial on students' apparent preference for apartments, remarked, "People will put up with a lot when on their own, as compared to being at home or in a dorm."

Many of the more recent college housing programs rely

on the concept of "natural" social groupings as the basis for dormitory design. They assume that there are optimum group sizes for various activities, and that collections of small groups comprise progressively larger groups. At the bottom of this planning hierarchy of communities is the student room; a large dining commons or a central quadrangle is usually at the top.

Designers and administrators disagree about the ideal size of the various groups within the hierarchy and about how the groups should interrelate. Despite their concern with establishing optimum group sizes, housing administrators seldom discuss the obvious question—optimum group size for what purpose? Size is generally determined, therefore, solely according to the criteria of managerial efficiency.

Our research suggests that among the several weaknesses of the natural grouping concept is its creation of a self-fulfilling prophecy. A rigidly conceived hierarchy of social groupings encourages a static, clique-ridden social structure. In planning for a rigid, predictable social order, the designer sets up obstacles to varying that order.

Each student belongs to many groups—groups that function differently and that change in structure, number and style. The formation of such groups may be facilitated by proximity and shared space. If it is intelligently conceived, design can engineer space in such a way that students will have a wide choice of group affiliation. It will take into consideration the fact that group activities tend to overlap and that they cannot therefore be linked permanently to a single space. Space for social interaction must reflect the needs and objectives of its users.

Our observations show that casual or routine activities are better social integrators than more formal ones. We found that each dormitory floor becomes a cohesive social group, whose members tend to stick together even in the large commons and dining room. Most of the students we interviewed found this clannishness oppressive at times. One girl said, "I get along with the girls on my floor, but they all think I'm a snob because I don't do *everything* with them."

The main lounge and library do little to develop overlapping social groups. They are generally frequented by loners and occasional couples seeking a private spot. Students report that casual small groups avoid the lounges because they are intimidated by the formal furniture and the general vastness. The fishbowl atmosphere, generated by the lounges' bright lights and the complete visibility of their occupants, makes them awkward as dating parlors and impossible as study rooms.

The large dining and recreation commons, which serve four residence halls—some 800 students—also fail to provide a suitable setting for coed social and intellectual exchanges. (Men and women are provided with separate entrances!) In fact, the dining hall compromises many of the positive social functions associated with group dining. Intellectual or intimate conversations are thwarted by the prevailing noise and confusion and by the "hurry up" atmosphere. Such conversations are vitally important to students. But unfortunately, facilities for mass feeding give priority to efficiency and easy maintenance over intangibles such as adaptability to conversation.

We have discerned five distinct social patterns in the dining hall. Each might be reflected in the design program.

□ *Gorge and go*
The student is in a hurry and needs a quick meal; he does not want to be detained by meeting friends, waiting in lines, or having to dress up for meals.

□ *Casual dining—making new friends*
Students try to use meal and snack times to meet people and to exchange ideas and community information. Vari-

ations in table shapes and methods of food dispensing can encourage social exchange. Psychologist Robert Sommer's work indicates that long tables are conducive to meeting new people, while circular tables are best for groups already formed. Self-service counters give students a chance to start conversations with strangers.

□ *Intimate conversation with friends*

Students need facilities for an occasional quiet, leisurely meal and conversation with a girl friend or an old buddy.

□ *Solitary meals while reading*

The coffee bar/news rack combination is often patronized by students who want to read while eating alone. They want a relatively quiet, unhurried atmosphere and adequate reading light.

□ *Snacking*

Students would like to be able to get or prepare a bite to eat at any time of the day or night, without necessarily getting dressed up for the public. Innovations in vending machine service may change traditional snacking habits.

At Berkeley, as at many other schools, studying occupies more student time than any other single activity—about six hours a day. It is not surprising, then, that "quiet for study" was the most frequent response to a question asking students to list the most important requirements for good housing.

The quality of an individual's intellectual effort is partially related to the environment in which the work is done. Clearly, the typical Berkeley dormitory fails to provide a good study environment. The double-occupancy room, with its lack of privacy, its noise, interruptions, its conflicts in roommate schedules, and its inadequate study equipment, is not conducive to concentration. Yet most students do all their studying in their rooms. A recent survey at the University of Wisconsin showed that over 75 percent of the students interviewed did all their studying in their rooms.

And in his observations at the Davis campus in 1966, Robert Sommer reported that 80 percent of all studying was done by students in their own residences.

Although some studying can be done in groups, the student's main need is for a personal space in which he can work alone, a need which has been confirmed by other researchers throughout the country.

In equipping the rooms for study, administrators and designers seem to have forgotten their own college days. Such activities as writing research papers and reading from various source materials require generously proportioned horizontal surfaces and storage areas. Almost half of the residents we questioned complained that their desk tops (24 inches by 40 inches) were too small for their work. Sixty-eight percent noted that they have to move books, radio, lamps and clocks off their desks whenever they want to study. The one desk drawer (12 inches by 15 inches by 8 inches) provides inadequate storage. One student said that his desk was "certainly too small for any comprehensive assignments consisting of several pages and using two or three books."

Forty percent of the questionnaire respondents said they used the bed rather than the desk for reading and writing; others preferred the floor. The study by Robert Sommer at the Davis campus showed that about 50 percent of the students regularly use the bed for study; moreover no correlation was found between grade-point average and study habits at bed or desk.

These findings suggest at least one possible solution— just as hospital beds have developed along specialized lines, student beds might be designed with study in mind. They could include an adjustable headrest, writing surface, storage, and lighting.

Our investigation revealed four types of study behavior:
□ Casual study, in which the student seeks relative isolation during study time but stays in touch with the social

situation during frequent breaks.

☐ The waiting-for-something-to-happen study. This usually occurs in a group setting where some social exchange is considered permissible; it is often associated with a lounge, library reading room or even a coffee shop.

☐ Small group study—"semming"—when a seminar-size group of three to seven students seeks isolation from others in order to swap class information.

☐ Intense study out of the room, when cramming or library assignments require extensive use of references.

Obviously, the student housing facilities cannot be expected to supply special areas for all the different kinds of study we have outlined. In any case, each student tends to develop his own inventory of favorite study places outside the dorm: the library, a carrel in the stacks, a quiet corner of the coffee shop, a vacant classroom, a shady place on the grass.

Decisions about how student housing will accommodate the various kinds of study should be made only after a realistic appraisal of study locations available on campus. Because the amount of gross space allowed each student varies according to discipline, an intelligently planned design for study should be done on a campus-wide basis; in such a plan, the dormitory or apartment, which serves as home base, should provide the perfect setting for individual and small-group study.

The breakdown of informal faculty-student contact in large multiversities is another problem engendered by the intellectual environment in large dormitories. Students interviewed said that the dorms tend to sustain the split between learning and living. The notion that housing can foster an interplay between academic and nonacademic lives has by now become cliché among housing planners.

Close communities of teachers and students can be created by building environments in which the two groups can live and work together. A recent example of a successful residential living-learning program was the one conceived by members of Berkeley's University Students Cooperative Association and held in its facilities in the summer of 1967.

There will undoubtedly be continuing exploration of residential living-learning concepts. Any planning along these lines should take into account the matter of faculty loyalties, interests and aims at a large university. Because a professor's loyalties, particularly in his developing years, lie predominantly with his discipline and his department, it may be difficult to sustain his interest in undergraduate teaching away from his home base.

The mobility of the modern student calls for the creation of a network of scattered informal settings where faculty and students can meet on neutral ground.

A recent survey of 5,000 Berkeley students revealed the following considerations for choosing living space, listed in order of importance: cost, location, size, character and privacy. The most preferred student residences were: private houses, fraternities and sororities, and large apartments. All three share the following characteristics: they provide generous living space; they are occupied by groups of students in more or less voluntary association; their residents are free to socialize and entertain, with some degree of privacy; the rooms are highly individual and students may personalize them according to their own tastes and needs.

The least preferred residences were dormitories, cooperatives and boarding houses. Their common characteristics contrast sharply with the highly preferred units. They provide a smaller amount of living space in multiple, institutionalized settings. Each facility is occupied by a large number of students—usually more than 30—who are thrown together arbitrarily and for relatively short periods of time; they therefore provide little opportunity for group cohesion. The rooms themselves are similar or identical, and the residents are generally forbidden to personalize them. And finally, students find it difficult to entertain in private.

Our evaluation at Berkeley and additional surveys of student housing conditions across the country suggest some conclusions about how student housing needs can be met through design and construction. The kind of housing that students want is no more expensive than the accommodations that are generally being built at present. The single room we propose, together with its common living space and circulation, would require less gross space per student than the 250 square feet that is presently allotted.

In addition to innovations in the design and construction of student housing, new financing mechanisms are required. Much of the student housing built in the last decade was financed through long-term, low-interest federal loans to institutions. Why shouldn't a loan program similar to the one for senior citizens (another group with specialized needs) be made available to nonprofit student housing cooperatives? Students know their needs better than the institutions that serve them, and cooperatives generally operate lower-cost housing to the greater satisfaction of students. For example, Berkeley's University Student Cooperative Association provides room and board for more than 800 students at one-third the cost of dormitory accommodations. The greatest impetus to better student housing would be "easy money" for legitimate student associations to build, rehabilitate or rent their own housing.

SOME DESIGN PROPOSALS
Furniture and Equipment
Needs:
Students want to rearrange their furniture occasionally. Beds should be made adaptable for studying.

Desks must permit comfortable study involving two or three books, typewriter and papers.

Desk chair must permit free and comfortable shifting, tilting, leg stretching, etc.

Students want visual barriers so that they can "break up" their room space.

In order to personalize their rooms, students want to be able to tack, paint, and hang decorations on wall surfaces.

To accommodate regular student turnover, housing administrators want to restore rooms to original conditions periodically and at minimum cost.

Specifications:

All components are movable; all furnishings could readily be rearranged by two freshman girls.

The bed unit can be free-standing or hung from the wall (at the student's discretion); it includes adjustable backrest, integral lighting fixture, and swing-away night table.

Desk's minimum dimensions are 45 inches long, 24 to 30 inches wide, 28 to 30 inches high. Adequate space underneath allows for stretching and crossing legs. A soft-covered, tilt-back desk chair can double as an easy chair.

The clothes unit is free-standing and movable; it may contain drawers and double as a dresser. An optional free-standing bureau the same height as the desk could provide added work surface. Minimum dimensions for closet unit are: 60 inches high and 20 to 30 inches wide for full-length hanging space; 30 inches high and 16 inches wide for half-length hanging space. Both full-closet and half-closet would be 24 inches deep.

The back, sides and front of the closet can be used as tackboard surface.

Movable wall-surface panels are provided for painting, hanging, etc.; their dimensions are 7 feet 6 inches by 4 feet or 7 feet 6 inches by 8 feet. Panels may be installed and removed without complicated tools.

Room
Needs:

For the most part, students want single rooms; a few, usually incoming freshmen, prefer double rooms. Some students will accept roommates to reduce costs; some will want to change from double to single accommodations as they progress through school.

Students want to be able to choose from a variety of living conditions according to their financial straits.

Students want to put up an occasional overnight visitor; off-campus commuters may want to rent dormitory space for one or two days a week only.

Even when sharing a room, students want a personal space that can accommodate all their furnishings and equipment and that is visually separate from their roommate.

Students prefer privacy in bathrooms and they generally resent "gang bathrooms."

Students want to entertain visitors in their quarters without inconveniencing others.

Acoustical privacy is an essential.

Students may want to leave and enter their private space without running into others from their shared living space.

Specifications:

All rooms are of three types:

a) strictly single

b) optional single or double

c) strictly double

Types b and c can accommodate visitors or transient students.

All rooms are based on a 7-foot, 6-inch module; each module provides complete personal territory for one student with bed, storage units and desk in a visually protected space.

Each room has its own bathroom core.

Each room has two entrances: one directly onto public

passageway and the other to common living space shared by several other rooms.

Each entrance has two doors separated by an acoustical buffer space.

Each room receives natural light from at least one eye-level window.

Total space allotment per student should not exceed 250 square feet, budgeted at $5,000.

Common Living Space

Needs:

Students like a shared living room for occasional parties, study seminars, etc.

Many students want to make an occasional meal or snack for themselves or in the company of several friends.

Students preparing food will want to be able to see and converse with friends in the living space.

Since more than one student will want to use the galley at a given time, work areas will have to be accessible from both sides.

Students don't want to be more than seconds away from their rooms when they are working in the galley.

Students will want to have coed privileges in the common space; in loco parentis rules may require a special entrance into common space from public passageway.

Specifications:

One common living space (with kitchen galley) for every four to eight students; the common space contains two alcoves, each seating four to six people for eating, visiting, group study, etc.

A student cooking in the galley can see and talk to others in the living space.

Galley counters, sinks, etc. are of the "island" type; they allow work to go on around them, and not from one side only.

The galley has two distinct preparation areas along with two hotplate burners, two sinks, one oven, individual cupboards and one two-cubic-foot refrigerated locker for each student room.

The common living space opens directly onto public passageway or stairs, as well as to each individual room it serves (through double doors).

September 1969

FURTHER READING

Dorms at Berkeley: An Environmental Analysis by Sim Van der Ryn (University of California Center for Planning and Development, 1968) is a more detailed treatment of the subject in the article.

Students for McCarthy—
What Unites Them

MELVIN KAHN

The college students working so diligently for the nomination of Senator Eugene McCarthy have several things in common. Most of them are affluent. They are solidly against the war in Vietnam, and strongly favor civil rights for Negroes. They are very mistrustful of the Johnson administration. And although they are devoted to Senator McCarthy, they could have easily transferred their support to Robert F. Kennedy, or to Nelson Rockefeller. Yet to consider these students a homogeneous unit would be erroneous. By and large they do not share a common ideology.

These findings come from a survey I made of 1,228 volunteers working for McCarthy in Milwaukee during the Wisconsin primary (form March 29 to March 31, 1968). This was, of course, before President Johnson's withdrawal from the race, before Vice President Hubert H. Humphrey's entrance, and before the assassination of Senator Kennedy. Of the volunteers, I focused on the 986 who were college students.

49

Most of these young campaigners, I learned, have middle-class backgrounds. The median income of their fathers was $13,000; some 28 percent of their fathers had incomes of $18,000 or more.

Not surprisingly, these students showed a slight leaning to liberal viewpoints. They were, for instance, very much in favor of enacting and enforcing open-housing legislation. Regarding organized labor, they had divided feelings. Three-fourths went so far as to uphold the right of public employees—teachers, firemen and so on—to strike. At the same time, a majority felt that American labor unions possess too much power.

Another finding was that McCarthy's student supporters are not especially "alienated." Although 50 percent believe that college administrators are not really interested in their students, 80 percent believe that college teachers are. Of course, these McCarthy volunteers were more mature than most students—56 percent were old enough to vote.

On the other hand, most agree that President Johnson and his administration have a credibility gap. Some 82 percent said that they "seldom" or "rarely" believe what the administration says. Only three of the 986 "almost always" believe the administration.

What is important to note is how deeply these students were divided on several vital issues. Half thought that public officials are seriously concerned about what young people think; the other half thought that public officials did not care. The students also divided equally when asked what the government should do about the Ku Klux Klan, half saying that it should take no action, half saying that it should. The lack of a consensus on these issues, and on many others, suggests that, among other factors, McCarthy's students are not a New Left organization.

One anecdote is illustrative. A Harvard student refused to

take part in my survey on the grounds that he was not really working for McCarthy. "Actually," he explained, "I'm a member of the New Left and find McCarthy far too bland. But my people are very well off, and since I don't object to their financial aid, I have to go along with them more often than I would like. They've been objecting to my New Left associates, and last week my old man called me and said he wanted me to come out to Milwaukee to associate with respectable Leftists. So here I am."

These students, then, are not so alienated as many may think, and they are not, for the most part, New Leftists. In addition, they are not even especially rebellious.

Some 52 percent identify as Democrats; 75 percent consider their fathers Democrats. Of the student Democrats, two-thirds say they are independent Democrats, rather than moderate or strong ones. Six percent identify with the Republican Party; 6 percent perceive of their fathers as Republicans. One-fourth of all the students say they are independents; 14 percent claim their fathers are independents.

Another interesting finding was that, at this point in the campaign at least, the McCarthy supporters were not really true diehards. If McCarthy dropped out, they would have supported Senator Kennedy—even though many were bitter about Senator Kennedy's having entered the race.

As a part of the survey, the volunteers were given an opportunity to vote on a ballot pitting the then five major candidates against one another. Included on the ballot was a column headed, "Would not vote." Running against Nixon, Kennedy received 95 percent of the votes. Indeed, the one consistent loser was Nixon. He was swamped not only by Kennedy and McCarthy, but by Governor Rockefeller. Rockefeller, in fact, received 95 percent of the votes against both Nixon and Johnson.

But the New York Governor, when pitted against the two

top Democrats, lost heavily. Against Rockefeller, Kennedy received 77 percent of the votes; McCarthy did even better. Perhaps the students saw Rockefeller as less of a hawk than either Johnson or Nixon, but less of a dove than either McCarthy or Kennedy. Or perhaps, despite the students' claim that they are independent, they will simply vote Democratic when given a choice between men who are not hawks.

It was clear that the overriding issue to these students was the Vietnam war. In the Johnson versus Nixon race, 62 percent of the students were so unhappy with a choice between two hawks that they refused to vote for either man. Among the remainder, slightly more than half favored Johnson over Nixon.

Over half of the students, asked to give the most important reason why they had flocked to Senator McCarthy, cited his stand on the Vietnam war. That reason was given by more students than all the other reasons put together— opposition to President Johnson in general, opposition to Robert Kennedy, the desire to express their own viewpoint through McCarthy, and their admiration of McCarthy's courage.

Thus, for these students the Vietnam war transcends everything else. With their varying attitudes about different aspects of liberalism and conservatism, they do not constitute a common ideological movement. It is the Vietnam war, and virtually that alone, that provides cohesion for McCarthy's student supporters.

July/August 1968

Universities
on Collision Course

DAVID RIESMAN

When one considers the plight of our mental hospitals, of our prisons, of our inadequate welfare and our other starved public services, it is clear that higher education has been in many states the secular cathedral of our time. One wonders, though, whether colleges would have enjoyed all the public support they received in the past if people were as ashamed of having their children in college as they are of having relatives in mental hospitals or in jail, or if state legislators, trustees and others concerned with higher education got as little enjoyment and prestige from their involvements with colleges as they do from other public facilities.

The question is not entirely fanciful. For, as everyone knows, at the same time that higher education is under tremendous pressures to increase its services to its diverse constituencies, the taxpaying public, as represented in legislatures and boards of regents and the like, is growing somewhat disenchanted with at least some aspects of the whole enterprise. The result, as yet, is not an absolute diminution of support, but rather a relative falling off when measured against the expectations of rapidly rising support that most people in higher education have become accustomed to since World War II.

The faculties perhaps most of all. They assume the payroll will somehow be met and, in a remarkable example of self-fulfilling prophecy, that their courses will not be cut out and that the plateau on which they have been living will continue to rise. Indeed, as academic salaries have risen, teaching loads have dropped (which does not mean, necessarily, that less work is being done), and, because of the boom market for Ph.D.'s, colleges have had to offer faculty increasing amenities in order to recruit and retain them. In the 13th grade (that is, the freshman year of college), the faculty's teaching load tends to be half, or less, of what it was in the 12th grade (or senior year of high school), and the salary generally somewhat higher. Also, as one goes on to the post-graduate level, the faculty/student ratio grows closer and closer to one-to-one. The result, when combined with the fact that it is rapidly becoming easier for almost every young person to go to college than not to, is a really enormous rise in the cost of higher education. Even the conservative projections of the Carnegie Commission on Higher Education put the increase in these costs at about twice the national rise of wages, and maybe three times the level of inflation.

This general pattern of escalating costs persists at a time when students and communities are demanding more and more from academic institutions. Many of the affluent students who often lead the protest movements at colleges seem persuaded that the society is fully abundant and that nothing really costs anything. And many other people have also been persuaded, overpersuaded in my opinion, of the contributions that institutions of higher learning can make to the problems of contemporary society. Much of the overpersuasion has been done by the universities themselves, especially by the people in the social sciences. Having responded to so many demands in the past, especially from defense-related agencies, and having often overstated their claim to "relevance" to justify themselves to Philistine critics, the universities may now, however, be driven to bankruptcy by the demand for Urban Studies, Black Studies, courses that will help prepare students for the Peace Corps—all the new relevancies—while neither outside constituencies nor the faculty are prepared to cut down on the older ones.

At Chapel Hill, at Duke and many other places, I have noticed that black and white radical students are organizing the cafeteria workers and the buildings and grounds people to demand higher salaries. Medical students, once very conservative and now often radicalized, are making similar demands of the medical schools for more service in the ghettos. The trouble is that none of these and other like demands are self-sealing; all are self-escalating.

The most dramatic example is, perhaps, the effort of the colleges to expand greatly their recruitment of black students and, in many cases, to set up Black Studies programs as well. But recruitment is expensive, and so is the increasingly elaborate system of orientation and counseling that colleges find necessary to help students, black and white alike, to cope with the often new situation they encounter in college. And Black Studies programs are expensive, too. The problem of resources is made almost desperate by the fact that it is not easy to cut down on Far Eastern Studies, for example, just because one is developing a program in Ethnic Studies; and after a point, one cannot visibly do less for, let us say, Italians, just because one wants to do more for blacks, for Spanish Americans and for other deprived groups.

A subtler but no less costly demand for reform is for more imaginative teaching. Because of what I have come to think of as a contemporary cult of intimacy, pressures in the general society, as well as within the university, tend to drive both students and faculty to demand small groups. I suspect that research would show that there has been a general decline in the span of control (i.e., the number of individuals to whom a person feels he can relate) that individuals feel they can manage and in which they believe they can learn and grow. There is a decline of belief in the vicarious, such as the big lecture provides; and our current ideology, in my judgment, often confuses the authoritative with the authoritarian and dispenses with both. At the University of New Hampshire and elsewhere it has been proposed that the senior faculty give freshmen seminars with 15 or fewer students, but rarely do these proposals cope with the logistical problems of where the money will come from or recognize that there is no educational reform that does not cost money and take its toll of faculty time (which also of course costs money).

All this is happening as an extraordinary tacit alliance between the Right and the Left puts pressure on the universities from both sides. Paranoia is a convenient state of mind because one is never disappointed. If one is on the Left and can prove to oneself that the "power structure" is invariably racist and fascist, then he will never be surprised, even by the most desperate efforts of the university to accede to his demands. And if right-wing paranoids can prove to themselves that the lapse in authoritarian controls leads to "anarchy," they need not distinguish between Clark Kerr and Mark Rudd in deciding which better represents the university his taxes or contributions are supporting.

For all of us, the world is perplexing and disorienting. How are we to interpret the war in Vietnam, or the intervention in the Dominican Republic, or the hegemony over the budget that the military and their civilian allies, including the labor unions, possess? Do these things represent the true reactionary nature of our society, which can only be corrected by revolution? Or are we to see them as evils that perhaps can be moderated through existing democratic and institutional channels? Many young radicals are not sure of the answer to this, nor of their own courage and beliefs. By acting dramatically and decisively, they seek to persuade themselves of their solidarity with each other; by getting a reaction from adults, they sometimes feel confirmed in what they are only tentatively seeking to become. The adults whom they confront in the universities are even more evidently unsure of themselves: We often lack a feeling of legitimacy. In our defensiveness, we sometimes become *like* the young, and sometimes we overreact to their defiance of us.

I do not myself believe that the Left can gain in the United States by forcing the Right to act repressively. If one raises the issue of long-range consequences with the students who are helping to bring about this repression, they are apt to say that their violent tactics work. They do sometimes work, locally; the problem is in their cumulative and national impact. In 1964, I talked to some FSM activists in Berkeley, who also said that their tactics—mild enough in hindsight—worked. I commented that maybe they did work at Berkeley but that they might make Ronald Reagan governor, or perhaps President. Some students only replied. "That's fine. That will uncover the fascist face of our society." But underneath that euphoria about confrontation, it seems to me, is a terrible despair that would find release in an apocalyptic showdown.

A consequence of these combined developments, in which higher education becomes more and more omnivorous of resources while it becomes less and less able to elicit community support, is a collision course. The most obvious casualties now appear to be the great state universities where overcommitment and underfinancing go hand in hand as bond issues are defeated and as state legislators respond in often punitive ways to white and black student protests and to the alleged softness of faculty and administration in seeking to control them. But the private colleges, too, are already facing at least equally severe financial pressures. Those that depend on tuition and have miniscule endowments may find themselves in the position of Sarah Lawrence College, where students sat in to enforce their demands for lower tuition, the recruitment of more impoverished black and white girls, and the maintenance of small class size. Andrew Greeley of NORC has done a recent study of private college alumni seven years out, work that indicates a certain amount of resentment against institutions of higher learning on the part of their recent beneficiaries. Certainly in the endowed private prestige colleges, some alumni are disenchanted when they find that their sons and daughters cannot get in, while places are being found for what they feel are ungrateful blacks and cantankerous whites.

The balancing act, in all these situations, has to be performed by the administration; yet it seems to me that one of the consequences of what is happening in universities today is a loss of administrative flexibility. Top administrators would like to experiment with cost-cutting devices, but experience has taught them that what they may gain in dollar savings they more than lose in faculty and student morale. Departmental power, and now student power, tend to rob administrators of whatever residual room for maneuver they have to resist outside pressures and cope with budgetary stringencies. Students and faculty are in the American grain in finding the enemy in administrative "bureaucracy"; but actually the undernourished and understaffed academic administrations often behave inflexibly because lack of personnel means that decisions cannot be individuated but must be handled by rules. In a recent book, *Mirror of Brass*, Mark Ingraham observes that administrators lack the fringe benefits that faculty have, receive few vacations, get no sabbaticals, and have no way of retiring gracefully.

In his much abused but penetrating book, *The Uses of the University*, Clark Kerr described a new breed of academic administrators who were in effect brokers among the various commitments and constituencies of higher education. He saw these men much as I see them, as having minimal power and limited leverage over their departments, their students, their alumni, and their sources of financial and other public support. But if we are to get through the years ahead and preserve some of the autonomous functions of the university, where the commitment to action is oblique rather than direct, I think we will need to find a still newer breed of administrators, men who will be capable of resisting some constituencies in order to satisfy others. They will have to inspire students and faculty and others in the university to accept their leadership in making these choices, and their leadership will have to be persuasive rather than arbitrary. They will have to help institutions to make a better division of academic labor, to decide for example that a particular university will continue its mission to foreign students even if it is at the cost of blocking more forceful pressures for more black students. Another administrator may decide that he will go ahead with a concentration on the needs of black students and resist pressures to do something for the Chicanos; and so on around the ethnic map and the wider map of possible commitments to action.

The academic leaders who can help institutions make these hard decisions are going to be even more unpopular and unfashionable than the men who now wish they could step gracefully out of office. If we do not find these other leaders, however, we will see higher education spread increasingly thin over the landscape, seldom committed to reflection, often committed to impulse, often ending in the bankruptcy both of treasuries and of hopes.

September 1969

Why All of Us
May Be Hippies Someday

FRED DAVIS

And thus in love we have declared the purpose of our hearts plainly, without flatterie, expecting love, and the same sincerity from you, without grumbling, or quarreling, being Creatures of your own image and mould, intending no other matter herein, but to observe the Law of righteous action, endeavoring to shut out of the Creation, the cursed thing, called Particular Propriety, which is the cause of all wars, bloud-shed, theft, and enslaving Laws, that hold the people under miserie.

Signed for and in behalf of all the poor oppressed people of England, and the whole world.

Gerrard Winstanley and others
June 1, 1649

This quotation is from the leader of the Diggers, a millenarian sect of communistic persuasion that arose in England at the time of Oliver Cromwell. Today in San Francisco's hippie community, the Haight-Ashbury district, a group of hippies naming themselves after this sect distributes free food to fellow hippies (and all other takers, for that matter) who congregate at about four o'clock every afternoon in the district's Panhandle, an eight-block strip of urban green, shaded by towering eucalyptus trees, that leads into Golden Gate Park to the west. On the corner of a nearby street, the "Hashbury" Diggers operate their Free Store where all—be they hip, straight, hostile, curious or merely in need—can avail themselves (free of charge, no questions asked) of such used clothing, household articles, books and second-hand furniture as find their way into the place on any particular day. The Diggers also maintained a large flat in the district where newly arrived or freshly dispossessed hippies could stay without charge for a night, a week, or however long they wished—until some months ago, when the flat was condemned by the San Francisco Health Department. Currently, the Diggers are rehabilitating a condemned skid-row hotel for the same purpose.

Not all of Haight-Ashbury's 7,500 hippies are Diggers, although no formal qualifications bar them; nor, in one sense, are the several dozen Diggers hippies. What distinguishes the Diggers—an amorphous, shifting and sometimes contentious amalgam of ex-political radicals, psychedelic mystics, Ghandians and Brechtian avant-garde thespians—from the area's "ordinary" hippies is their ideological brio, articulateness, good works and flair for the dramatic event. (Some are even rumored to be over 30.) In the eyes of many Hashbury hippies, therefore, the Diggers symbolize what is best, what is most persuasive and purposive about the surrounding, more variegated hippie subculture —just as for certain radical social critics of the American scene the hippies are expressing, albeit elliptically, what is best about a seemingly ever-broader segment of American youth; its openness to new experience, puncturing of cant, rejection of bureaucratic regimentation, aversion of violence and identification with the exploited and disadvantaged. That this is not the whole story barely needs saying. Along with the poetry and flowers, the melancholy smile at passing and ecstatic clasp at greeting, there is also the panicky incoherence of the bad LSD trip, the malnutrition, a startling rise in VD and hepatitis, a seemingly phobic reaction to elementary practices of hygiene and sanitation, and—perhaps most disturbing in the long run—a casualness about the comings and goings of human relationships that must verge on the grossly irresponsible.

But, then, social movements—particularly of this expressive-religious variety—are rarely of a piece, and it would be unfortunate if social scientists, rather than inquiring into the genesis, meaning, and future of the hippie movement, too soon joined ranks (as many are likely to, in any case) with solid burghers in an orgy of research into the "pathology" of it all: the ubiquitous drug use (mainly marijuana and LSD, often amphetamines, rarely heroin or other opiates), the easy attitudes toward sex ("If two people are attracted to each other, what better way of showing it than to make love?"), and the mocking hostility toward the middle-class values of pleasure-deferral, material success and—ultimately—the whole mass-media-glamorized round of chic, deodorized, appliance-glutted suburban existence.

Clearly, despite whatever real or imagined "pathology" middle-class spokesmen are ready to assign to the hippies, it is the middle-class scheme of life that young hippies are reacting against, even though in their ranks are to be found some youth of working-class origin who have never enjoyed the affluence that their peers now so heartily decry. To adulterate somewhat the slogan of Marshall McLuhan, one of the few non-orientalized intellectuals whom hippies bother to read at all, *the hip scene is the message*, not the elements whence it derives or the meanings that can be assigned to it verbally. (Interestingly, this fusion of disparate classes does not appear to include any significant number of the Negro youths who reside with their families in the integrated Haight-Ashbury district or in the adjoining Negro ghetto, the Fillmore district. By and large, Negroes view with bewilderment and ridicule the white hippies who flaunt, to the extent of begging on the streets, their rejection of what the Negroes have had scant opportunity to attain. What more revealing symbol of the Negro riots in out nation's cities than the carting off of looted TV sets, refrigerators and washing machines? After all, aren't these things what America is all about?)

But granting that the hippie scene is a reaction to middle-class values, can the understanding of any social movement—particularly one that just in the process of its formation is so fecund of new art forms, new styles of dress and demeanor, and (most of all) new ethical bases for human relationships—ever be wholly reduced to its reactive aspect? As Ralph Ellison has eloquently observed in his critique of the standard sociological explanation of the American Negro's situation, a people's distinctive way of life is never solely a reaction to the dominant social forces that have oppressed, excluded or alienated them from the larger society. The cumulative process of reaction and counterreaction, in its historical unfolding, creates its own ground for the emergence of new symbols, meanings, purposes and social discoveries, none of which are ever wholly contained in embryo, as it were, in the conditions that elicited the reaction. It is, therefore, less with an eye toward explaining "how it came to be" than toward explaining what it may betoken of life in the future society that I now want to examine certain facets of the Hasbury hippie subculture. (Of course, very similar youth movements, subcultures and settlements are found nowadays in many parts of the affluent Western world—Berkeley's Telegraph Avenue teeny-boppers; Los Angeles' Sunset Strippers; New York's East Village hippies; London's mods; Amsterdam's Provos; and the summer *Wandervögel* from all over Europe who chalk the pavement of Copenhagen's main shopping street, Strøget, and sun themselves on the steps of Stockholm's Philharmonic Hall. What is culturally significant about the Haight-Ashbury hippies is, I would hazard, in general significant about these others as well, with—to be sure—certain qualifications. Indeed, a certain marvelous irony attaches itself to the fact that perhaps the only genuine cross-national culture found in the world today builds on the rag-tag of beards, bare feet, bedrolls and beads, not on the cultural-exchange programs of governments and universities, or tourism, or—least of all—ladies' clubs' invocations for sympathetic understanding of one's foreign neighbors.)

What I wish to suggest here is that there is, as Max Weber would have put it, an elective affinity between prominent styles and themes in the hippie subculture and certain incipient problems of identity, work and leisure that loom ominously as Western industrial society moves into an epoch of accelerated cybernation, staggering material abundance, and historically-unprecedented mass opportunities for creative leisure and enrichment of the human personality. This is not to say that the latter are the hidden causes or tangible motivating forces of the former. Rather, the point is that the hippies, in their collective yet radical break with the constraints of our present society, are—whether they know it or not (some clearly do intuit a connection) —already rehearsing *in vivo* a number of possible cultural solutions to central life problems posed by the emerging society of the future. While other students of contemporary youth culture could no doubt cite many additional emerging problems to which the hippie subculture is, willy-nilly, addressing itself (marriage and family organization, the character of friendship and personal loyalties, the forms of political participation), space and the kind of observations I have been able to make require that I confine myself to three: the problems of compulsive consumption, of passive spectatorship, and of the timescale of experience.

What working attitude is man to adopt toward the potential glut of consumer goods that the new technology will make available to virtually all members of the future society? Until now, modern capitalist society's traditional response to short-term conditions of overproduction has been to generate—through government manipulation of fiscal devices—greater purchasing power for discretionary consumption. At the same time, the aim has been to cultivate the acquisitive impulse—largely through mass advertising, annual styling changes and planned obsolescence—so that, in the economist's terminology, a high level of aggregate demand could be sustained. Fortunately, given the great backlog of old material wants and the technologically-based creation of new wants, these means have, for the most part worked comparatively well—both for advancing (albeit unequally) the mass standard of living and ensuring a reasonably high rate of return to capital.

But, as Walter Weisskopf, Robert Heilbroner and other economists have wondered, will these means prove adequate for an automated future society in which the mere production of goods and services might easily outstrip man's desire for them, or his capacity to consume them in satisfying ways? Massive problems of air pollution, traffic congestion and waste disposal aside, is there no psychological limit to the number of automobiles, TV sets, freezers and dishwashers that even a zealous consumer can aspire to, much less make psychic room for in his life space? The spector that haunts postindustrial man is that of a near workerless economy in which most men are constrained, through a variety of economic and political sanctions, to frantically purchase and assiduously use up the cornucopia of consumer goods that a robot-staffed factory system (but one still harnessed to capitalism's rationale of pecuniary profit) regurgitates upon the populace. As far back as the late 1940s sociologists like David Riesman were already pointing to the many moral paradoxes of work, leisure, and interpersonal relations posed by a then only nascent society of capitalist mass abundance. How much more perplexing the paradoxes if, using current technological trends, we extrapolate to the year 2000?

Hippies, originating mainly in the middle classes, have been nurtured at the boards of consumer abundance. Spared their parents' vivid memories of economic depression and material want, however, they now, with what to their elders seems like insulting abandon, declare unshamefacedly that the very quest for "the good things of life" and all that this entails—the latest model, the third car, the monthly credit payments, the right house in the right neighborhood—are a "bad bag." In phrases redolent of nearly all utopian thought of the past, they proclaim that happiness and a meaningful life are not to be found in things, but in the cultivation of the self and by an intensive exploration of inner sensibilities with like-minded others.

Extreme as the antimaterialistic stance may seem, and despite its probable tempering should hippie communities develop as a stable feature on the American landscape, it nonetheless points a way to a solution of the problem of material glut; to wit, the simple demonstration of the ability to live on less, thereby calming the acquisitive frenzy that would have to be sustained and even accelerated, if the present scheme of capitalist production and distribution were to remain unchanged. Besides such establishments as the Diggers' Free Store, gleanings of this attitude are even evident in the street panhandling that so many hippies engage in. Unlike the street beggars of old, there is little that is obsequious or deferential about their manner. On the contrary, their approach is one of easy, sometimes condescending casualness, as if to say. "You've got more than enough to spare, I need it, so let's not make a degrading charity scene out of my asking you." The story is told in the Haight-Ashbury of the patronizing tourist who, upon being approached for a dime by a hippie girl in her late teens, took the occasion to deliver a small speech on how delighted he would be to give it to her—provided she first told him what she needed it for. Without blinking an eye she replied, "It's my menstrual period and that's how much a sanitary napkin costs."

As social historians are forever reminding us, modern man has—since the beginnings of the industrial revolution—become increasingly a spectator and less a participant. Less and less does he, for example, create or play music, engage in sports, dance or sing; instead he watches professionally-trained others, vastly more accomplished than himself, perform their acts while he, perhaps, indulges in Mitty-like fantasies of hidden graces and talents. Although this bald statement of the spectator thesis has been challenged in recent years by certain social researchers—statistics are cited of the growing numbers taking guitar lessons, buying fishing equipment, and painting on Sunday—there can be little doubt that "doing" kinds of expressive pursuits, particularly of the collective type, no longer bear the same integral relationship to daily life that they once did or still do in primitive societies. The mere change in how they come to be perceived, from what one does in the ordinary course of life to one's "hobbies," is in itself of profound historical significance. Along with this, the virtuoso standards that once were the exclusive property of small aristocratic elites, rather than being undermined by the oft-cited revolutions in mass communications and mass education, have so diffused through the class structure as to even cause the gifted amateur at play to apologize for his efforts with some such remark as, "I only play at it." In short, the cult of professionalism, in the arts as elsewhere, has been institutionalized so intensively in Western society that the ordinary man's sense of expressive adequacy and competence has progressively atrophied. This is especially true of the college-educated, urban middle classes, which —newly exposed to the lofty aesthetic standards of high culture—stand in reverent if passive awe of them.

Again, the problem of excessive spectatorship has not proved particularly acute until now, inasmuch as most men have had other time-consuming demands to fill their lives with, chiefly work and family life, leavened by occasional vacations and mass-produced amusements. But what of the future when, according to such social prognosticators as Robert Theobald and Donald Michael, all (except a relatively small cadre of professionals and managers) will be faced with a surfeit of leisure time? Will the mere extension of passive spectatorship and the professional's monopoly of expressive pursuits be a satisfactory solution?

Here, too, hippies are opening up new avenues of collective response to life issues posed by a changing sociotechnological environment. They are doing so by rejecting those virtuoso standards that stifle participation in high culture; by substituting an extravagantly eclectic (and, according to traditional aestheticians, reckless) admixture of materials, styles, and motifs from a great diversity of past and present human cultures; and, most of all, by insisting that every man can find immediate expressive fulfillment provided he lets the socially-suppressed spirit within him ascend into vibrant consciousness. The manifesto is: All men are artists, and who cares that some are better at it than others; we can all have fun! Hence, the deceptively crude antisophistication of hippie art forms, which are, perhaps, only an apparent reversion to primitivism. One has only to encounter the lurid art nouveau contortions of the hippie posters and their Beardsleyan exoticism, or the mad melange of hippie street costume—Greek-sandaled feet peeking beneath harem pantaloons encased in a fringed American Indian suede jacket, topped by pastel floral decorations about the face—or the sitar-whining cacophony of the folk-rock band, to know immediately that one is in the presence of expressiveness for its own sake.

In more mundane ways, too, the same readiness to let go, to participate, to create and perform without script or forethought is everywhere evident in the Hashbury. Two youths seat themselves on the sidewalk or in a store entranceway; bent beer can in hand, one begins scratching a bongo-like rhythm on the pavement while the other tattoos a bell-like accompaniment by striking a stick on an empty bottle. Soon they are joined, one by one, by a tambourinist, a harmonica player, a penny-whistler or recorder player and, of course, the ubiquitous guitarist. A small crowd collects and, at the fringes, some blanket-bedecked boys and girls begin twirling about in movements vaguely resembling a Hindu dance. The wailing, rhythmic beating and dancing, alternately rising to peaks of intensity and subsiding, may last for as little as five minutes or as long as an hour, players and dancers joining in a dropping out as whim moves them. At some point—almost any—a mood takes hold that "the happening is over"; participants and onlookers disperse as casually as they had collected.

Analogous scenes of "participation unbound" are to be observed almost every night of the week (twice on Sunday) at the hippie's Parnassus, the Fillmore Auditorium where a succession of name folk-rock bands, each more deafening than the one before, follow one another in hour-long sessions. Here, amidst the electric guitars, the electric organs, and the constantly metamorphizing show of lights, one can see the gainly and the graceless, the sylph bodies and rude stompers, the crooked and straight—all, of whatever condition or talent, dance as the flickering of a strobe light reduces their figures in silhouette to egalitarian spastic bursts. The recognition dawns that this, at last, is dancing of utterly free form, devoid of fixed sequence or step, open to all and calling for no Friday after-school classes at Miss Martha's or expenxive lessons from Arthur Murray. The sole requisite is to tune in, take heart and let go. What follows must be "beautiful" (a favorite hippie word) because it is *you* who are doing and feeling, not another to whom you have surrendered the muse.

As with folk-rock dancing, so (theoretically, at least) with music, poetry, painting, pottery and the other arts and crafts: expression over performance, impulse over product. Whether the "straight world" will in time heed this message of the hippies is, to be sure, problematical. Also, given the lavish financial rewards and prestige heaped upon more talented hippie artists by a youth-dominated entertainment market, it is conceivable that high standards of professional performance will develop here as well (listen to the more recent Beatles' recordings), thus engendering perhaps as great a participative gulf between artist and audience as already exists in the established arts. Despite the vagaries of forecasting, however, the hippies— as of now, at least—are responding to the incipient plenitude of leisure in ways far removed from the baleful visions of a Huxley or an Orwell.

In every society, certain activities are required to complete various tasks and to achieve various goals. These activities form a sequence—they may be of short duration and simple linkage (boiling an egg); long duration and complex linkage (preparing for a profession); or a variety of intermediate combinations (planting and harvesting a crop). And the activity sequences needed to complete valued tasks and to achieve valued goals in a society largely determine how the people in that society will subjectively experience time.

The distinctive temporal bent of industrial society has

been toward the second of these arrangements, long duration and complex linkage. As regards the subjective experience of time, this has meant what the anthropologist Florence Kluckhohn has termed a strong "future orientation" on the part of Western man, a quality of sensibility that radically distinguishes him from his peasant and tribal forebears. The major activities that fill the better part of his life acquire their meaning less from the pleasure they may or may not give at the moment than from their perceived relevance to some imagined future state of being or affairs, be it salvation, career achievement, material success, or the realization of a more perfect social order. Deprived of the pursuit of these temporally distant, complexly modulated goals, we would feel that life, as the man in the street puts it, is without meaning.

This subjective conception of time and experience is, of course, admirably suited to the needs of post-eighteenth century industrial society, needs that include a stable labor force; work discipline; slow and regular accumulation of capital with which to plan and launch new investments and to expand; and long, arduous years of training to provide certain people with the high levels of skill necessary in so many professions and technical fields. If Western man had proved unable to defer present gratifications for future rewards (that is, if he had not been a future-oriented being), nothing resembling our present civilization, as Freud noted, could have come to pass. Yet, paradoxically, it is the advanced technology of computers and servo-mechanisms, not to overlook nuclear warfare, that industrial civilization has carried us to that is raising grave doubts concerning this temporal ordering of affairs, this optimistic, pleasure-deferring and magically rationalistic faith in converting present effort to future payoff. Why prepare, if there will be so few satisfying jobs to prepare for? Why defer, if there will be a superabundance of inexpensively-produced goods to choose from? Why plan, if all plans can disintegrate into nuclear dust?

Premature or exaggerated as these questions may seem, they are being asked, especially by young people. And merely to ask them is to prompt a radical shift in time-perspective—from what will be to what is, from future promise to present fulfillment, from the mundane discounting of present feeling and mood to a sharpened awareness of their contours and their possibilities for instant alteration. Broadly, it is to invest present experience with a new cognitive status and importance: a lust to extract from the living moment its full sensory and emotional potential. For if the present is no longer to be held hostage to the future, what other course than to ravish it at the very instant of its apprehension?

There is much about the hippie subculture that already betokens this alteration of time-perspective and concomitant reconstitution of the experienced self. Hippie argot—some of it new, much of it borrowed with slight connotative changes from the Negro, jazz, homosexual and addict subcultures—is markedly skewed toward words and phrases in the active present tense: "happening," "where it's at," "turn on," "freak out," "grooving," "mind-blowing," "be-in," "cop out," "split," "drop acid" (take LSD), "put on," "uptight" (anxious and tense), "trip out" (experience the far-out effects of a hallucinogenic drug). The very concept of a happening signifies immediacy: Events are to be actively engaged in, improvised upon and dramatically exploited for their own sake, with little thought about their origins, duration, or consequences. Thus, almost anything—from a massive be-in in Golden Gate Park to ingesting LSD to a casual street conversation to sitting solitarily under a tree—is approached with a heightened awareness of its happening potential. Similarly, the vogue among Hashbury hippies for astrology, tarot cards, I Ching and other forms of thaumaturgic prophecy (a hippie conversation is as likely to begin with "What's your birthday?" as "What's your name?") seems to be an attempt to denude the future of its temporal integrity—its unknowability and slow unfoldingness—by fusing it indiscriminately with present dispositions and sensations. The hippie's structureless round-of-day ("hanging loose"), his disdain for appointments, schedules and straight society's compulsive parceling out of minutes and hours, are all implicated in his intense reverence for the possibilities of the present and uninterest in the future. Few wear watches, and as a colleague who has made a close participant-observer study of one group of hippies remarked, "None of them ever seems to know what time it is."

It is, perhaps, from this vantage point that the widespread use of drugs by hippies acquires its cultural significance, above and beyond the fact that drugs are easily available in the subculture or that their use (especially LSD) has come to symbolize a distinctive badge of membership in that culture. Denied by our Protestant-Judaic heritage the psychological means for experiencing the moment intensively, for parlaying sensation and exoticizing mundane consciousness, the hippie uses drugs where untutored imagination fails. Drugs impart to the present—or so it is alleged by the hippie psychedelic religionists—an aura of aliveness, a sense of union with fellow man and nature, which—we have been taught—can be apprehended, if not in the afterlife that few modern men still believe in, then only after the deepest reflection and self-knowledge induced by protracted experience.

A topic of lively debate among hippie intellectuals is whether drugs represent but a transitory phase of the hippie subculture to be discarded once other, more self-generating, means are discovered by its members for extracting consummatory meaning from present time, or whether drugs are the *sine qua non* of the subculture. Whatever the case, the hippies' experiment with ways to recast our notions of time and experience is deserving of close attention.

As of this writing, it is by no means certain that Haight-Ashbury's "new community," as hippie spokesmen like to call it, can survive much beyond early 1968. Although the "great summer invasion" of emigre hippies fell far short of the 100,000 to 500,000 forecast, the influx of youth from California's and the nation's metropolitan suburbs was, despite considerable turnover, large enough to place a severe strain on the new community's meager resources. "Crash pads" for the night were simply not available in sufficient quantity; the one daily meal of soup or stew served free by the Diggers could hardly appease youthful appetites; and even the lure of free love, which to young minds might be construed as a substitute for food, tarnished for many—boys outnumbered girls by at least three to one, if not more. Besides, summer is San Francisco's most inclement season, the city being shrouded in a chilling, wind-blown fog much of the time. The result was hundreds of youths leading a hand-to-mouth existence, wandering aimlessly on the streets, panhandling, munching stale doughnuts, sleeping in parks and autos and contracting virulent upper-respiratory infections. In this milieu cases of drug abuse, notably involving methedrine and other "body-wrecking" amphetamines, have showed an alarming increase, beginning about mid-summer and continuing up to the present. And, while the city fathers were not at first nearly so repressive as many had feared, they barely lifted a finger to ameliorate the situation in the Haight-Asbury. Recently, however, with the upcoming city elections for Mayor and members of the Board of Supervisors, they have given evidence of taking a "firmer" attitude toward the hippies: Drug arrests are on the increase, many more minors in the area are being stopped for questioning and referral to juvenile authorities, and a leading Haight Street hippie cultural establishment, the Straight Theatre, has been denied a dance permit.

It has not, therefore, been solely the impact of sheer numbers that has subjected the new community to a difficult struggle for survival. A variety of forces, internal and external, appear to have conjoined to crush it. To begin with, there is the hippies' notorious, near-anarchic aversion to sustained and organized effort toward reaching some goal. Every man "does his own thing for as long as he likes" until another thing comes along to distract or delight him, whereupon the hippie ethos enjoins him to drop the first thing. (Shades of the early, utopian Karl Marx: ". . . in the communist society it [will be] possible for me to do this today and that tomorrow, to hunt in the morning, to fish in the afternoon, to raise cattle in the evening, to be a critic after dinner, just as I feel at the moment; without ever being a hunter, fisherman, herdsman, or critic." From *The German Ideology*.) Even with such groups as the Diggers, projects are abandoned almost as soon as they are begun. One of the more prominent examples: An ongoing pastoral idyll of summer cultural happenings, proclaimed with great fanfare in May by a group calling itself the Council for the Summer of Love, was abandoned in June when the Council's leader decided one morning to leave town. Add to this the stalling and ordinance-juggling of a city bureaucracy reluctant to grant hippies permits and licenses for their pet enterprises, and very little manages to get off the ground. With only a few notable exceptions, therefore, like the Haight-Ashbury Free Medical Clinic, which—though closed temporarily—managed through its volunteer staff to look after the medical needs of thousands of hippies during the summer, the new community badly failed to provide for the hordes of youth drawn by its paeans of freedom, love and the new life.

Perhaps there is some ultimate wisdom to "doing one's own thing"; it was, however, hardly a practical way to receive a flock of kinsmen.

Exacerbating the "uptightness" of the hippies is a swelling stream of encounters with the police and courts, ranging from panhandling misdemeanors to harboring runaway minors ("contributing to the delinquency of a minor") to, what is most unnerving for hip inhabitants, a growing pattern of sudden mass arrests for marijuana use and possession in which as many as 25 youths may be hauled off in a single raid on a flat. (Some hippies console themselves with the thought that if enough middle-class youths get "busted for grass," such a hue and cry will be generated in respectable quarters that the marijuana laws will soon be repealed or greatly liberalized.) And, as if the internal problems of the new community were not enough, apocalyptic rumors sprung up, in the wake of the Newark and Detroit riots, that "the Haight is going to be burned to the ground" along with the adjoining Fillmore Negro ghetto. There followed a series of ugly street incidents between blacks and whites—assaults, sexual attacks, window smashing—which palpably heightened racial tensions and fed the credibility of the rumors.

Finally, the area's traffic-choked main thoroughfare, Haight Street, acquired in the space of a few months so carnival and Dantesque an atmosphere as to defy description. Hippies, tourists, drug peddlers, Hell's Angels, drunks, speed freaks (people high on methedrine), panhandlers, pamphleteers, street musicians, crackpot evangelists, photographers, TV camera crews, reporters (domestic and foreign), researchers, ambulatory schizophrenics and hawkers of the underground press (at least four such papers are produced in the Haight-Ashbury alone) jostled, put-on and taunted one another through a din worthy of the Tower of Babel. The street-milling was incessant, and all heads remained cocked for "something to happen" to crystallize the disarray. By early summer, so repugnant had this atmosphere become for the "old" hippies (those residing there before—the origins of Hashbury's new community barely go back two years) that many departed; those who remained did so in the rapidly fading hope that the area might revert to its normal state of abnormality following the expected post-Labor Day exodus of college and high-school hippies. And, while the exodus of summer hippies has indeed been considerable, the consensus among knowledgeable observers of the area is that it has not regained its former, less frenetic, and less disorganized ambience. The transformations wrought by the summer influx—the growing shift to methedrine as *the* drug of choice, the more general drift toward a wholly drug-oriented subculture, the appearance of hoodlum and thrill-seeking elements, the sleazy tourist shops, the racial tensions—persist, only on a lesser scale.

But though Haight-Ashbury's hippie community may be destined to soon pass from the scene, the roots upon which it feeds run deep in our culture. These are not only of the long-term sociohistoric kind I have touched on here, but of a distinctly contemporary character as well, the pain and moral duplicity of our Vietnam involvement being a prominent wellspring of hippie alienation. As the pressures mount on middle-class youth for ever greater scholastic achievement (soon a graduate degree may be mandatory for middle-class status, as a high-school diploma was in the 1940s), as the years of adolescent dependence are further prolonged, and as the accelerated pace of technological change aggravates the normal social tendency to intergenerational conflict, an increasing number of young people can be expected to drop out, or opt out and drift into the hippie subculture. It is difficult to foresee how long they will remain there and what the consequences for later stages of their careers will be, inasmuch as insufficient time has passed for even a single age cohort of hippies to make the transition from early to middle adulthood. However, even among those youths who "remain in" conventional society in some formal sense, a very large number can be expected to hover so close to the margins of hippie subculture as to have their attitudes and outlooks substantially modified. Indeed, it is probably through some such muted, gradual and indirect process of social conversion that the hippie subculture will make a lasting impact on American society, if it is to have any at all.

At the same time, the hippie rebellion gives partial, as yet ambiguous, evidence of a massiveness, a universality and a density of existenial texture, all of which promise to transcend the narrowly-segregrated confines of age, occupation, and residence that characterized most bohemias of the past (Greenwich Village, Bloomsbury, the Left Bank). Some hippie visionaries already compare the movement to Christianity sweeping the Roman Empire. We cannot predict how far the movement can go toward enveloping the larger society, and whether as it develops it will—as have nearly all successful social movements—significantly compromise the visions that animate it with the practices of the reigning institutional system. Much depends on the state of future social discontent, particularly within the middle classes, and on the viable political options governments have for assuaging this discontent. Judging, however, from the social upheavals and mass violence of recent decades, such options are, perhaps inevitably, scarce indeed. Just possibly, then, by opting out and making their own kind of cultural waves, the hippies are telling us more than we can now imagine about our future selves.

December 1967

FURTHER READING

It's Happening by J. L. Simmons and Barry Winograd (Santa Barbara, Calif.: Marc-Laird Publications, 1966).

Looking Forward: The Abundant Society by Walter A. Weisskopf, Raghavan N. Iyer, and others (Santa Barbara, Calif.: Center for the Study of Democratic Institutions, 1966).

The Next Generation by Donald N. Michael (New York: Vintage Books-Random House, 1965).

The Future as History by Robert L. Heilbroner (New York: Grove Press, 1961).

Hippie Morality—
More Old Than New

For a few months I've been going around the San Francisco Bay Area asking hippies what the New Morality is all about, and for more than a few months I've been reading and listening to their sympathizers and spokesmen, present and former: Paul Goodman, Edgar Friedenberg, Herbert Marcuse, Norman O. Brown, John Seeley, Alan Watts, Tim Leary and Ken Kesey, among others. I read the *East Village Other* and the *Berkeley Barb,* and the *San Francisco Oracle* (when I can bear to), and I've been doing more than my share of cafe-sitting, digging the moral feeling of the young as it comes across through their talk. On the basis of these—forgive the expression—data, it would be very easy to argue (as I will) that there isn't much, if any, New Morality around, and certainly none that warrants upper-case letters (although how unprecedented or unheard of a morality must be to be regarded as "new" is a question too difficult for me to attempt to answer here).

81

But the conclusion that there isn't much new morality around is one I am reluctant to come to, because it almost inevitably functions as a put-down of various activities, some of which I actually want to encourage. Thus I am confronted with the very old problem of whether to speak the truth when it may have undesired consequences. To love the truth is no doubt a great virtue; but to love to speak the truth is a small vanity, and I should like to be very explicit that it is my vanity that constrains me to risk dampening the ardor of some of those who belong to a movement, which in many respects I admire, by attempting to speak the truth about it. People whose spirit may rest on an erroneous conviction that they are doing something new and revolutionary may be unhappy when told that they are (only) the most recent expression of what is by now an old tradition, even if it is, as I believe, an important and honorable tradition as well.

More than 30 years ago (a "generation," as Karl Mannheim reckoned social time, two generations as José Ortega y Gasset reckoned it, and three, four, or more as contemporary journalists and other grabbers of the main literary chance reckon it), the literary critic Malcolm Cowley wrote *Exile's Return,* a book about the experience of American literary expatriates in Europe in the 1920s. In it he treats to some extent the history of bohemianism, starting back in the middle of the nineteenth century with that important document of bohemian history, Henry Murger's *Scenes of Bohemian Life.* By 1920, Cowley says, bohemia had a relatively formal doctrine, "a system of ideas that could be roughly summarized as follows" (and as I go through these eight basic ideas, please keep in mind the hippies—and the fact that these ideas were formulated 33 years ago about phenomena that were then more than a hundred years old):

☐ The first point in the bohemian doctrine is what Cowley

calls "The idea of salvation by the child.—Each of us at birth has special potentialities which are slowly crushed and destroyed by a standardized society and mechanical modes of teaching. If a new educational system can be introduced, one by which children are encouraged to develop their own personalities, to [listen!] blossom freely like flowers, then the world will be saved by this new, free generation." The analogues here are hippie innocence (more on this later), flower power and the educational revolution.

☐ "The idea of self-expression.—Each man's, each woman's, purpose in life is to express himself, to realize his full individuality through creative work and beautiful living in beautiful surroundings." This, I believe, is identical with the hippies' moral injunction to "do your thing."

☐ "The idea of paganism.—The body is a temple in which there is nothing unclean, a shrine to be adorned for the ritual of love." Contemporary paganism, by no means limited to the hippies but especially prevalent among them, is manifest in the overpowering eroticism that their scene exudes: the prevalence of female flesh (toe, ankle, belly, breast and thigh) and male symbols of strength (beards, boots, denim, buckles, motorcycles), or the gentler and more restrained versions of these, or the by-now hardly controversial assumption that fucking will help set you free.

☐ "The idea of living for the moment.—It is stupid to pile up treasures that we can enjoy only in old age. . . . Better to seize the moment as it comes. . . . Better to live extravagantly . . . 'burn [your] candle at both ends. . . .' " Today, this might be formulated as something like being super WOW where the action is in the NOW generation, who, like, know what's happening and where it's at. (It was a gentle English cleric who said many years ago that the man who marries the spirit of his own age is likely to be a widower in the next. Prophets of rapid social change, please take notice.)

☐ "The idea of liberty.—Every law . . . that prevents self-expression or the full enjoyment of the moment should be shattered and abolished. Puritanism is the great enemy." Today, this is manifest in the movement to legalize marijuana, to render ecstasy respectable (dancing in the park, orgiastic sex, turning everybody on, etc.) and to demonstrate the absurdity of laws against acts that harm no one and the hypocrisy of those who insist on the enforcement of these laws.

☐ "The idea of female equality.—Women should be the economic and moral equals of men . . . same pay . . . same working conditions, the same opportunity for drinking, smoking, taking or dismissing lovers." For the hippies, insistence on equality in smoking and the taking and dismissing of lovers is already quaint, and drinking is increasingly irrelevant. But the theme of sexual equality is still important with respect to cultural differences between the sexes, and evident in the insistence that men may be gentle and women aggressive, and in the merging of sexually related symbols of adornment (long hair, beads, bells, colorful clothes and so on).

☐ Hippies often tell me that it is really quite difficult, if not impossible, to understand their scene without appreciating the importance of psychedelic drugs in it. Although I am inclined to believe this, the importance of mind-expansion in the bohemian doctrine was plain to Cowley 33 years ago. The references are dated but the main point of his seventh basic idea is unmistakable: "The idea of psychological adjustment.—We are unhappy because . . . we are repressed." To Cowley, the then-contemporary version of the doctrine prescribed that repression could and should be overcome by Freudian analysis, or by the mystic qualities of George Ivanovich Gurdjieff's psychophysical disciplining, or by a daily dose of thyroid. Today, repression may be uptightness or "game reality," and it is not Freud but Reich, not thyroid but LSD, nor Gurdjieff but yoga, I Ching, *The Book of the Dead* or some other meditational means of transcending the realities that hang one up.

☐ Cowley's final point in the bohemian doctrine is the old romantic love of the exotic. "The idea of changing place.— 'They do things better in . . .' " (you name it). At some times the wisdom of old cultures has been affirmed, at other times, wild and primitive places—anything that will break the puritan shackles. Paris, Mexico, Tahiti, Tangier, Big Sur. The contemporary hippie fascination with American Indians has a triple attraction: They were oppressed, they were nobly savage, and by a symbolic act of identification they became a part of one's American collective unconscious, reachable under the influence of drugs.

Hippie morality, then, at least that part of it perceivable from the outside, seems to be only the most recent expression of a long tradition. Having said this, I don't want to just leave it there, because if my saying that the morality isn't new functions as a put-down of what it actually is, then my statement is misleading. Let me try to clarify what I am getting at.

Some months ago I gave a talk on "black culture" to what I then mistakenly thought was the usual sort of polite, university-extension audience of culture-hungry schoolteachers and social workers—in this case, many of them Negro. I argued—tentatively, without much conviction, in the dispassionate style I have argued so far in this article—that although the idea of black culture seemed useful to me as a myth to bind Negroes together in a way that would enhance their ability to press their political demands, there seemed to be little in what the nationalists and other militants were touting as "black culture" that couldn't be understood as a combination of Southern regional patterns, evangelical Christianity, and lower-class patterns of the metropolitan ghetto. I had hardly finished when I found myself facing an angry and shouting group of people who felt they had been insulted, and who, in other circumstances, might simply have killed me as an enemy of the people (I am not being melodramatic). Later, it was pointed out to me that black culture was in the process of being formed, and if I didn't see it, that was because I didn't know where it was at (both of which may be true). Besides, my implying that there wasn't any was likely not only to weaken the myth but to impede the actual growth and development of the reality—which made me an enemy.

The logical form of this problem is an old one for sociologists who deal with issues of public resonance: the problem of self-fulfilling and self-denying assertions. So although I do not see among the hippies any system of values that warrants the pretentious solemnity of the phrase "New Morality," I believe that moralities old *and* new rise and fall in part through self-fulfilling and self-denying processes that may be activated by descriptive statements innocent of prescriptive intent. But knowing this destroys the possibility of innocence for those who make statements that affect outcomes they are interested in. There are, that is, always potentially ascendant, deviant or subterranean moralities around, the numbers of whose adherents are subject to expansion or contraction partly on the basis of how persuasively the morality is talked up or down, glamorized or mystified, vitalized or stultified, and its prevalence exaggerated or minimized. Such processes affect the rigor with which sanctions are or are not applied, and therefore obstruct or facilitate not merely moral deviance but the prospect that deviance will become legitimate and proclaim its own propriety. Joseph Conrad, that famous Polish sociologist, used as an epigraph for his very sociological

Lord Jim the following words: "It is certain that my conviction increases the moment another soul will believe it."

Hippie morality is not new, but I think that more souls
are believing it. The proportions of the age-grade may not
be any larger, but the absolute numbers are enormous—
for two very good and rather new reasons. First, there is
the unprecedented, colossal size of the cohort between, say,
13 and 25, even a small percentage of which produces very
large numbers indeed. Second, this cohort of morally deviant youth has been further swelled by the group known as
"teeny-boppers"—pre-adolescents and early adolescents
who have not, to my knowledge, previously played any
significant role in bohemian movements. Their presence on
the contemporary scene is, I think, a function of the institutionalization of adolescence, not simply as the traditional
"transitional stage," but as a major period of life. This
period may last as long as 20 years, and therefore evokes
its own orientational phenomena and behavior, which we
have learned to understand as "anticipatory socialization."

In addition to the hippies' large numbers, their peculiar
visibility is playing an important part in the gradual legitimation of their traditionally subterranean morality. Exactly *un*like Michael Harrington's invisible poor, the
hippies are unequally distributed in ways that magnify
their visibility. They are concentrated—segregated in
universities, or recently out of them and into the bohemian
ghettos of the more glamorous big cities. They are colorful,
disturbing, and always newsworthy. Moreover, they have a
substantial press of their own and radio stations that play
their music almost exclusively. And not only are many of
them the children of relatively affluent and influential people, but they have their sympathizers (secret and not so
secret) in the universities, and let's not forget the ballet,
and in the mass media.

How do I know the bohemian morality is gradually being legitimated? I don't for sure, but when John Lennon said the Beatles were more popular than Jesus—something that probably wasn't even quite true—he got away with it, and helped make it truer by getting away with it. There's better evidence. Take sex, which in this country seems to be the quintessence of morality. More important and more reliable than survey data reporting premarital sexual experience are the revealing attitudes of more or less official moral spokesmen. Hollywood films, for example, are as good an indicator of acceptable morality as one is likely to find (appealing, as their producers say they must, to mass sentiments), and these films not only affirm unmarried sex but even suggest that your life may be ruined by the decision *not* to climb into bed with the person you love. It is still news when Christian ministers refuse to condemn unchastity, but it makes the inside pages now, and it is not nearly so startling an event as it was a few years ago. And now, finally, the topic is ready for discussion in the public schools: *Is* premarital intercourse wrong? William Graham Sumner gave us the answer: The moment the mores are questioned, they have lost their authority. And when they are questioned publicly by official representatives of the major institutions, they not only have lost their authority but are ready to be replaced—not, let me repeat, by a "new morality" but by an old one that has been underground, and that now, like Yeats' rough beast, its hour come round at last, slouches toward Bethlehem to be born.

So what else is new? Well, several things that express traditional bohemian virtues in so fresh, unusual, and potentially consequential a manner that they are worth noting.

□ A few words about hippie innocence. Clearly, the symbols of childhood and innocence are very much in: flowers, ice cream, kites, beads, bells, bubbles and feathers, and sitting on the ground, like Indians, or legs outstretched in front of one, like Charlie Brown and his friends (perhaps reflecting the guilelessness of the prose styles of Paul Goodman and Alan Watts?). Just recently, hippie innocence was a major theme in a CBS documentary oddly titled "The Hippie Temptation." CBS (Harry Reasoner, that is) disapproved, pointing out that the innocence is used in a hostile way (a girl taunts an annoyed policeman by insistently offering him flowers), and concluding with the (smug?) observation that people who can grow beards and make love ought to go beyond innocence to wisdom. What CBS apparently chose to ignore (and I say "chose" because it seems so obvious) was the fact that innocence as wisdom and the child as moral leader are two ideas that go back a couple of thousand years to very respectable sources. Harry Reasoner, a man with a usually reliable sense of irony, also chose to ignore the irony of network TV prescribing wisdom—and to the "TV generation"! Of course, hippie innocence is provocative; it angers the police, it angers CBS, and it is potentially consequential because authority finds it difficult to fight. Wisdom might be a good antidote, but there's very little wisdom around (and more people pleading incompetence to preach it). There's only sophistication, and not too much of that.

□ Another interesting development in the hippie milieu is the panhandling. It's interesting because of its relation to the innocence theme, and because of the peculiar moral relevance of the interaction. The approach is usually the standard "Do you have any spare change?" But it is often consciously winsome and "charming." A teen-age girl, for example, asks me to lend her 15 cents for an ice-cream cone, then asks for 2 cents more so she can have the ice cream in a sugar cone. The mood of the interaction is different from skid-row panhandling, where the bum plays humble and subservient, thus allowing his mark to feel generous or powerful—or even contemptuous—which is what the giver gets in return for giving. Hippie panhandling is innocent, offhand, as if to say "You've got it and can spare it, I haven't; all men are brothers, and if you don't give, you're a kind of fink; or, if you think it's principle that prevents you from giving, it reveals only your uptightness about money, your enslavement to an obsolete ethic about the virtue of *earning* what you get." Indeed, one of the things one may learn from being approached is the shocking discovery that one does truly believe in that virtue. Whatever the specific character of one's response, the people I have spoken to invariably find it obscurely disturbing, an occasion for reflection, and this is important.

□ The hippies have also played an important role in the gradual institutionalization of the use of formerly obscene and other taboo language in public, even on ceremonial occasions. This trend is part of the general eroticization of public life, from print, to advertising, to film, to styles of dress and undress, and it has within it the potential for changing the quality of public life through its effect on spoken rhetoric, which may help reclaim the language from the depths to which public speech has sunk it. Lenny Bruce was a prophet of this trend. The so-called filthy-speech movement at Berkeley in the summer of 1965 is well-known, and so are the rather severe sanctions invoked against the offenders. What is not so well-known is that, shortly after this controversy, the university sponsored a poetry conference on the campus. For almost a whole week, there were daily and nightly readings, by, among others, several of the more successful beat poets of the 1950s, as well as by many very young and relatively unknown hippie poets. I remember sitting in the hallowed halls of Wheeler Auditorium and the only slightly less hallowed Dwinelle Hall, amidst little old ladies with knitting, suburban housewives from Orinda, and cashmere-sweatered undergraduates holding tight to their boyfriends' hands. And I remember listening to Allen Ginsberg rhapsodize about waking up with his cock in the mouth of his friend Peter Orlovsky; I remember listening to other poets wax eloquent about cunnilingus and about what they repeatedly insisted upon calling "fucking." Now, because I am a sociologist as well as a person interested in poetry, I remember not only sitting and listening to the poets, but I also remember observing that the ladies hardly looked up from their knitting and the undergraduates listened raptly (with that almost oppressive quiet reminiscent of museums), and I heard neither a titter nor a gasp of shock. I saw no outraged exits, and not an indignant word in the press that week about pornography or obscenity. Nor was I aware of any other complaints against the use of university facilities for such goings-on—although the organizer of the conference told me, when I spoke to him about it later, that there had been one or two letters of complaint. One or two. And, I must confess, it is the improbability of negative sanctions that encourages me, here, to contribute to the tendency I am describing, that is, to show you my point rather than argue it: that formerly taboo language is increasingly used in public, and that, yes, Virginia, it is erotic. Nor is the poetry conference the only example at hand. As Bay Area residents well know, Lenore Knadel's *The Love Book,* shortly after being banned by the San Francisco police, was read aloud at a mass meeting of faculty and students at San Francisco State. And I have been told by the cast of *The Beard*—a one-act play that had a long run in San Francisco before its New York opening, which uses all the four-letter words and winds up with an act of cunnilingus on stage—that their performances on campuses before college groups have been invariably successful: The audiences laugh in the funny places, not in the dirty ones. Only the Saturday night audiences in their San Francisco theater still leave a good deal to be desired.

□ The music (rock, folk-rock, etc.), of course, is new, but I will not discuss it at any length except to point to some features of it that I think may have important social consequences. First of all, the lyrics of many of the songs are—for the first time in the history of popular music in this country—lyrics that a thoughtful person of some sensibility and taste can sing without embarrassment. Think of it! Intelligent people singing popular songs seriously! Cole Porter was an exception to the rule of banality. Bob Dylan is not an exception because there is no longer a rule. Dylan is no great poet; he's not even a very good one. But he *is* a poet in a country where lyricists have usually been versifiers rather than poets. Second, I am struck by the fact that few, if any, of the traditional popular baritones sing rock well, or sing good rock well, or sing rock at all. It seems apparent that rock songs are not made for deep or mature voices; there is a prevalence of high, reedy, thin, sometimes even falsetto male voices—indeed, when listening to rock songs, one often finds it difficult to tell the difference between a male and a female voice. Enunciation, when it can be understood at all, is often childlike, sometimes even infantile. Postures tend to be limp, and facial expressions unformed and vulnerable. All this tends to identify the music with an age-group and a life-style, a distinctive kind of music for a distinctive kind of people— music that outsiders may admire, if they do, only as a tourist admires an exotic scene, but closer intimacy with which exposes one to the dangers of infection by other aspects of the life-style. Finally, there is the fact that rock groups typically do their own material almost exclusively, something—as far as I know—unprecedented in American popular music. And even when a song is very successful, other groups do not generally perform it. This may well express the importance of the idea of authenticity in the subculture, that doing your thing should be doing *your* thing, which would discourage a rock group from doing something that wasn't "theirs."

It is, of course, easy to deflate the authenticity balloon by pointing out that certain "things" can be authentically evil, and that doing your thing can be indirectly damaging to lots of people, including yourself. Qualifications, then, are necessary, but they are not usually made by moralists; the great moral dicta are typically stated in absolute terms, and never with all of the qualifications necessary to live with them. The commandment prohibiting homicide does not, after all, say except in self-defense, or except at the order of the commander-in-chief; and we all know that we may be pardoned our inability to honor our mothers and fathers if they push heroin in the high-school cafeteria.

This brings me to the question of the value of the not-so-new hippie morality. Unfortunately, we sociologists are among those least likely to speak with sympathy about expressive morality, because, of all data, data on morality reveal the greatest disparity between the point of view of the participant and that of the observer. The participant sees consummation, whereas we observers typically treat expressive morality as social facts whose prime significance lies in the institutional functions they facilitate or obstruct. As sociologists, we avoid moral discourse and resist indulging our moral feelings—because our scientific education has taught us that all moralities are ultimately arbitrary, and as men of science we have learned to abhor arbitrariness. Moralists frequently embarrass or bore sociologists: Their moralists' passion keeps demanding a like response from us, whereas our impulse is to look only for latent functions. But, like Philoctetes, the moralist has a magic bow as well as a festering wound, for one of the important manifest functions of the moralist's passion is to define or affirm or redefine the standards with reference to which expressive satisfactions are achieved. And to the extent that scientists get expressive satisfactions through their work, these standards are never irrelevant.

The closest that sociologists usually get to real moral judgment is when they invoke comparative data as a source or norms to appraise morally relevant situations. This angers and frustrates moralists, because their mission is utopian. In moral discourse, reliance on norms of evaluation derived from comparative data leaves one impotent to affect the standards in terms of which the evaluations are made; it renders one morally acted upon rather than morally active. For moralists, the invocation of comparative norms is irrelevant. If the moralists appear fanatical, intransigent, and unreasonable, it is because they must believe that moral feeling is not negotiable, that half a consummation is no consummation at all. It makes no difference that Americans are freer than Peruvians or Iranians and more humane that Guatemalans or Guineans; in terms of some current moral vision of human possibility, America may still stink. Where expressive values rather than facts or judicious estimates are at stake, the utopian standard is more relevant than the comparative norm, and therefore sociologists make poor moral leaders. Let me conclude with an old Jewish joke that may clarify this somewhat. Jake says, "So nu, Sam, how's your wife?" And Sam says, "Compared to what?" It's funny because of the inappropriateness of the comparative norm. How, then, is the hippie morality? Compared to what? No worse than anybody else's, better than many, but still not good enough.

December 1967

FURTHER READING:

Berkeley Barb, East Village Other, San Francisco Oracle. Weekly or occasional "underground" newspapers catering to the disaffected young and to voyeurs. *Barb* is less hippie than it is New Left; *Oracle* is a psychedelic orgy of print and picture.

Time, Life, CBS, ABC, *Newsweek,* and other media that define what "news" is. If one knew why the hippies are so consistently newsworthy, one would have the answer to a very important question. The hippies don't know. Only the media know, and they aren't telling.

The Condemnation and
Persecution of Hippies

MICHAEL E. BROWN

This study is about persecution and terror. It speaks of the hippie and the temptations of intimacy that the Myth of Hippie has made poignant, and it does this to discuss the institutionalization of repression in the United States.

When people are attacked as a group, they change. Individuals in the group may or may not change, but the organization and expression of their collective life will be transformed. When the members of a gathering believe that there is a grave danger imminent and that opportunities for escape are rapidly diminishing, the group loses its organizational quality. It becomes transformed in panic. This type of change can also occur outside a situation of strict urgency: When opportunities for mobility or access to needed resources are cut off, people may engage in desperate collective actions. In both cases, the conversion of social form occurs when members of a collectivity are about to be hopelessly locked into undesired and undesirable positions.

The process is not, however, automatic. The essential ingredient for conversion is social control exercised by external agents on the collectivity itself. The result can be benign, as a panic mob can be converted into a crowd that makes an orderly exit from danger. Or it can be cruel.

The transformation of groups under pressure is of general interest; but there are special cases that are morally critical to any epoch. Such critical cases occur when pressure is persecution, and transformation is destruction. The growth of repressive mechanisms and institutions is a key concern in this time of administrative cruelty. Such is the justification for the present study.

Four aspects of repressive social control such as that experienced by hippies are important. First, the administration of control is suspicious. It projects a dangerous future and guards against it. It also refuses the risk of inadequate coverage by enlarging the controlled population to include all who might be active in any capacity. Control may or may not be administered with a heavy hand, but it is always a generalization applied to specific instances. It is a rule and thus ends by pulling many fringe innocents into its bailiwick; it creates as it destroys.

Second, the administration of control is a technical problem which, depending on its site and object, requires the bringing together of many different agencies that are ordinarily dissociated or mutually hostile. A conglomerate of educational, legal, social welfare and police organizations is highly efficient. The German case demonstrates that. Even more important, it is virtually impossible to oppose control administered under the auspices of such a conglomerate since it includes the countervailing institutions ordinarily available. When this happens control is not only efficient and widespread, but also legitimate, commanding a practical, moral and ideological realm that is truly "one-demensional."

Third, as time passes, control is applied to a wider and wider range of details, ultimately blanketing its objects' lives. At that point, as Hilberg suggests in his *The Destruction of the European Jews*, the extermination of the forms of lives leads easily to the extermination of the lives themselves. The line between persecution and terror is thin. For the oppressed, life is purged of personal style as every act becomes inexpressive, part of the struggle for survival. The options of a life-style are eliminated at the same time that its proponents are locked into it.

Fourth, control is relentless. It develops momentum as organization accumulates, as audiences develop, and as unofficial collaborators assume the definition of tasks, expression and ideology. This, according to W. A. Westley's "The Escalation of Violence Through Legitimation," is the culture of control. It not only limits the behaviors, styles, individuals and groups toward whom it is directed, it suppresses all unsanctioned efforts. As struggle itself is destroyed, motivation vanishes or is turned inward.

These are the effects of repressive control. We may contrast them with the criminal law, which merely prohibits the performance of specific acts (with the exception, of course, of the "crimes without victims"—homosexuality, abortion and drug use). Repression converts or destroys an entire social form, whether that form is embodied in a group, a style or an idea. In this sense, it is terror.

These general principles are especially relevant to our understanding of tendencies that are ripening in the United States day by day. Stated in terms that magnify it so that it can be seen despite ourselves, this is the persecution of the hippies, a particularly vulnerable group of people who are the cultural wing of a way of life recently emerged from its quiet and individualistic quarters. Theodore Roszak, describing the hippies in terms of their relationship to the culture and politics of dissent, notes that "the underlying unity of youthful dissent consists . . . in the effort of beat-hip bohemianism to work out the personality structure, the total life-style that follows from New Left social criticism." This life-style is currently bearing the brunt of the assualt on what Roszak calls a "counter-culture"; it is an assault that is becoming more concentrated and savage every day. There are lessons for the American future to be drawn from this story.

Near Boulder, Colorado, a restaurant sign says "hippies not served here." Large billboards in upstate New York carry slogans like "Keep America Clean: Take a Bath." and "Keep America Clean: Get a Haircut." These would be as amusing as ethnic jokes if they did not represent a more systematic repression.

The street sweeps so common in San Francisco and Berkeley in 1968 and 1969 were one of the first lines of attack. People were brutally scattered by club-wielding policemen who first closed exits from the assaulted area and then began systematically to beat and arrest those who were trapped. This form of place terror, like surveillance in Negro areas and defoliation in Vietnam, curbs freedom and forces people to fight or submit to minute inspection by hostile forces. There have also been one-shot neighborhood pogroms, such as the police assault on the Tompkins Square Park gathering in New York's Lower East Side on Memorial Day, 1967: "Sadistic glee was written on the faces of several officers," wrote the *East Village Other*. Some women became hysterical. The police slugged Frank Wise, and dragged him off, handcuffed and bloody, crying, "My God, my God, where is this happening? Is this America?" The police also plowed into a group of hippies, Yippies, and straights at the April, 1968, "Yip-in" at Grand Central Station. The brutality was as clear in this action as it had been in the Tompkins Square bust. In both cases, the major newspapers editorialized against the police tactics, and in the first the mayor apologized for the "free wielding of nightsticks." But by the summer of 1968, street sweeps and busts and the continuous presence of New York's Tactical Police Force had given the Lower East Side an ominous atmosphere. Arrests were regularly accompanied by beatings and charges of "resistance to arrest." It became clear that arrests rather than subsequent procedures were the way in which control was to be exercised. The summer lost its street theaters, the relaxed circulation of people in the neighborhood and the easy park gatherings.

Official action legitimizes nonofficial action. Private citizens take up the cudgel of law and order newly freed from the boundaries of due process and respect. After Tompkins Square, rapes and assaults became common as local toughs assumed the role, with the police, of defender of the faith. In Cambridge, Massachusetts, following a virulent attack on hippies by the mayor, *Newsweek* reported that vigilantes attacked hippie neighborhoods in force.

Ultimately more damaging are the attacks on centers of security. Police raids on "hippie pads," crash pads, churches and movement centers have become daily occurrences in New York and California over the past two and a half years. The usual excuses for raids are drugs, runaways and housing violations, but many incidents of unlawful entry by police and the expressions of a more generalized hostility by the responsible officials suggests that something deeper is involved. The Chief of Police in San Francisco put it bluntly; quoted in the *New York Times* magazine in May 1967, he said:

> Hippies are no asset to the community. These people do not have the courage to face the reality of life. They are trying to escape. Nobody should let their young children take part in this hippy thing.

The Director of Health for San Francisco gave teeth to this counsel when he sent a task force of inspectors on a door-to-door sweep of the Haight-Ashbury—"a two-day blitz" that ended with a strange result, again according to the *Times*: Very few of the hippies were guilty of housing violations.

Harrassment arrests and calculated degradation have been two of the most effective devices for introducing uncertainty to the day-to-day lives of the hippies. Cambridge's mayor's attack on the "hipbos" (the suffix stands for body odor) included, said *Newsweek* of October 30, 1967, a raid on a "hippie pad" by the mayor and "a platoon of television cameramen." They "seized a pile of diaries and personal letters and flushed a partially clad girl from the closet." In Wyoming, the *Times* reported that two "pacifists" were "jailed and shaved" for hitchhiking. This is a fairly common hazard, though Wyoming officials are perhaps more sadistic than most. A young couple whom I interviewed were also arrested in Wyoming during the summer of 1968. They were placed in solitary confinement for a week during which they were not permitted to place phone calls and were not told when or whether they would be charged or released. These are not exceptional cases. During the summer of 1968, I interviewed young hitchhikers throughout the country; most of them had similar stories to tell.

In the East Village of New York, one hears countless stories of apartment destruction by police (occasionally reported in the newspapers), insults from the police when rapes or robberies are reported, and cruel speeches and even crueler bails set by judges for arrested hippies.

In the light of this, San Francisco writer Mark Harris' indictment of the hippies as paranoid seems peculiar. In the September 1967 issue of *The Atlantic*, he wrote,

The most obvious failure of perception was the hippies' failure to discriminate among elements of the Establishment, whether in the Haight-Ashbury or in San Francisco in general. Their paranoia was the paranoia of all youthful heretics. . . .

This is like the demand of some white liberals that Negroes acknowledge that they (the liberals) are not the power structure, or that black people must distinguish between the good and the bad whites despite the fact that the black experience of white people in the United States has been, as the President's Commission on Civil Disorder suggested, fairly monolithic and racist.

Most journalists reviewing the "hippie scene" with any sympathy at all seem to agree with *Newsweek* that "the hippies do seem natural prey for publicity-hungry politicians—if not overzealous police," and that they have been subjected to varieties of cruelty that ought to be intolerable. This tactic was later elaborated in the massive para-military assault on Berkeley residents and students during a demonstration in support of Telegraph Avenue's street people and their People's Park. The terror of police violence, a constant in the lives of street people everywhere, in California carries the additional threat of martial law under a still-active state of extreme emergency. The whole structure of repression was given legitimacy and reluctant support by University of California officials. Step by step, they became allies of Reagan's "dogs of war." Roger W. Heyns, chancellor of the Berkeley campus, found himself belatedly reasserting the university's property in the lot. It was the law and the rights of university that trapped the chancellor in the network of control and performed the vital function of providing justification and legitimacy for Sheriff Madigan and the National Guard. Heyns said: "We will have to put up a fence to re-establish the conveniently forgotten fact that this field is indeed the university's, and to exclude unauthorized personnel from the site. . . . The fence will give us time to plan and consult. We tried to get this time some other way and failed—hence the fence." And hence "Bloody Thursday" and the new regime.

And what of the hippies? They have come far since those balmy days of 1966-67, days of flowers, street-cleaning, free stores, decoration and love. Many have fled to the hills of Northern California to join their brethren who had set up camps there several years ago. Others have fled to communes outside the large cities and in the Middle West. After the Tompkins Square assault, many of the East Village Hippies refused to follow the lead of those who were more political. They refused to develop organizations of defense and to accept a hostile relationship with the police and neighborhood. Instead, they discussed at meeting after meeting, how they could show their attackers love. Many of those spirits have fled; others have been beaten or jailed too many times; and still others have modified their outlook in ways that reflect the struggle. Guerrilla theater, Up Against the Wall Mother Fucker (UAWMF), the Yippies, the urban communes; these are some of the more recent manifestations of the alternative culture. One could see these trends growing in the demonstrations mounted by hippies against arrests of runaways or pot smokers, the community organizations, such as grew in Berkeley for self-defense and politics, and the beginnings of the will to fight back when trapped in street sweeps.

It is my impression that the hippie culture is growing as it recedes from the eye of the media. As a consequence of the destruction of their urban places, there has been a redistribution of types. The flower people have left for the hills and become more communal; those who remained in the city were better adapted to terror, secretive or confrontative. The hippie culture is one of the forms radicalism can take in this society. The youngsters, 5,000 of them, who came to Washington to counter-demonstrate against the Nixon inaugural showed the growing amalgamation of the New Left and its cultural wing. The Yippies who went to Chicago for guerrilla theater and learned about "pigs" were the multi-generational expression of the new wave. A UAWMF drama, played at Lincoln Center during the New York City garbage strike—they carted garbage from the neglected Lower East Side and dumped it at the spic 'n' span cultural center—reflected another interpretation of the struggle, one that could include the politically militant as well as the culturally defiant. Many hippies have gone underground—in an older sense of the word. They have shaved their beards, cut their hair, and taken straight jobs, like the secret Jews of Spain; but unlike those Jews, they are consciously an underground, a resistance.

What is most interesting and, I believe, a direct effect of the persecution, is the enormous divergence of forms that are still recognizable by the outsider as hippie and are still experienced as a shared identity. "The Yippies," says Abbie Hoffman, "are like hippies, only fiercer and more fun." The "hippie types" described in newspaper accounts of drug raids on colleges turn out, in many cases, to be New Leftists.

The dimensions by which these various forms are classified are quite conventional: religious-political, visible-secret, urban-hill, communal-individualistic. As their struggle intensifies, there will be more efforts for unity and more militant approaches to the society that gave birth to a real alternative only to turn against it with a mindless savagery. Yippie leader Jerry Rubin, in an "emergency letter to my brothers and sisters in the movement" summed up:

Huey Newton is in prison.

Eldridge Cleaver is in exile.

Oakland Seven are accused of conspiracy.

Tim Leary is up for 30 years and how many of our brothers are in court and jail for getting high?

Campus activists are expelled and arrested.
War resisters are behind bars.
Add it up!

Rubin preambles his summary with:

From the Bay Area to New York, we are suffering the greatest depression in our history. People are taking bitterness in their coffee instead of sugar. The hippie-yippie-SDS movement is a "white nigger" movement. The American economy no longer needs young whites and blacks. We are waste material. We fulfill our destiny in life by rejecting a system which rejects us.

He advocates organizing "massive mobilizations for the spring, nationally coordinated and very theatrical, taking place near courts, jails and military stockades."

An article published in a Black Panther magazine is entitled "The Hippies Are Not Our Enemies." White radicals have also overcome their initial rejection of cultural radicals. Something clearly is happening, and it is being fed, finally, by youth, the artists, the politicos and the realization, through struggle, that America is not beautiful.

The persecution of the Jews destroyed both a particular social form and the individuals who qualified for the Jewish fate by reason of birth. Looking at the process in the aggregate, Hilberg describes it as a gradual coming together of a multitude of loose laws, institutions and intentions, rather than a program born mature. The control conglomerate that resulted was a refined engine "whose devices," Hilberg writes, "not only trap a larger number of victims; they also require a greater degree of specialization, and with that division of labor, the moral burden too is fragmented among the participants. The perpetrator can now kill his victims without touching them, without hearing them, without seeing them. . . . This ever growing capacity for destruction cannot be arrested anywhere." Ultimately, the persecution of the Jews was a mixture of piety, repression and mobilization directed against those who were in the society but suddenly not of it.

The early Christians were also faced with a refined and elaborate administrative structure whose harsh measures were ultimately directed at their ways of life: their social forms and their spiritual claims. The rationale was, and is, that certain deviant behaviors endanger society. Therefore, officials are obligated to use whatever means of control or persuasion they consider necessary to strike these forms from the list of human possibilities. This is the classical administrative rationale for the suppression of alternative values and world views.

As options closed and Christians found the opportunities to lead and explore Christian lives rapidly struck down, Christian life itself had to become rigid, prematurely closed and obsessed with survival.

The persecution of the early Christians presents analogies to the persecution of European Jews. The German assault affected the quality of Jewish organizations no less than it affected the lives of individual Jews, distorting communities long before it destroyed them. Hilberg documents some of the ways in which efforts to escape the oppression led on occasion to a subordination of energies to the problem of simply staying alive—of finding some social options within the racial castle. The escapist mentality that dominated the response to oppression and distorted relationships can be seen in some Jewish leaders in Vienna. They exchanged individuals for promises. This is what persecution and terror do. As options close and all parts of the life of the oppressed are touched by procedure, surveillance and control, behavior is transformed. The oppressed rarely retaliate (especially where they have internalized the very ethic that rejects them), simply because nothing is left untouched by the persecution. No energy is available for hostility, and, in any case, it is impossible to know where to begin. Bravery is stoicism. One sings to the cell or gas chamber.

The persecution of hippies in the United States involves, regardless of the original intentions of the agencies concerned, an assault on a way of life, an assault no less concentrated for its immaturity and occasional ambivalence. Social, cultural and political resources have been mobilized to bring a group of individuals into line and to prevent others from refusing to toe the line.

The attractiveness of the hippie forms and the pathos of their persecution have together brought into being an impressive array of defenders. Nevertheless theirs has been a defense of gestures, outside the realm of politics and social action essential to any real protection. It has been verbal, scholarly and appreciative, with occasional expressions of horror at official actions and attitudes. But unfortunately the arena of conflict within which the hippies, willy-nilly, must try to survive is dominated not by the likes of Susan Sontag, but by the likes of Daniel Patrick Moynihan whose apparent compassion for the hippies will probably never be translated into action. For even as he writes (in the *American Scholar*, Autumn, 1967) that these youths are "trying to tell us something" and that they are one test of our "ability to survive," he rejects them firmly, and not a little ex cathedra, as a "truth gone astray." The hippie remains helpless and more affected by the repressive forces (who will probably quote Moynihan) than by his own creative capacity or the sympathizers who support him in the journals. As John Kifner reported in the *Times*, " 'This scene is not the same anymore,' said the tall, thin Negro called Gypsy. '. . . There are some very bad vibrations.' "

But it's just another murder. A hippie being killed is just like a housewife being killed or a career girl being killed or a hoodlum being killed. None of these people, notice, are persons; they're labels. Who cares who Groovy was; if you know he was a 'hippie,' then already you know more about him than he did about himself.

See, it's hard to explain to a lot of you what a hippie is because a lot of you really think a hippie IS something. You don't realize that the word is just a convenience picked up by the press to personify a social change thing beginning to happen to young people. (*Paul William, in an article entitled "Label Dies—But Not Philosophy,"* Open City, *Los Angeles, November 17-23, 1967.*)

Because the mass media have publicized the growth of a fairly well-articulated hippie culture, it now bears the status of a social form. Variously identified as "counter-culture," "hippiedom," "youth" or "underground," the phenomenon centers on a philosophy of the present and takes the personal and public forms appropriate to that philosophy. Its values constitute a heresy in a society that consecrates the values of competition, social manipulation and functionalism, a society that defines ethical quality by long-range and general consequences, and that honors only those attitudes and institutions that affirm the primacy of the future and large-scale over the local and immediately present. It is a heresy in a society that eschews the primary value of intimacy for the sake of impersonal service to large and enduring organizations, a society that is essentialist rather than existentialist, a society that prizes biography over interactive quality. It is a heresy in a country whose President could be praised for crying, "Ask not what your country can do for you, but what you can do for your country!" Most important, however, it is heresy in a society whose official values, principles of operation and officials themselves are threatened domestically and abroad.

For these reasons the hippie is available for persecution. When official authority is threatened, social and political deviants are readily conjured up as demons requiring collective exorcism and thus a reaffirmation of that authority. Where exorcism is the exclusive province of government, the government's power is reinforced by the adoption of a scapegoat. Deviant style and ideals make a group vulnerable to exploitation as a scapegoat, but it is official action which translates vulnerability into actionable heresy.

By contrast, recent political developments within black communities and the accommodations reached through bargaining with various official agencies have placed the blacks alongside the Viet Cong as an official enemy, but not as a scapegoat. As an enemy, the black is not a symbol but a source of society's troubles. It is a preferable position. The hippie's threat lies in the lure of his way of life rather than in his political potential. His vulnerability as well as his proven capacity to develop a real alternative life permits his selection as scapegoat. A threatened officialdom is all too likely to take the final step that "brings on the judge." At the same time, by defining its attack as moderate, it reaffirms its moral superiority in the very field of hate it cultivates.

We are speaking of that which claims the lives, totally or in part, of perhaps hundreds of thousands of people of all ages throughout the United States and elsewhere. The number is not inconsiderable.

The plausibility of the hippie culture and its charisma can be argued on several grounds. Their outlook derives from a profound mobilizing idea: Quality resides in the present. Therefore, one seeks the local in all its social detail—not indulgently and alone, but openly and creatively. Vulnerability and improvisation are principles of action, repudiating the "rational" hierarchy of plans and stages that defines, for the grounded culture, all events as incidents of passage and means to an indefinitely postponable end—as transition. The allocation of reality to the past and the future is rejected in favor of the present, and a present that is known and felt immediately, not judged by external standards. The long run is the result rather than the goal of the present. "Psychical distance," the orientation of the insulated tourist to whom the environment is something forever foreign or of the administrator for whom the world is an object of administration, is repudiated as a relational principle. It is replaced by a principal of absorption. In this, relationships are more like play, dance or jazz. Intimacy derives from absorption, from spontaneous involvement, to use Erving Goffman's phrase, rather than from frequent contact or attraction, as social psychologists have long argued.

This vision of social reality makes assumptions about human nature. It sees man as only a part of a present that depends on all its parts. To be a "part" is not to play a stereotyped role or to plan one's behavior prior to entering the scene. It is to be of a momentum. Collaboration, the overt manifestation of absorption, is critical to any social arrangement because the present, as experience, is essentially social. Love and charisma are the reflected properties of the plausible whole that results from mutual absorption. "To swing" or "to groove" is to be of the scene rather than simply at or in the scene. "Rapping," an improvised, expansive and collaborative conversational form, is an active embodiment of the more general ethos. Its craft is humor, devotion, trust, openness to events in the process of formation and the capacity to be relevant. Identity is neither strictly personal nor something to be maintained, but something always to be discovered. The individual body is the origin of sounds and motions, but behavior, ideas, images and reflective thought stem from interaction itself. Development is not of personalities but of situations that include many bodies but, in effect, one mind. Various activities, such as smoking marijuana, are disciplines that serve the function of bringing people together and making them deeply interesting to each other.

The development of an authenic "counterculture," or, better, "alternative culture," has some striking implications. For one, information and stress are processed through what amounts to a new conceptual system—a culture that replaces, in the committed, the intrapersonal structures that Western personality theories have assumed to account for intrapersonal order. For example, in 1966, young hippies often turned against their friends and their experience after a bad acid trip. But that was the year during which "the hippie thing" was merely one constructive expression of dissent. It was not, at that point, an alternative culture. As a result, the imagery cued in by the trauma was the imagery of the superego, the distant and punitive authority of the Western family and its macrocosmic social system. Guilt, self-hatred and the rejection of experience was the result. Many youngsters returned home filled with a humiliation that could be forgotten, or converted to a seedy and defensive hatred of the dangerously deviant. By 1968 the bad trip, while still an occasion for reconversion for some, had for others become something to be guarded against and coped with in a context of care and experienced guidance. The atmosphere of trust and new language of stress-inspired dependence rather than recoil as the initial stage of cure. One could "get high with a little help from my friends." Conscience was purged of "authority."

Although the ethos depends on personal contact, it is carried by underground media (hundreds of newspapers claiming hundreds of thousands of readers), rock music, and collective activities, artistic and political, which deliver and duplicate the message; and it is processed through a generational flow. It is no longer simply a constructive expression of dissent and thus attractive because it is a vital answer to a system that destroys vitality; it is culture, and the young are growing up under the wisdom of its older generations. The ethos is realized most fully in the small communes that dot the American urbscape and constitute an important counter-institution of the hippies.

This complex of population, culture, social form, and ideology is both a reinforcing environment for individuals and a context for the growth and elaboration of the complex itself. In it, life not only begins, it goes on; and, indeed, it must go on for those who are committed to it. Abbie Hoffman's *Revolution for the Hell of It* assumes the autonomy of this cultural frame of reference. It assumes that the individual has entered and has burned his bridges.

As the heresy takes an official definition and as the institutions of persecution form, a they-mentality emerges in the language which expresses the relationship between the oppressor and the oppressed. For the oppressed, it distinguished life from nonlife so that living can go on. The they-mentality of the oppressed temporarily relieves them of the struggle by acknowledging the threat, identifying its agent, and compressing both into a quasi-poetic image, a cliche that can accomodate absurdity. One young man said, while coming down from an amphetamine high: "I'm simply going to continue to do what I want until they stop me."

But persecution is also structured by the they-mentality of the persecutors. This mentality draws lines around its objects as it fits them conceptually for full-scale social action. The particular uses of the term "hippie" in the mass media—like "Jew," "communist," "Black Muslim" or "Black Panther"—cultivates not only disapproval and rejection but a climate of opinion capable of excluding hippies from the moral order altogether. This is one phase of a subtle process that begins by locating and isolating a group, tying it to the criminal, sinful or obscene, developing and displaying referential symbols at a high level of abstraction which depersonalize and objectify the group, defining the stigmata by which members are to be known and placing the symbols in the context of ideology and readiness for action.

At this point, the symbols come to define public issues and are, consequently, sources of strength. The maintenance of power—the next phase of the story—depends less on the instruction of reading and viewing publics than on the elaboration of the persecutory institutions which demonstrate and justify power. The relationship between institution and public ceases to be one of expression or extension (of a public to an institution) and becomes one of transaction or dominance (of a public with or by an institution). The total dynamic is similar to advertising or the growth of the military as domestic powers in America.

An explosion of hippie stories appeared in the mass media during the summer of 1967. Almost every large-circulation magazine featured articles on the hippie "fad" or "subculture." *Life's* "The Other Culture" set the tone. The theme was repeated in the *New York Times Magazine,* May 14, 1967, where Hunter Thompson wrote that "The 'Hashbury' (Haight-Asbury in San Francisco) is the new capital of what is rapidly becoming a drug culture." *Time's* "wholly new subculture" was "a cult whose mystique derives essentially from the influences of hallucinogenic drugs. By fall, while maintaining the emphasis on drugs as the cornerstone of the culture, the articles had shifted from the culturological to a "national character" approach, reminiscent of the World War II anti-Japanese propaganda, as personal traits were piled into the body of the symbol and objectification began. The hippies were "acid heads," "generally dirty," and "visible, audible and sometimes smellable young rebels."

As "hippie" and its associated terms ("long-haired," "bearded") accumulated pejorative connotation, they began to be useful concepts and were featured regularly in news headlines: for example, "Hippie Mother Held in Slaying of Son, 2" (*New York Times,* Nov. 22, 1967); "S Squad Hits Four Pads" (*San Francisco Chronicle,* July 27, 1967). The articles themselves solidified usage by dwelling on "hippie types," "wild drug parties" and "long-haired, bearded" youths (see, for example, *The New York Times* of February 13, 1968, September 16, 1968 and November 3, 1967).

This is a phenomenon that R. H. Turner and S. J. Surace described in 1956 in order to account for the role of media in the development of hostile consciousness toward Mexicans. The presentation of certain symbols can remove their referents from the constraints of the conventional moral order so that extralegal and extramoral action can be used against them. Political cartoonists have used the same device with less powerful results. To call Mexican-Americans "zootsuiters" in Los Angeles, in 1943, was to free hostility from the limits of the conventional, though fragile, antiracism required by liberal ideology. The result was a wave of brutal anti-Mexican assaults. Turner and Surace hypothesized that:

To the degree, then, to which any symbol evokes only one consistent set of connotations throughout the community, only one general course of action with respect to that object will be indicated, and the union of diverse members of the community into an acting crowd will be facilitated . . . or it will be an audience prepared to accept novel forms of official action.

First the symbol, then the accumulation of hostile connotations, and finally the action-issue: Such a sequence appears in the news coverage of hippies from the beginning of 1967 to the present. The amount of coverage has decreased in the past year, but this seems less a result of sympathy or sophistication and more one of certainty: The issue is decided and certain truths can be taken for granted. As this public consciousness finds official representation in the formation of a control conglomerate, it heralds the final and institutional stage in the growth of repressive force, persecution and terror.

The growth of this control conglomerate, the mark of any repressive system, depends on the development of new techniques and organizations. But its momentum requires an ideological head of steam. In the case of the hippie life, the ideological condemnation is based on several counts: that it is dangerous and irresponsible, subversive to authority, immoral and psychopathological.

Commenting on the relationship between beliefs and the development of the persecutory institutions for witch-control in the 16th century. Trevor-Roper, in an essay on "Witches and Witchcraft," states:

> In a climate of fear, it is easy to see how this process could happen: how individual deviations could be associated with a central pattern. We have seen it happen in our own time. The "McCarthyite" experience of the United States in the 1950s was exactly comparable: Social fear, the fear of an incompatible system of society, was given intellectual form as a heretical ideology and suspect individuals were persecuted by reference to that heresy.

The same fear finds its ideological expression against the hippies in the statement of Stanley F. Yolles, director of the National Institute of Mental Health, that "alienation," which he called a major underlying cause of drug abuse, "was wider, deeper and more diffuse now than it has been in any other period in American history." The rejection of dissent in the name of mental health rather than moral values or social or political interest is a modern characteristic. Yolles suggested that if urgent attention is not given the problem:

> there are serious dangers that large proportions of current and future generations will reach adulthood embittered towards the larger society, unequipped to take on parental, vocational and other citizen roles, and involved in some form of socially deviant behavior. . . .

Seymour L. Halleck, director of student psychiatry at the University of Wisconsin, also tied the heresy to various sources of sin: affluence, lack of contract with adults, and an excess of freedom. Henry Brill, director of Pilgrim State Hospital on Long Island and a consultant on drug use to federal and state agencies, is quoted in the *New York Times,* September 26, 1967:

> It is my opinion that the unrestricted use of marijuana type substances produces a significant amount of vagabondage, dependency and psychiatric disability.

Yolles, Halleck and Brill are probably fairly representative of psychiatric opinion. Psychiatry has long defined normality and health in terms of each other in a "scientific" avoidance of serious value questions. Psychiatrists agree in principle on several related points which could constitute a medical rational foundation for the persecution of hippies: They define the normal and healthy individual as patient and instrumental. He plans for the long range and pursues his goals temperately and economically. He is an individual with a need for privacy and his contacts are moderate and respectful. He is stable in style and identity, reasonably competitive and optimistic. Finally, he accepts reality and participates in the social forms which constitutes the givens of his life. Drug use, sexual pleasure, a repudiation of clear long-range goals, the insistence on intimacy and self-affirmation, distrust of official authority and radical dissent are all part of the abnormality that colors the hippies "alienated" or "disturbed" or "neurotic."

This ideology characterizes the heresy in technical terms. Mental illness is a scientific and medical problem, and isolation and treatment are recommended. Youth, alienation and drug use are the discrediting characteristics of those who are unqualified for due process, discussion or conflict. The genius of the ideology has been to separate the phenomenon under review from consideration of law and value. In this way the mutual hostilities that ordinarily divide the various agencies of control are bypassed and the issue endowed with ethical and political neutrality. Haurek and Clark, in their "Variants of Integration of Social Control Agencies," described two opposing orientations among social control agencies, the authoritarian-punitive (the police, the courts) and the humanitarian-welfare (private agencies, social workers), with the latter holding the former in low esteem. The hippies have brought them together.

The designation of the hippie impulse as heresy on the grounds of psychopathology not only bypasses traditional enmity among various agencies of social control, but its corollaries activate each agency. It is the eventual coordination of their efforts that constitutes the control conglomerate. We will briefly discuss several of these collaries before examining the impact of the conglomerate. Youth, danger and disobedience are the major themes.

Dominating the study of adolescence is a general theory which holds that the adolescent is a psychosexual type. Due to an awakening of the instincts after a time of relative quiescence, he is readily overwhelmed by them. Consequently, his behavior may be viewed as the working out of intense intrapsychic conflict—it is symptomatic or expressive rather than rational and realistic. He is idealistic, easily influenced and magical. The idealism is the expression of a threatened superego; the susceptibility to influence is an attempt to find support for an identity in danger of diffusion; the magic, reflected in adolescent romance and its rituals, is an attempt to get a grip on a reality that shifts and turns too much for comfort. By virtue of his entrance into the youth culture, he joins in the collective expression of emotional immaturity. At heart, he is the youth of Golding's *Lord of the Flies,* a fledgling adult living out a transitional status. His idealism may be sentimentally touching, but in truth he is morally irresponsible and dangerous.

As the idealism of the young is processed through the youth culture, it becomes radical ideology, and even radical practice. The attempts by parents and educators to break the youth culture by rejecting its symbols and limiting the opportunities for its expression (ranging from dress regulations in school to the censorship of youth music on the air) are justified as a response to the dangerous political implications of the ideology of developed and ingrown immaturity. That these same parents and educators find their efforts to conventionalize the youth culture (through moderate imitations of youthful dress and attempts to "get together with the kids") rejected encourages them further to see the young as hostile, unreasonable and intransigent. The danger of extremism (the New Left and the hippies) animates their criticism, and all intrusions on the normal are read as pointing in that direction. The ensuing conflict between the wise and the unreasonable is called (largely by the wise) the "generation gap."

From this it follows that radicalism is the peculiar propensity of the young and, as Christopher Jencks and David Riesman have pointed out in *The Academic Revolution,* of those who identify with the young. At its best it is not considered serious; at its worst it is the "counterculture." The myth of the generation gap, a myth that is all the more strongly held as we find less and less evidence for it, reinforces this view by holding that radicalism ends, or should end, when the gap is bridged—when the young grow older and wiser. While this lays the groundwork for tolerance or more likely, forbearance, it is a tolerance limited to youthful radicalism. It also lays the groundwork for a more thorough rejection of the radicalism of the not-so-young and the "extreme."

Thus, the theory of youth classifies radicalism as immature and, when cultivated, dangerous or pathological. Alienation is the explanation used to account for the extension of youthful idealism and paranoia into the realm of the politically and culturally adult. Its wrongness is temporary and trivial. If it persists, it becomes a structural defect requiring capture and treatment rather than due process and argument.

Once a life-style and its practices are declared illegal, its proponents are by definition criminal and subversive. On the one hand, the very dangers presupposed by the legal proscriptions immediately become clear and present. The illegal life-style becomes the living demonstration of its alleged dangers. The ragged vagabondage of the hippie is proof that drugs and promiscuity are alienating, and the attempts to sleep in parks, gather and roam are the new "violence" of which we have been reading. Crime certainly is crime, and the hippies commit crime by their very existence. The dangers are: (1) crime and the temptation to commit crime; (2) alienation and the temptation to drop out. The behaviors that, if unchecked, become imbedded in the personality of the suspectible are, among others, drug use (in particular marijuana), apparel deviance, dropping out (usually of school), sexual promiscuity, communal living, nudity, hair deviance, draft resistance, demonstrating against the feudal oligarchies in cities and colleges, gathering, roaming, doing strange art and being psychedelic. Many of these are defused by campaigns of definition; they become topical and in fashion. To wear bell-bottom pants, long side-burns, flowers on your car and beads, is, if done with taste and among the right people, stylish and eccentric rather than another step toward the brink or a way of lending aid and comfort to the enemy. The disintegration of a form by co-opting only its parts is a familiar phenomenon. It is tearing an argument apart by confronting each proposition as if it had no context, treating a message like an intellectual game.

Drugs, communalism, gathering, roaming, resisting and demonstrating, and certain styles of hair have not been defused. In fact, the drug scene is the site of the greatest concentration of justificatory energy and the banner under which the agencies of the control conglomerate unite. That their use is so widespread through the straight society indicates the role of drugs as temptation. That drugs have been pinned so clearly (despite the fact that many hippies are nonusers) and so gladly to the hippies, engages the institutions of persecution in the task of destroying the hippie thing.

The antimarijuana lobby has postulated a complex of violence, mental illness, genetic damage, apathy and alienation, all arising out of the ashes of smoked pot. The hypothesis justifies a set of laws and practices of great harshness and discrimination, and the President recently recommended that they be made even more so. The number of arrests for use, possession or sale of marijuana has soared in recent years: Between 1964 and 1966 yearly arrests doubled, from 7,000 to 15,000. The United States Narcotics Commissioner attributed the problem to "certain groups" which give marijuana to young people, and to "false information" about the danger of the drug.

Drug raids ordinarily net "hippie-type youths" although lately news reports refer to "youths from good homes." The use of spies on campuses, one of the bases for the original protest demonstrations at Nanterre prior to the May revolution, has become common, with all its socially destructive implications. Extensive spy operations were behind many of the police raids of college campuses during 1967, 1968 and 1969. Among those hit were Long Island University's Southampton College (twice), State University College at Oswego, New York, the Hun School of Princeton, Bard College, Syracuse University, Stony Brook College and Franconia College in New Hampshire; the list could go on.

It is the "certain groups" that the Commissioner spoke of who bear the brunt of the condemnation and the harshest penalties. The laws themselves are peculiar enough, having been strengthened largely since the hippies became visible, but they are enforced with obvious discrimination. Teenagers arrested in a "good residential section" of Naugatuck, Connecticut, were treated gently by the circuit court judge:

> I suspect that many of these youngsters should not have been arrested. . . . I'm not going to have these youngsters bouncing around with these charges hanging over them.

They were later released and the charges dismissed. In contrast, after a "mass arrest" in which 15 of the 25 arrested were charged with being in a place where they knew that others were smoking marijuana, Washington's Judge Halleck underscored his determination "to show these long-haired ne'er-do-wells that society will not tolerate their conduct" (*Washington Post,* May 21, 1967).

The incidents of arrest and the exuberance with which the laws are discriminatorily enforced are justified, although not explained, by the magnifying judgment of "danger." At a meeting of agents from 74 police departments in Connecticut and New York, Westchester County Sheriff John E. Hoy, "in a dramatic stage whisper," said, "It is a frightening situation, my friends . . . marijuana is creeping up on us."

One assistant district attorney stated that "the problem is staggering." A county executive agreed that "the use of marijuana is vicious," while a school superintendent argued that "marijuana is a plague-like disease, slowly but surely strangling our young people." Harvard freshmen were warned against the "social influences" that surround drugs and one chief of police attributed drug use and social deviance to permissiveness in a slogan which has since become more common (*St. Louis Post-Dispatch*, August 22, 1968).

Bennett Berger has pointed out that the issue of danger is an ideological ploy (*Denver Post*, April 19, 1968): "The real issue of marijuana is ethical and political, touching the 'core of cultural values.'" The *New York Times* of January 11, 1968, reports "Students and high school and college officials agree that 'drug use has increased sharply since the intensive coverage given to drugs and the hippies last summer by the mass media.'" It is also supported by other attempts to tie drugs to heresy: The *New York Times* of November 17, 1968, notes a Veterans Administration course for doctors on the hippies which ties hippies, drugs, and alienation together and suggests that the search for potential victims might begin in the seventh or eighth grades.

The dynamic relationship between ideology, organization and practice is revealed both in President Johnson's "Message on Crime to Insure Public Safety" (delivered to Congress on February 7, 1968) and in the gradual internationalizing of the persecution. The President recommended "strong new laws," an increase in the number of enforcement agents, and the centralization of federal enforcement machinery. At the same time, the United Nations Economic and Social Council considered a resolution asking that governments "deal effectively with publicity which advocates legalization or tolerance of the non-medical use of cannabis as a harmless drug." The resolution was consistent with President Johnson's plan to have the Federal Government of the United States "maintain world-wide operations . . . to suppress the trade in illicit narcotics and marijuana." The reasons for the international campaign were clarified by a World Health Organization panel's affirmation of its intent to prevent the use or sale of marijuana because it is "a drug of dependence, producing health and social problems." At the same time that scientific researchers at Harvard and Boston University were exonerating the substance, the penalties increased and the efforts to proscribe it reached international proportions. A number of countries, including Laos and Thailand, have barred hippies, and Mexico has made it difficult for those with long hair and serious eyes to cross its border.

The assumption that society is held together by formal law and authority implies in principle that the habit of obedience must be reinforced. The details of the hippie culture are, in relation to the grounded culture, disobedient. From that perspective, too, their values and ideology are also explicitly disobedient. The disobedience goes far beyond the forms of social organization and personal presentation to the conventional systems of healing, dietary practice and environmental use. There is virtually no system of authority that is not thrown into question. Methodologically, the situationalism of pornography, guerrilla theater and place conversion is not only profoundly subversive in itself; it turns the grounded culture around. By coating conventional behavioral norms with ridicule and obscenity, by tying radically different meanings to old routines, it challenges our sentiments. By raising the level of our self-consciousness it allows us to become moral in the areas we had allowed to degenerate into habit (apathy or gluttony). When the rock group, the Fugs, sings and dances "Group Grope" or any of their other songs devoted brutally to "love" and "taste," they pin our tender routines to a humiliating obscenity. We can no longer take our behavior and our intentions for granted. The confrontation enables us to disobey or to reconsider or to choose simply by forcing into consciousness the patterns of behavior and belief of which we have become victims. The confrontation is manly because it exposes both sides in an arena of conflict.

When questions are posed in ways that permit us to disengage ourselves from their meaning to our lives, we tolerate the questions as a moderate and decent form of dissent. And we congratulate ourselves for our tolerance. But when people refuse to know their place and, what is worse, our place, and they insist on themselves openly and demand that we re-decide our own lives, we are willing to have them knocked down. Consciousness permits disobedience. As a result, systems threatened from within often begin the work of reassertion by an attack on consciousness and chosen forms of life.

Youth, danger and disobedience define the heresy in terms that activate the host of agencies that, together, comprise the control conglomerate. Each agency, wrote Trevor-Roper, was ready: "The engine of persecution was set up before its future victims were legally subject to it." The conglomerate has its target. But it is a potential of the social system as much as it is an actor. Trevor-Roper comments further that:

> once we see the persecution of heresy as social intolerance, the intellectual difference between one heresy and another becomes less significant.

And the difference, one might add, between one persecutor and another becomes less significant. Someone, it does not matter who, tells Mr. Blue (in Tom Paxton's song): "What will it take to whip you into line?"

How have I ended here? The article is an analysis of the institutionalization of persecution and the relationship between the control conglomerate which is the advanced form of official persecution and the hippies as an alternative culture, the target of control. But an analysis must work within a vision if it is to move beyond analysis into action. The tragedy of America may be that it completed the technology of control before it developed compassion and tolerance. It never learned to tolerate history, and now it is finally capable of ending history by ending the change that political sociologists and undergroups understand. The struggle has always gone on in the mind. Only now, for this society, is it going on in the open among people. Only now is it beginning to shape lives rather than simply shaping individuals. Whether it is too late or not will be worked out in the attempts to transcend the one-dimensionality that Marcuse described. That the alternative culture is here seems difficult to doubt. Whether it becomes revolutionary fast enough to supersede an officialdom bent on its destruction may be an important part of the story of America.

As an excercise in over-estimation, this essay proposes a methodological tool for going from analysis to action in areas which are too easily absorbed by a larger picture but which are at the same time too critical to be viewed outside the context of political action.

The analysis suggests several conclusions:

☐ Control usually transcends itself both in its selection of targets and in its organization.
☐ At some point in its development, control is readily institutionalized and finally institutional. The control conglomerate represents a new stage in social organiza-

tion and is an authentic change-inducing force for social systems.

□ The hallmark of an advanced system of control (and the key to its beginning) is an ideology that unites otherwise highly differing agencies.

□ Persecution and terror go in our society. The hippies, as a genuine heresy, have engaged official opposition to a growing cultural-social-political tendency. The organization of control has both eliminated countervailing official forces and begun to place all deviance in the category of heresy. This pattern may soon become endemic to the society.

September 1969

FURTHER READING:

The Politics of Protest (The Report to the National Commission on the Causes and Prevention of Violence) by Jerome H. Skolnick (New York: Clarion, Simon and Schuster, 1969).

The Destruction of the European Jews by Raul Hilberg (Chicago: Quadrangle Books, 1961).

The Religions of the Oppressed by Vittorio Lanternari (New York: Alfred A. Knopf, 1963) deals with the emergence of political and cultural underlife.

Revolution for the Hell of It by Abbie Hoffman (New York: Dial Press, 1968).

Bomb Culture by Jeff Nuttall (London: MacGibbon and Kee Ltd., 1968) is an historical description of the emergence of the underground currents of the sixties.

PART II

The Generation Gap

JEROME H. SKOLNICK

The dramatic events of recent days and months—the riot in Chicago, the protests at Columbia, and so forth—are properly analyzable as both symptom and cause of a deeper and more profound revolution, a revolution in some people's conception of social reality. Let me illustrate the significance of a conceptual revolution by quoting from Thomas Kuhn's classic book, *The Structure of Scientific Revolution:*

> Examining the record of past research from the vantage of contemporary historiography, the historian of science may be tempted to exclaim that when paradigms change, the world itself changes with them. Led by a new paradigm, scientists adopt new interests and look in new places. Even more important, during revolutions scientists see new and different things when looking with familiar instruments in places they have looked before. . . . Insofar as their only recourse to [the] world is through what they see and do, we may want to say that after a

revolution scientists are responding to a different world.

Perhaps the most famous and most consequential illustration of a scientific revolution was the Copernican revolution. It affected not only the direction of scientific inquiry, but touched off a continuing conflict over the authoritativeness of religious dogma. Once it was understood that the earth revolves around the sun, the social institutions of the earth could never be the same.

In social life, as well as in the social sciences, what is truly revolutionary is a fresh paradigm of how social reality might be or ought to be. In fact, new forms of protest may be considered attempts to hammer home newly perceived conceptions of reality, conceptions which themselves have frequently been forged and sharpened through crises. Changes of a paradigmatic order are now taking place in conceptions of the administration of criminal justice, in the black communities over America and among America's youth. Let me illustrate what these paradigmatic revisions suggest with reference to student protest. Although it is not only students who protest against the war and are disenchanted with America, the new vision of the young has educated their elders. In the matter of protest, the students are the teachers and the teachers are the students.

During the 1930s and the 1940s, the effect of a widely revered president and an enemy who symbolized absolute evil was to affirm the United States as the ethical center of the universe for American liberals. Although the rest of the world might have been somewhat skeptical about this status, it appeared to fulfill earlier conceptions of the superiority and "manifest destiny" of the country. In the 1950s, domestic failings such as racial injustice and McCarthyism were overshadowed by the dismal realities of life behind the Iron Curtain, and especially Khrushchev's validation of the crimes of the Stalin era.

In the late 1950s, however, the image of the United

States began to tarnish. The U-2 incident, which exposed America and its President as being capable of provocative military acts and public deceit, in the supposed interests of national policy; the Bay of Pigs incident, which revealed full-blown the extensive power and corrupting potential of the CIA in international affairs; the assassination of the President, the assassination of the President's accused assassin on the TV screens of the nation; the Warren Commission, which failed to quash gnawing doubts; the Dominican intervention, which dramatized the history of United States support for anti-Communist regimes, no matter how reactionary and brutal; and finally, the escalation of the minor conflict in Vietnam into a large and exceedingly horrible war, each step accompanied by an official denial that the war was in fact expanding—these major incidents made possible a revolution of Copernican proportions in the position of the United States in the ethical universe.

From the shining center of this universe in the 1940s, the United States fell first to the status of an "ordinary" country in the 1950s, and then—as the war in Vietnam being increasingly brutal and destructive—the United States, to many of its own young, plunged into outer darkness. To some it became an ethical outlaw, to others a fallen angel, and—to a portion of the New Left in America—the devil incarnate.

Most informed studies suggest that student activists are *not* rebelling against the values of their parents, but instead are trying to implement these values through action. For example, Richard Flacks found that student-activist tendencies were especially related to parents' beliefs that intellectual and esthetic pursuits are more worthy than material success, and that the really important things in life are opportunities for free expression and humanitarian concern.

I believe that there are even subtler causes, difficult to measure. For example, the political consciousness of a human being born into a "liberal" household after the World War II was formed in the Eisenhower years. How many "liberal" fathers, at least in the privacy of their homes, were denouncing Joe McCarthy, bemoaning the fate of Adlai Stevenson in the electoral process, and railing against, or at least poking fun at, the stupidity and banality of constituted authority—in those years, the Eisenhower administration? In brief, then, I am suggesting that children of "liberal" parents did not have the experience during 1952-60 of the government as a positive and progressive force. Furthermore, their parents adopted a style of private attack and public prudence, of private animosity and public acceptance—a style vulnerable to the charge of hypocrisy.

In examining the issue of why student activists are the way they are, I cannot help but be influenced by the revolutionary transformation in perspective that has occurred in the sociology of crime and deviance. The new outlook of this sociology has sensitized us to understand that the structure of an inquiry implies a whole set of assumptions about what is "normal" or reprehensible. I think that this novel perspective probably was given its greatest impetus as a result of national Prohibition. Prior to that time, a criminologist typically studied criminals and what made them do the sorts of things they did. But Prohibition developed a new consciousness. The manufacture, sale, and drinking of alcoholic beverages was a crime, yet all sorts of otherwise "respectable" people were committing it. From this perspective, at least two major consequences flowed, which students of crime and deviance have been building upon ever since: that "criminals" are human beings responding to definitions of what is right and wrong as they learned them, not necessarily as they are given by higher authority; and that when you study people as "problems," you stigmatize them. In the case of Prohibition, it is surely arguable just who needed to be studied, the "criminals" who persisted in patronizing speakeasies, or the people who decided that drinking was criminal.

If we apply this perspective to the "new forms of protest," we observe that the very posing of the issue may bias the answer. For the issue as presented assumes that what is problematic is protest, when it might be just as reasonable to assume that what is problematic is the failure to protest; that more concern should be generated over political apathy, in light of contemporary political events, than over political activism.

From this perspective, it might be argued that the expeience of the United States as the center of the ethical universe, the experience of Hitler and World War II, has induced in the older generation not wisdom or insight, but rather an incapacity to assess the true character of the current world situation. Older generations not uncommonly romanticize the impressions and loyalties of their own youth. The Roosevelt years may have been years of "the politics of joy" when America was the center of the ethical universe. Today, such an expression sounds as willfully ignorant to many young people as the continued insistence of papal authorities that the earth was the center of the universe must have sounded to Copernicus and his followers.

The student generation is not a generation of "romantics," a charge often hurled at them. The older generation that waves the flag, that sees America as a country of manifest destiny saving the world for democracy—they are the romantics. The younger generation is by contrast a generation of realists who are not willing to kill and be killed unless the cause is unmistakably honorable. In this perspective, the issue today is not what is wrong with the younger generation in trying to overturn established institutions, but what is wrong with the older generations in trying to conduct business as usual.

When stability disruption becomes part of a larger strategy for achieving power, it becomes increasingly difficult for a social analyst to draw a line between crime and political activity. This is not to suggest that legal authorities cannot draw such a line. A young black man who set fire to a Vietnamese hut is lawfully considered to be serving his country. A young black man who sets fire to a downtown department store is engaged in an act of arson, or an act of revolutionary heroism, depending upon his view of constituted authority. The meaning of the concept of crime is under continuous revision and when that happens the related concepts, "political action" and "civil liberties," receive associated shock waves.

Revolutionary situations pose a terrible dilemma for a liberal social scientist or other professional when he finds himself in sympathy with the motives of the revolutionaries, deplores violent means, and at the same time recognizes that an emphasis upon order may impede necessary and desirable social change. The dilemma is particularly agonizing when he finds himself increasingly unable to distinguish between contemporary morality and immorality. Which is perferable, the violent revolutionary act or the severe social sanctions that slowly, sometimes negligently, impinge upon masses of human beings on the basis of their racial or ethnic characteristics?

In this perspective, what should be our response to the black struggle? Principally, it must be to recognize that the needs and concerns of black people in our society are different from those of the comfortably-situated white liberal. The black man living in the inner city is not so concerned with freedom of expression as an abstract ideal, or in drawing fine distinctions between expression and action. He has pressing and immediate concerns—housing, medical care, police brutality—that are not being attended to by established institutions in the social order.

American liberty now costs more than its former price, eternal vigilance. The price of liberty has been raised to include both social knowledge and social justice. This point is not merely rhetorical; it means that liberty depends upon the capacity to gain and use social knowledge to create just social conditions. It also means that the traditional role of the social scientist and other professionals must be expanded to encompass the achievement of social justice. For if we do not achieve social justice in America, and soon, we are not long for liberty.

November 1968

Rock, Recordings and Rebellion

IRVING LOUIS HOROWITZ

In the sociology of music, most analysis seems to start with the musician instead of his music. That is, standard stratification variables of class and racial backgrounds, urban life styles, regional and sectional characteristics and so forth are generally employed. Some very useful work has been done within these categories, but my own feeling is that to arrive at a somewhat deeper understanding of the sociology of music, we should begin with the musical product and end with the social sources and background of music. Aside from the priority of the art object over the art producer or art consumer, there is an additional strategic advantage: namely, establishing a bona fide among those who know the music you are talking about, even though they may know little or no sociology.

The gap between the esoteric knowledge held by musicians and the exoteric belief systems held by listeners is exceptionally wide. Unlike the fields of politics, psychology and economics in which everyone fancies himself an expert, professional distance between musician and listener is easily established. In music, the notational system by which the creative process is expressed is so removed from the knowledge of ordinary listeners that communication between artist and audience, at the verbal level at least, is difficult and sometimes quite impossible. My starting point, then, will be the product and the place where artist and audience interest meet most significantly—the market, the recording. The record is to the musician what the book is to the academic scholar. It is the recognition of his importance to a wider public. It is the focus of his musical energies, all directed toward making the recording different from all others, or at least different enough to be purchased. The musician measures success precisely in terms of the aesthetic worth of the product and the sales of that product to a non-musician audience, or at least an audience beyond his known circle of friends in the muscial world.

The recording represents the transformation of an ephemeral idea into a copyrighted product; a musical moment into a durable commodity. Jazz, and especially rock, are both essentially twentieth century aesthetic concepts, but they emerge coincidentally with a market system that defines worth in terms of salability—specifically, the sale of the recording. The jazz ambience has been less willing to accept this fact, and has therefore hesitated to fully exploit the medium through which the artist speaks to a wider audience. The rock subculture, being thoroughly convinced that the recording is an expression of worth, has been more innovative; the use of electric guitars, Moog synthesizers, the use of amplifiers as musical instruments, and so forth, are all clearly pegged to the product as record. Thus, what starts as an effort at bottling and selling the ephemeral idea, ends with the market product, the record, beginning to determine the musical structure, and the ephemeral idea itself.

The recording not only provides legitimacy to rock performers, by proving their worth in market terms, but also warrants their authenticity. Rock music listeners usually hear a group first on recordings; then, later on, they see the group in person. The recording provides the audience with an objective standard of measurement for determining whether the live performance is better than, the same as, or worse than the recorded performance. The live performance also enables the performing artist to advertise his new disc, or new album. Few performances fail to include an announcement to the effect that "the next number is from our new album on our very own label, and can be heard again if you like the live performance." In other words, the crucial item of exchange between artist and audience is clearly the recording, rather than, as it was 50 years ago, sheet music.

The recording is important to rock groups for other reasons as well. In their live performances, musicians are constantly involved in electronic processes. Though the music is reasonably, or as some may declare, unreasonably simplistic, the electronic apparatus they must learn to manipulate is quite complex. Because of this relative isomorphism between rock music and technology, the impulse to define success in terms of the recording is not simply or even primarily a desire for wide communication with an amorphous audience, not is it a pecuniary drive unique to musicians; rather, it stems from realization that the gap between the engineering of sound and the creation of music has narrowed to a remarkable degree. Thus, the legacy of dodecaphonic and electronic music has not been lost in classical experimentation, but has been absorbed, though largely unconsciously, in the rock tradition. The recording situation allows the musician maximum control in the manipulation of technology, and thus, in his artistic creation.

Finally, by starting with the recording, we can encompass the whole gamut of social actors in the music business: the recording company, the booking agents, the performing artists, the engineering and recording experts, publicists and propagandists and pushers of all sorts. For this reason, I shall simply examine a series of recordings that illustrate the theme of this paper: the relationship of modern jazz to hard rock. The selection of recordings will not be exhaustive or exclusive; but rather representative and illustrative of major trends and tendencies. But first, let me review the background of jazz and of rock, and the similarities and discontinuities between the two.

There is a parallel between the history of societies and the history of their arts. Just as there is a historical continuity in science, there is also a historical continuity in the scientific-technical aspect of the arts (it was not mere chance that perspective became consolidated during the Renaissance—Europe was discovering the third dimension in painting).

While the sociologist studies the social, historical, economic and cultural events which account for the development of an intellectual and artistic movement such as the Renaissance, the musician can translate the manifestations of that movement into specific expressions: Humanism gives birth to tonal language, and ecclesiastic modes which lack the lyricism of the new language are rejected. The counterpoint extends its methods toward new horizons which are a part of that expression. Another example might be provided by the translation of Enlightenment absolutism into music in the form of the homophony of the classical period. Or the ideas of freedom in the French Revolution which are echoed in the chromatics and the gradual development from sonata form to the cyclical form of the Romantic movement.

Jazz also underwent, in the course of 80 years, the

changes of a dynamic society, reflected in its schools and innovations. The jazz musician—black or white—gradually acquired a certain lucidity regarding the sound materials with which he was working. The mixture of rhythms and modes of African polyphony mingled with the tonal homophony of the European colonizers. The resulting synthesis was jazz, and the perception of musicians (who are always in the forefront of society regarding the apprehension of sounds materials) became wider. What makes such an analysis difficult is the fact that jazz never existed in pure form. (For example, Bix Beiderbecke "discovered" Debussy.) The important thing is that musicians such as Thelonious Monk, Charlie Parker and Dizzy Gillespie achieved results similar to those of Bartok and Stravinsky by way of instinct and the extension of tradition. Lennie Tristano and Ornette Coleman, on the other hand, opened the door to tonal dissolution. They were all the product of a complex period—from World War Two until the present.

But this tonal dissolution involved, in extramusical terms, the dissolution of the musical audience. The deeper the music, the further removed jazz became from the dance tradition. Into this void of a music without audience, and a form without content, the rock musician emerged. At first clumsily, almost foolishly in the form of sexual exhibitionism and musical inanities—such as in the performances of Elvis Presley and Jerry Lee Lewis. Indeed, the Sha-Na-Na now make a living parodying such "music of the fifties." Yet, even in its early days, rock provided direct percussive expression to dance needs, and reestablished communion between artist and audience without retreating to the absurd banalities of the fox trot, the Vienna waltz and the Virginia Reel.

The first stage in the development of rock was the sacrifice of musical complexity for the sake of capturing an audience; the second step was to solidify that audience by message music—by an appeal to the rising political consciousness of a generation no less than by an appeal to dance forms that were clearly generational in character. Only when both these stages were reached, did the third stage of musical innovation involving atonalities, electronics and art music became possible. It might well be that rock is doomed to replicate the cycle of jazz, with its attendant separation from the dance form and its ultimate loss of mass audience, but in the meantime a new art form has been born.

Although technical perfection for the most part remains an unfulfilled goal in rock music, there are notable successes. Among them are the rejection of complication for its own sake, the return to a more direct expression of emotions, and an attempt to move beyond a jazz scene thoroughly lacking in extramusical direction (with the possible exception of men like Archie Shepp and John Coltrane—although they have yet to generate a significant audience for their message) by introducing lyrics of political and personal significance.

More significantly, the history of every art form can be formulated as the following: Each new form of expression requires a new technology for its fulfillment. And here there is a complicated syndrome at work. For on the one hand, the young harbor a powerful resentment for a technological idiocy that has brought mankind to the brink of nuclear, bacteriological and chemical warfare. On the other hand, the musical requisites of rock involve a remarkably advanced form of technology, the implications of which are only now being drawn. In the larger societal situation, there is a demand on the part of many radical young people for simplicity, and a utopian longing for nature and mother earth, rather than society and grandfather pollution. But the young's rejection of these aspects of the larger society is radically different from their response to the new music. The rock scene is extraordinarily concerned with technological innovation.

A young sociologist, Paul M. Hirst, has recently taken note of this fact in an article entitled "The Economics of Rock" that appeared in *The Nation* in March 1970. His summary comment is quite appropriate to our discussion:

The contribution of modern technology is important. All phases of rock music have become increasingly tied to technology, from concert staging and recording techniques to record retailing and audience management. Musicians and their audiences regard better amplifiers, microphones, tape recorders, film techniques, record packaging, outdoor festivals and speaker systems as a natural and desirable part of their environment. They assume, with accustomed indifference, that the gadgets they've grown up with are to be used when needed, and simply ignored when irrelevant. Most young people including "dropouts" and "dissenters," are neither alienated, as some have argued, by such signs of the age as television, moon shots and atomic weapons, nor are they particularly impressed. They seem only "natural" to a generation which has always known them. While this attitude is now starting to be challenged by a growing concern for our environment, it is still too early to pronounce today's vanguard youth seriously hostile to modern gadgetry. Persuasive evidence that we are still far from a wholesale "back to nature" movement is the overwhelming popularity of rock and roll, and all the technology it encompasses.

The importance of this youth ambivalence to technology can hardly be overestimated. It points up their dialectical attitudes toward technology, not simply a foolish concern on the part of the young for a return to musical primitivism or sectional chauvinism.

The jazz musicians, especially the followers of Gillespie

and Monk, are most resistant to technological invention. Some musicians like Freddie Hubbard and Ornette Coleman have openly stated their opposition to electronic music. In fact, they tend to think that any device not to be found in a nineteenth century symphony orchestra is by definition not a musical instrument. However, it is not primarily at the technological level that objections are registered, but rather at the sociological level. The new electronic phase upsets the existing professional status arrangements. It introduces new personnel and makes new demands on established performers. Only the recent herculean efforts of Miles Davis, that ever-inventive figure, have moved beyond this technological Ludditism; and interestingly, as the composition of his new group shows, beyond racial exclusivism as well.

With respect to the tonal dissolution that jazz is said to have exhibited, my own feeling is that this is more myth than reality. The jazz musican has tended to use shifting tonal centers rather than to move toward the kind of tonal dissolution advocated by Berg or Schoenberg. In this connection, I would say that many rock musicians have done much the same kind of things as their jazz predecessors. They have not worried about formal invention as much as they should have. But this may be because musicians in active creation rarely concern themselves with their place in the history of modern popular music.

The problem here is not one of integrity but of musicality. The rock musician is concerned about the dance elements in his output—that is, the relationship between sound and movement. I have the distinct impression that the modern jazz musician has come to envision himself very much like a chamber ensemble. This is reflected in the behavior of the Modern Jazz Quartet and in the Charles Mingus quintet, which often make outrageous demands of silence on the audience. The jazz musician has come to expect a non-emotional response to emotion; which in some sense is precisely what the rock culture is in rebellion against. The jazz generation has become the older generation. It has done so inadvertently by absorbing the general culture (and the genteel values) of classical music, with its fixed separation of artist and audience.

Music expresses its times and its anxieties, but certain expressions of these anxieties are more effective and others less effective. The anomaly, the contradiction, of an all-black group like that run by Archie Schepp or John Handy is that they are listened to by a largely white audience. This certainly lends a note of doubt to the belief that theirs is an effective form of black protest. It more likely alleviates white guilt. In this sense, the rock scene, being generational rather then racial, suffers less from the kind of black-white contradiction that has plagued jazz from its inception. Unlike jazz, hard rock is basically a white music. A strong connection does exist between soul music and hard rock, but hard rock is a sound apart: white, youthful, disengaged, sexually blunt and for the most part ideologically closer to pantheism than to socialism. But even though rock music is a white music, it makes no affirmation of being white, nor does it even covertly affirm supremacist tendencies that were prevalent in previous white sounds from Paul Whiteman in the twenties to Elvis Presley in the fifties. The best rock musicians have been unabashed in their praise of the black traditions of their craft, and unashamed to express such continuities in musical terms. This makes it possible for rock to achieve an intellectual integrity, and perhaps ultimately a synthesis, that has always been one giant step beyond the nonideological and undisturbed jazz musician.

No more than a decade ago, recordings were being made for "square" audiences who loved the classics and hated jazz. It is a sign of new generational fissures that the jazz audience has moved over into the camp of the squares, seeking comfort and solace in its "art" music over and above "pop" music. The tradition of the new, it seems, must always be less than welcomed by participants and advocates of established cultural traditions. This only proves that staying young beyond one's chronology is a complex and often painful undertaking and that those who even make the attempt subject themselves to criticism if not downright ridicule. As Marty Balin and Paul Kanter of the Jefferson Airplane explain: "One generation got old / One generation got soul."

The following selection of rock albums is based on considerations of innovation and invention that hopefully reveal certain jazz qualities: high improvisation, solid arrangement, awareness of social roots and tradition, novel harmonies and rhythmic patterns and so forth. It may not be the best hard rock of the last few years but my own guess is that were such a list compiled, even the *cogniscenti* would agree that the following albums are outstanding. *Country Joe and the Fish! Electric Music for the Mind and Body* (Vanguard VRS09244). Like many groups, this one is uneven; but some of the cuts, like "Grace" and "Porpoise Mouth" are a remarkable cross between Ravel of the Bolero and Schifrin of the Jazz Mass. This group has come a long way from its original adolescent recordings. They retain a radicalism of extramusical purpose with a certain musical integrity which prevents them from becoming commercial in the bad sense. They have the old jazz concern for the negative consequences of being popular without point. And they act out that concern by wonderfully outrageous assaults on political moguls of Americana. Perhaps this group sounds fresh because they manage to be political without falling into pre-packaged ideological traps. This group has the unique ability to "secularize" rather than "sacralize" their sound and lyrics. Direct assault is made on all forms of mystification from astrology to drugs to political conformism. And by the careful avoidance of a simple-minded "heavy" sound, the lyrical aspects of their performances remain clear and uncluttered. Because of their premature radicalism, Country Joe and the Fish have not had the advantages of a big recording label, but rather have joined performers like Joan Baez and Pete Seeger on a label of distinction and taste. The young listeners have caught up to this group politically, and it has now become a question whether this group can meet the pace in creative musical terms.

Barry Goldberg: Two Jews Blues (Buddah Records BDS05029). Goldberg is a major figure from the musical underground, who never quite surfaced. His arrangements and work for the Mother Earth group make them rise beyond the pedestrian. In this particular album, he is free to experiment much more. He knows more about jazz and is better able to integrate the jazz tradition than nearly any other hard rock soloist (with the possible exception of John Kahn and Skip Prokop). The key cut here is "Spirit of Trane"—a veritable review of Coltrane and the movement from "waves of sound" hard jazz to a similar technique in hard rock. The title of the album is strange. This is not a religious mish-mash of talmudism; but the work of a hard-driving, alienated third generation Jewish soul who knows where it's at from the streetblack viewpoint. He is an important ideological variation on the theme of Jewish alienation from wealth and Jewish identification with suffering of the poor.

Rolling Stones: Beggars Banquet (London PL-539). This is probably the key album by the Stones—musically and politically. Everything works well, especially the lyrics by Mick Jagger and Keith Richard. I doubt that this group will ever replicate this achievement; certainly their more recent album performances are much weaker, more eclectic and confused in direction. It is hard to remain a "Street Fighting Man" when one is so rich and famous, or fall in love with a "Factory Girl" and make cheap Hollywood films. But this album is a direct musical assault on the conservatism of the Beatles, on the freakout and copout approach they have come to represent. The Stones remain a real group, while the Beatles have become a recording session. The quality of their performance reveals the difference between gigging musicians and studio musicians. Perhaps the jazz element is less profound than the traditional blues and folk elements in the Rolling Stones—but the roots are there; and this is a critical album to an understanding of what the hard rock revolution is about, and particularly how that musical revolution develops a political awareness.

The juxtaposition of the Stones with the Beatles is hardly accidental. They compare and contrast in critical respects. Both represented the two major British groups of most of the sixties; both developed international reputations by simulating an amalgam of American sounds from rock to jazz; and both produced individual performers of such noteworthiness as to transcend the customary group identities. But the gulfs and the gaps are even more noteworthy: The Stones represented radicalism in extramusical content, while the Beatles moved steadily toward a conservative ideology disguised by a continuing faith in the drug scene. The Stones record for London Records while the Beatles record for Electric Musical Industries, a subsidiary of the American-owned Capitol Record Company. Once the level of musical capabilities of the Stones became equal to that of the Beatles, the choice between them had to be made on extramusical grounds; and in effect the two groups came to symbolize the two main tendencies of the youth culture, at least within an Anglo-American context. Needless to say, beneath the manipulation of conflicting political symbols was the common drive for financial payoff. Radical lyrics and conservative lyrics, the political culture versus the drug culture, the folk style in contrast to the mystical style—all seemed to coalesce in these two groups and in this way their audiences were able to simulate as well as absorb the larger political and economic struggles going in the world.

The Beatles: Revolver (Capitol T-2576). The one really great album the Beatles made, *Revolver* holds together musically, without the freakish, bizarre qualities of the later albums, and the amateurish childishness of the early *werke*. It has things that hard rock needs more of: above all, a sense of humor and a range of emotions that fall somewhere between love and hate, rather than at the poles of expression and the precipice of emotion. From a jazz viewpoint, the best cut is "Tomorrow Never Knows"—although the entire album swings hard and clean. Also this recording is not overengineered, the way nearly every Beatle album has been since 1966.

The tragedy of the Beatles is commercialism with a vulgar vengeance. Business interests, pressures to make movies, discover new talent, all the mawkish things that musicians are better off leaving to their press agents have come, sadly, to be the hallmarks of the Beatles. The choice between a drug culture and a political culture has become increasingly urgent. And the Beatles have, in the main, opted in favor of heroin and against heroism.

The Beatles evolved from a hip youth cult, strongly identified with the aspirations of English working class sectors, to an international recording and commercial combine. In this not so mysterious magical tour, they created the basis of their disolution as a group. Individual performers became key, personal mawkish styles became exaggerated, and the process of arranging and orchestrating became completely detached from the group itself. The collapse of the Beatles was heralded by their final album, in which a Mantovani-like string ensemble was dubbed into simple musical lines to create a thoroughly outmoded sound typical of the late forties and antithetical to the needs of the late sixties. And this drift signified a decisive break with a major portion of the youth culture as it exists, and a mystification of life processes that took on all but the formal apparatus of conservative Christian symbolism of a rather unsophisticated variety. The urge for peace was drowned by demands for piety; and under the circumstances, perhaps the dissolution of the most famous of all rock groups was inevitable.

Big Brother and the Holding Company: Cheap Thrills* (Columbia KCS-9700). This album presents a major event —the best jazz singer since Ma Rainey and Bessie Smith in the white form of Janis Joplin. She is the real thing, and her album illustrates a key facet of the new music: the role of the collective. Although Joplin is clearly the most viable commercial variable here, the group rather than the individual vocalist is featured. When this essential aspect of the new sound was forgotten, and Joplin attained dubious star status, the group dissolved; and in part, so did Joplin. "Piece of My Heart" and "Ball and Chain" are brilliant. If only Aretha Franklin could have such a supporting group instead of the cheap Mantovani style backup that makes a mockery of her great talent. The musicianship here is first class, and Joplin and the group led by Albin, Getz, Gurley *et al*, are really fine.

Perhaps the most revealing description of Joplin is contained in what probably was meant to be high flattery—the program notes for her Canadian "Festival Express" per-

---

*This article was written prior to Janis Joplin's death in October 1970.

formances in the summer of 1970:

> Janis Joplin will probably explode some day. It's inevitable. She'll be up there on stage, shrieking and stomping and wailing over some old Big Mama Thornton blues tune, a white girl trying to sound so black her voice comes in all colors. And she'll laugh her hooker laugh as she smooths down her hooker clothes, as she calls them, that erzatz combination of feathers and frills, ankle bracelets and satins and ribbons. It'll happen at one of those incredible moments when Janis suddenly sounds like she's singing in the wrong decade. It'll happen with a bottle of Southern Comfort nearby, and some guy nearby, and...well, you know. It'll happen when she'll be trying for that one note that's never been had before. When she'll be singing harder, higher and faster than anybody has sung before. It'll happen because it will be the only thing left for her to do. It'll happen that way.

In point of fact, Joplin is expected to "explode," since of all white singers, her conception of music comes closest to the black sound, and her extramusical conception of black life is the suicidal model so typical of past blues singers. That black life has changed, and black aspirations have become antithetical to such neurotic models only makes Joplin an anomaly, albeit a tragic one, living out in vicarious white form the long since dead "black experience."

The Iron Butterfly: Ball (Atco SD-33-280). This is an unusual group. They incorporate many elements from Bach to Shankar. They have an eclecticism that derives from a strong identification with the drug scene and the return to astrology and related anti-scientific trends. They have not quite jelled yet; perhaps they never will. Or perhaps they are into a mystical bag that a supreme rationalist must question if not reject. But the mystique of the new music is an important cultural element linking drugs to resistance. They are on the right track in terms of innovative possibilities. Listen to "In the Crowds," "Fill With Fear" and "Belda Beat" for some idea of the Butterfly's direction. This is not a polished group, but it is a major attempt to make a new music that integrates vocals, orchestration and invention, with the entire drug culture.

Creedence Clearwater Revival: Bayou Country (Fantasy 8387). This is a powerful group, coming out of the Arkansas country and blues tradition. They exhibit the benefits of amplification and engineering effects, at the same time leaving intact certain driving musical values. This is hard rock of the sixties, like the Jazz Messengers represented hard jazz in the fifties: uncompromising devotion to the role of rhythm, with melody and harmonic invention playing a lesser role. And like the Blakey machine, CCR tends to get themselves into a groove from which there is no escape. This is a highly repetitious group. But can they ever swing and drive! They have the conviction and uncompromising drive that the jazz feeling is all about. "Proud Mary," "Bootleg" and "Keep on Chooglin" are major attempts to universalize what in the past were regionalisms. This is the best of healthy nonsubjective hard rock; just as the Butterfly are the best of the subjective wing—if one can speak in such a strange language about music. Creedence's move backward to a Bill Haley's Comets sound indicates a return to musical history to escape from the hard tasks of creativity, not an unusual decision in this competitive environment.

The Band: The Band (Capital STAO 132). If the appelation "Bob Dylan's favorite group" or the publicity in *Time* Magazine does not do this group in, then we will have a major musical event. That we probably have already. It remains to be seen whether or not The Band can sustain themselves; for here the ideology of country and western music is fused with the more radical ideology of hard rock. "The Night They Drove Old Dixie Down" is perhaps one of the best and yet one of the most disquieting events in the rock scene—since it represents a veritable *Gone With the Wind* in musical terms. Like the book and movie, "The Night They Drove Old Dixie Down" portrays both the antiwar sentiments and regional passions that inflamed the South in the aftermath of the war.

The frustration of white rebellious youth with the black scene is nowhere better evident than in the current celebration of The Band. Dylan's integration of the country and western sound has also taken on elements of working class populism (listen to the Johnny Cash *San Quentin* album), but they remain poorly articulated in extramusical terms. Musically, there is no doubt, however, that The Band has it. This is a polished professional group in every way, with a universally appealing good story on every record side, and with a moral lesson behind every story— also near and dear to the youth culture of today. All of this is attractively presented in precise musical terms. This album grows and does not wear on the listener, because sophistication rather than simplicity underlies every note and every line of music. I cannot imagine a firmer grip on musical invention that relies so heavily on the country and western blues traditions. This is a "rural" music, and its extraordinary reception indicates a strong longing for utopia and the future that is really the past. But the music is worth paying attention to—since the elements of creativity are all present. No musical revolution is ever a perfect expression of the age—but some groups well express the longings and confused hopes of revolutionists—and this The Band does remarkably well.

Carlos Santana: Santana (Columbia CS-0891). Santana offers a hard rock equivalent to the Afro-Cuban jazz rhythms which gripped many of the more popular varieties of music in the fifties. It has a similar percussive emphasis, with a variegated, inventive use of bongos and congas augmenting a rich texture of guitar and organ. Unfortunately, like the Afro-Cuban materials, there is a tendency toward musical repetition, and the broad use of rhythmic color at the expense of the more serious elements in contemporary rock. Further, while the instrumental portions tend to be innovative, the vocal arrangements tend to be cheap and banal. This group would do well to distinguish between good taste and ethnicity. But this is a problem common to hard rock in general.

To get a good idea of what this group can do at their best, two sides stand out: "Treat," which offers very good jazz blues variations; and "Soul Sacrifice" where the work on piano and organ by Carlos Santana and Gregg Rolie is superb. The work of Santana, like that of Don Ellis, can better be appreciated in live performance than on recordings. Their fantastic percussive inventions too often transcribe poorly on records. Here too, this can probably just as easily be said about most top quality rock groups. Just as in jazz, the element of spontaneity and creativity of live performance is a central factor in the rock scene; groups that fail to innovate soon fail to attract wide audience support. What is important in Santana specifically, is the satisfactory marriage of different musical traditions. Santana is the "hard" equivalent of such "soft" musicians as Jose Feliciano. He represents, in a strange way, the emerging musical consciousness of the Chicano. He is doing for the California Spanish-speaking peoples what Mongo Santamaria, Machito, Prado, Puente, and others did for the Puerto Rican young a decade earlier in the New York area. These marginal outsider groups employ the dominant cultural expression of the age—be it rock or jazz—to give form to their special impoverished status in American society.

Ten Wheel Drive: Construction #1 and *Brief Replies* (Polydor 24-4008; 24-4024). This musical organization is probably the closest thing in the rock field to a pure jazz concept. They feature a brilliant, rough-hewn blues singer, Genya Raven, who manages to combine superb musicianship with her vocal talents. Like Janis Joplin and Bonnie Bramlett, she has listened closely to the black singers from Ma Rainey and Bessie Smith, to Billie Holiday and Ella Fitzgerald. The tenor saxophone of Dave Leibman is strongly reminiscent of Coltrane, and when given the opportunity to so, as in "Interlude: A View of the Soft," he is uniformly clean in his execution. The hard driving ensemble work at times overwhelms individual solo efforts, but the unusual Basie-type arrangements are so distinctive as to offset the absence of conventional rock progressions; although they are subtly expressed through the guitar work of the group.

The superior work of the ten-tet is enhanced by the trumpet, trombone, tenor sax and other instruments not customarily found in the rock band. The problem is a lack of integration: the winds and woodwinds want to play jazz, while the guitars want to play rock; and even the tight arrangements do not so much solve as disguise the disparity in traditions. On both these albums, which both emanate from the same period—1969-1970—there is an awareness of a unique attempt at "jazz rock"—a driving rock base over which is added a jazz chording with a rock or blues solo. On such tunes as "Tightrope" Genya sounds like Janis; while on "Candy Man Blues" she can sound like Bessie Smith might have with amplification.

Ten Wheel Drive is everything that Blood, Sweat and Tears is not: spontaneous, driving and yet highly disciplined. The group writes its own materials; and the work of Aram Schefrin and Mike Zager (two of the ten wheels) is very consciously attempting to bridge the jazz and rock traditions in a meaningful way. Even if all the pitfalls have not been cleared, the attempt is remarkably sound, and far beyond the usual cliche-ridden efforts to introduce simple blues phrasing into rock presentations. The lyrics also provide some good and tough East Coast elements; and these can be heard to advantage in "I Am A Want Ad" and "Home in Central Park." Like the West Coast counterparts, this group is archetypical of much that is happening, rather than a special musical force unto itself. If the East Coast sound is hard, intellectual and rationalistic, it still lacks one major ingredient of West Coast rock: a specified anger with direction.

Sly and the Family Stone: Stand! (Epic BN-26456). This is an exciting musical unit; one of the few interracial groups around, it manages to get beyond some stagemanaged rent-a-nigger or rent-a-whitey type of sound meant to appease naive liberal audiences. Musically, this is a hard swinging unit, strong on the blues tradition, and perhaps at times better in extramusical sentiment than in musical performance. Yet, this group has a tremendous driving quality, with a rich musical liturgy. Frankly, their less ideological materials are the most musically engaging, such as: "Sing a Simple Song," "Sex Machine," "You Can Make it if You Try." What a weird anomaly this group is: raising the banner of black and white forever, while everyone is running about taking up black separatism and cultural nationalism. Perhaps this is what makes the group so well-liked. They appeal to the middle class and essentially liberal youth-musical constituency who comprise a large part of the rock audience. However, their musical integrity would make them worth hearing whatever the peculiarity of their ideological or racial constellation. And who knows but that the slogan next year won't be togetherness instead of separateness. We old liberals clearly need such an option, and Sly and the Family Stone provide same.

The Grateful Dead: Workingman's Dead (Warner Bros. 1869). The Grateful Dead are perhaps more linked with the fate and fortune of California-base rock and roll than any other group. In that sense, their movement from funky Memphis-styled rock and roll, to an abstract expressionist "acid rock" phase, through a country-blues style is indicative of the toughening up of the rock sound generally, and the growing disenchantment of American youth with a purely nonpolitical and drug-oriented subculture. The *Workingmen's Dead* album, which, although not as "heady" in its solos as the earlier *Live Dead* album, has a sense of returning to the folk and blues traditions charted by The Band but with a firmer extramusical content. Many of the problems earlier encountered by the Grateful Dead: repetition in solo lines, lack of rythmic and melodic definition, absence of a clear extramusical statement in the lyrics, have been satisfactorily resolved in the newer Dead recordings. And if any group has demonstrated a selfless dedication to free concerts, free drugs, and free love, it has been the Dead - for ironically, although they lack the technical proficiency of the Jefferson Airplane, they seem to capture in their music the very probings, albeit partially understood, that characterize the most civilized city in America, which must yet remain ever part of the most uncivilized country in the industrial world.

Jefferson Airplane: Volunteers (RCA Victor LSP-4238). This is one of the most exciting and innovative recordings made by an American group. Grace Slick is a marvelous singer, and for this album, the regular members of the Airplane have been augmented by such superb performers as Steven Stills of Crosby, Stills and Nash and Jerry Garcia of The Grateful Dead. This group gets better with every album, and politically more serious. From "We Can Be Together" to "Volunteers (Got a Revolution)" this is powerful statement of radical youth. As a literary sentiment, the group might sound contrived, but not as a musical expression. They exhibit a sectional West Coast element—West Coast radicalism—fuzzy and even bizarre ("Up Against the Wall Motherfucker"), but nonetheless, generous and non-sectarian. Anyone can join the movement led by the Airplane. The West Coast with its culture of civility is remarkably receptive; and the militance ultimately becomes a part of humanism. But this album cannot and should not be reduced to ideological content; its musical essence is paramount. In so many ways, this recording summarizes the best of the hard rock scene—the professionalism of The Band, the drive of Creedence Clearwater Revival, the radicalism of the Rolling Stones, the racial egalitarianism of Sly, and so forth.

To understand the Airplane is to appreciate what the culmination of the moralizing sixties offered. That this moral energy may blow up into a paroxym of money-grubbing was made clear at the strange final "concert" turned mass-movement of the Rolling Stones on their recent United States tour. The group of Hell's Angels they hired "to protect them from the audience" beat to death a listener while the Stones were playing "Sympathy for the Devil" and while a member of the Jefferson Airplane was doing his best to save the victim's life. Theatricality has turned bitter and acrimonious in the seventies. The hard rockers, like the hard boppers before them, are not sure of their audience, either its size or substance. There are difficult years ahead, and maybe the music I have just been speaking of will appear obsolete and absurdly out of tune in the upcoming period, as jazz now seems to so many members of the present anti-American generation.

Clearly, any devotee of the rock music scene has his own favorites. The jazz aspects of Mike Bloomfield and Al Kooper, the endless inventiveness and seriousness of Eric Clapton, the Jelly Roll Morton piano playing of Leon

Russell, the remarkable early efforts of Canned Heat, or the "blue-eyed soul" of Delaney and Bonnie—all of these can and do have their partisans, and each can be said to reveal definite jazz sources for inspiration. But the individual performer or performance is secondary. The hard rock scene at its best is a musical trip that seeks to get beyond an ego trip. It is not a study in priestly "influences" (one of the most decadent and wasteful forms of energy among followers of jazz—and sometimes the musicians themselves—was to track down a musical ancestry with relentless energy, as if the absence of lineage was the same as the absence of legitimacy) but a vast movement toward the redefinition of American culture. And the redefinition is a task uniquely performed by the young, since it is they alone who combine invention and exaggeration, reason and motion, word and sound, music and politics.

Hard rock may be done in by popularity, commercialism and festivals. More likely it will collapse from internal ailments: becoming too artsy-craftsy or removed from the dance form that gave rise to jazz and rock alike, and thus distancing itself from the folk sources of its original inspiration. But in the meantime, this is the most significant music having a mass social base yet to appear in American society.

September 1970

Oversupply of the Young

HUGH FOLK

In recent years, the coming of spring to New York City has brought with it a now-familiar political drama involving the Neighborhood Youth Corps. The scenario is almost invariably the same. At some point, usually in April, the mayor announces that due to the stinginess of the federal authorities, the City will only - be able to afford, say, 43,000 young people on the Youth Corps rolls for the coming summer. Since this represents a cutback of perhaps 10,000 jobs, the guardians of the interests of New York City youth, among whom the staff of the Youth Corps figure very prominently, give vent to strong, well-publicized cries of protest and indignation, often mixed with dire predictions of rising political temperatures in the ghettos. These cries, contrapuntally answered by the administration's protests of helplessness, continue to be heard right up to the end of the school year. Then, as all parties knew would happen from the outset, the mayor lets it be known that he has somehow found the necessary funds

161

and the program can go forward much as it has in summers past.

The drama has much in common with the springtime discussions of middle-class Americans as they ponder their vacation plans, especially perhaps in the extent to which the provision of something useful or fun for the kids (such as camp) is thought of as an important condition of the parents' enjoyment of *their* summer. In the cities, however, the problem is considerably more intense. For underlying it is the widespread feeling that idle adolescents, if not given anything more constructive to do, will surely put their heads and hands to mayhem and riot; and this would spoil everyone's summer, no matter how far from the inner city they may contrive to be at the time.

Much less widespread is the realization that, at least in the cities and certainly for black and Puerto Rican youths, the only possible employer of these idle hands is the government. Still, there has been a certain amount of discussion about the employment problems of late teen-agers, and many people seem to be aware that for this age group getting a job in the private sector has become especially difficult, even in these times of prosperity. In what follows I want to look more closely at that and a few other assumptions about the nature of youth employment. If we can be a bit more precise about the problem, then perhaps our efforts to do something about it, such as they are, can be better planned. As will be seen, my analysis is concerned with unemployment among all young people enrolled in the labor market, not just the youth of the ghettos, and with youth employment as a year-round phenomenon, not just its summer crisis.

High youth unemployment in prosperous years has usually been viewed as a result of legal restrictions on the employment of young people, legal minimum wages, layoffs resulting from low seniority, discrimination on the part of employers and the floundering of young job seekers as they find places in a competitive labor market by a process of trial and error. More generally (and more dangerously), youths are often said to be the especial victims of what is known as "structural unemployment." This means that there is a growing mismatch between the nature of the youth labor pool and the needs of ever-increasing numbers of employers. It means, for example, that while there is a growing demand for highly trained workers, the average quality of the out-of-school youth labor force is probably falling, since many of the most able young people are continuing their schooling. Or it means, to take another example, that the rapid growth of the youth labor pool is experiencing increasing competition from such part-time workers as middle-aged women and older men. My analysis reaches findings that are in rather sharp contrast to much of the folklore of youth unemployment, although it does confirm much of the previous work of professional economists.

First of all, it is noteworthy that the high rate of unemployment among American young people is unique among industrialized countries, which suggest that we must look to the characteristics of the American labor market and American youth rather than to the fact of industrialization itself. In America, then, the normal pattern is for a young person to enter and leave the labor force several times before he permanently ceases his schooling. Not all of these entrances and exits show up on the unemployment indices, but they make a significant contribution. Another significant factor is that, unlike most groups in the labor pool, youth employment (and therefore unemployment) is highly seasonal in nature, owing to the school calendar. Unemployment usually reaches its peak in June and then declines, until by August it has reached a rate that is about the same as that during the school year.

For those who leave school permanently, whether through graduation or dropping out, the seasonal nature of the youth labor force adds a special complication to their efforts to find good work. In June the committed workers, those who want "good" jobs for keeps, must compete with those in their age group who are only looking for summer work. But the latter very often lie about their intentions to prospective employers, and as a result many employers are reluctant to hire the committed job hunters because of their past experiences with summer workers who had claimed to be seeking permanent jobs, and then quit.

By and large, however, the speed with which a school leaver finds employment depends on the state of the labor market, the thoroughness of his search, the available vacancies and the preferences of employers. In an ideal economy, there would be one suitable vacancy for each unemployed worker, but in the real world the search for a job is accompanied by a process of mutual accommodation by which employers gradually relax their requirements or increase the attraction of their job offers as vacancies persist, while job seekers scale down what they want from a job as unemployment persists.

Those who cannot find jobs regardless of the amount of search and accomodating they do are sometimes referred to as the "structurally unemployed." If, however, what one means by this is that the job hunter spends more than six months looking or waiting for employment, then one must conclude that very few younger workers can be considered structurally unemployed. It is true that between 1957 and 1963 large numbers of youth were unemployed for relatively long periods of time, but this cannot be attributed to structural factors such as a mismatch between vacancies and job seekers. Rather, it was due to the two recessions that occurred during this period. The fact is that most young workers do eventually find jobs. Even in 1963, a survey showed that among school leavers, nearly all the men found work and, of these, seven-tenths of the high-school dropouts, three-fourths of the high-school graduates, and seven-eighths of the college dropouts were employed within less than five weeks.

But eventual employment does not mean that the young worker thereby ceases to figure among the ranks of the unemployed of his age group. For the average youth enters the labor market initially as a part-time or summer worker. Typically, the jobs available to him are in nonunion firms or small companies, or he will work as a sales clerk in variety or food stores—anywhere at all in positions below the lowest rungs of occupational or career ladders. What this often means, for the committed worker at least, is that he must go through a period of floundering around while searching for the job that seems right for him and that shows some opportunity for advancement. In the process, he must change jobs fairly frequently and this will show up, though slightly, on the unemployment charts. The transition is neither smooth nor easy, and for most youths, high-school graduates or not, it does not occur until they are in their late teens or early twenties. "Good" jobs are commonly thought to be scarce, and job information is also scarce. Everyone seems to believe that "contacts" are very important here, and at least with respect to apprenticeship and other union-controlled work, the usefulness of family connections is amply documented. But the point is that even after the connection has been made and the job taken, many young workers quit. After all, one can really know what a job is like only after working at it. Moreover, this job changing gives free rein to a kind of opportunistic mendacity by which one can exaggerate one's past work experience and thereby get a job for which one might lack the formal qualifications.

The amount of unemployment that results from this sort

of shopping around is, however, very small. The principal problem in youth unemployment is that of finding the first job. But the fact that nearly all young job seekers finally do find work suggests that it is not their own characteristics, or "unemployability," that matters, but the attitudes of employers.

Employers discriminate against youth for several reasons. They may prefer not to hire them because of their age, education, arrest records, draft status, sex or race. And these standards may be rational in that they are based on experience, or irrational in that they result from mere prejudice. For instance, an employer may have to pay higher insurance or bonding rates if he employs ex-convicts, or he may have to face the obligation of rehiring a drafted worker after he completes his service. Discrimination for these reasons may be deplorable, but is certainly rational.

Employers may also discriminate against youthful applicants because they have inadequate experience. The good jobs in most firms are unavailable to young people in any case, because most employers promote from within. But even entry jobs often have a previous-experience requirement. Employers hope by this means to use other employers as screening devices. Another screening device used by employers is, of course, education. A large aircraft firm, for example, requires even its sweepers to be high-school graduates. This is an obvious absurdity, but such conditions abound, especially in governmental agencies and educational institutions.

The reasons that they do abound have a good deal to do with the size of the youth labor pool. Since the number of jobs to which this pool is restricted has grown more slowly than the number of job seekers, unemployment remains high while employers take advantage of the relative excess to make increasing demands on their job applicants. If, however, there were a shortage of workers for whom the discriminated-against youth were close substitutes, then we would see some diminution of this employer selectivity. Such a pattern of adjustment has indeed occured in the last few years. The unemployment rate of men 20-24 years old has dropped during this period, and the drop has been followed by slight decreases in the unemployment rates of younger workers. Even so, the unemployment rates of the least preferred groups, such as the younger non-whites, and especially girls, have remained very high. Even if, as economists assert, the mills of labor substitution grind exceedingly fine, they also grind slowly (as might be expected from the metaphor).

The excess supply of young workers permits employers considerable freedom to be discriminatory in their hiring policies, but it does not, oddly enough, permit the same freedom with respect to their wage policies. In theory, wages should fall under such conditions, but in fact they haven't done so. The reasons are not hard to find. Some employers have job-evaluation systems that set job rates without regard to the state of the labor market; others are bound into a negotiated wage pattern that makes entry rates unresponsive to the labor market. Most obviously, of course, there is the legal minimum wage. All of this results in entry wages that are far above the minimum necessary to attract suitable workers, but that is a far different thing from alleging, as some have done, that minimum wages, whether legal or customary, are a cause of unemployment. I can find no evidence for this bit of folklore.

Another type of legislation often held responsible for youth unemployment are the various laws protecting young people from supposedly hazardous work. While state laws differ, the general standard is that all wage employment is barred to those under 14, all employment during school hours is banned to those under 16, and certain so-called dangerous jobs are proscribed for anyone under 18. These restrictions do in fact limit the employment opportunities for many youths, and some employers prefer to avoid even the possibility of problems by hiring no one at all under 18. (This solicitude of the state for the safety of 17-year-olds contrasts strikingly with its willingness to let them drive automobiles or join the armed forces, since neither Vietnam nor the highways have been particularly safe places in recent years.)

I have been sketching here some of the most salient characteristics of the labor market for youth, but I have barely touched upon one of the most important aspects of that market, the differences in the careers of dropouts and graduates. The first point is, obviously, that dropouts have a higher rate of participation in the labor force than graduates. Even so, there is some movement into and out of the labor force by dropouts, but most of this movement appears to be voluntary. In September 1966, relatively few nonenrolled male dropouts reported that they were not in the labor force because the believe it would be impossible for them to find work.

One of the major problems of the school dropout is that he becomes committed to the labor force before he is eligible for most career jobs. In short, he must compete with students (who are often better qualified in the eyes of employers) for youth jobs, and he must grow older before he becomes eligible for career jobs. Even then, of course, he is relatively disadvantaged. Nearly all dropouts eventually become employed, however, and this is a point worth emphasizing, because it is one of the most persistent myths of our time that the unemployed dropout inevitably becomes the unemployed adult. This is not the case. For both graduate and dropout alike the unemployment rate decreases with increasing age, although at ages 20 and 21 the graduates show a 4.1 percent rate of unemployment as against a 7.5 percent rate for dropouts. Between the ages of 16 and 19, however, the two groups have very nearly the same rates of unemployment, which suggests that the importance of finishing high school has been somewhat exaggerated, at least for that period in one's life.

The high level of youth unemployment in post-recession 1966 was largely the result of youth's gradual and uncertain pattern of commitment to the labor market. Much of this coming and going grows out of extended duration of schooling. This is shown clearly in the figures for January and June, 1966. In January, the unemployment rate of youths 14 to 19 years was 11.8 percent, but only 3.0 percent of the youth labor force was unemployed because of losing jobs, and an additional 1.8 percent was unemployed because of leaving jobs voluntarily. Reentry to the labor force was the occasion for unemployment of 2.4 percent of the labor force, and new entrance was the occasion for 4.5 percent. Thus three-fifths of youth unemployment arose from entry and reentry in January 1966. The labor-force participation rate increased according to the regular seasonal pattern from 31.0 percent in January to 47.8 percent in June, and the unemployment rate consequently rose to 18.5 percent. More than one-half of this unemployment was attributable to new entry and about seven-eighths of unemployment in June arose from entry to reentry. Very similar results were observed for a few months in 1964 and 1965.

The role of inexperience or new entry into the labor force is shown quite clearly in the much lower unemployment rates of the experienced teen-age workers in 1966. For experienced boys 16 to 19 years old, the rate was 7.4 percent, contrasted to a total youth rate of 11.7 percent. The ratio of the unemployment rate for experienced workers to the total rates for the various age-sex groups shows how important new entry and reentry are for teen-agers in contrast to most of these other groups. Almost one-half of the unemployment of youth in 1966 was experienced by job seekers who had never before held a job and as shown above, reentry accounts for much of the unemployment of experienced youth.

One must also remember that even experienced youths are concentrated in those occupations that characteristically have high unemployment rates, such as laborers, service workers and operatives. Even within these occupation groups, however, youth unemployment rates are higher than for older groups. For instance, in 1966 the unemployment rate for "experienced" male laborers 16 to 19 was 9.8 percent compared to 7.3 percent for all ages, and for "experienced" young professional and technical workers it was 3.9 percent compared to 1.0 percent for all ages. Much of this higher occupational unemployment is attributable to reentry by youth.

If the new entrants and reentrants are excluded from the labor force and unemployment, the unemployment rate of the "permanent" youth labor force in 1966 would range between about 5 percent in January and 2.5 percent in June. These are not "high" rates of unemployment.

The unemployment that new entrants and reentrants experience is predominantly frictional, in that it does not result from a permanent or persistent mismatch of characteristics between jobs and job seekers, as it is necessary for "structural unemployment" by almost any of the currently used definitions. For most school leavers, the duration of the job search is only a few weeks. When the seasonal unemployment resulting from reentry and the frictional unemployment resulting from labor force turnover during the school year is added in, the result is a very high level of frictional unemployment.

It is hard to see how very many of the unemployed youth can be considered "structurally unemployed" because there are relatively few long-term unemployed and very few "discouraged youth" who are not also enrolled in school.

The problem of youth unemployment may also be treated in terms of demand and supply. The demand for labor as a whole increased over the last few years and the demand for youth labor increased even faster, because youth employment increased more than total employment in the period. In nearly all occupational and industry groups for which there are data available, the proportion of the total employment made up of youth increased. This suggests that there were no rigid and impenetrable barriers preventing the substitution of youth for older workers. Increased youth percentages were most noticeable in retail trade, private households, and laborers' occupations.

Youth, however, tend to be concentrated in the less rapidly growing occupations. As a result, even though their percentage of total employment in each group increased, the resulting increase in youth employment (or demand) was not as fast as the growth of the youth labor force. It does not appear possible to place all of the blame for this on the inadequate number of jobs. In view of the enormous growth of the youth labor force and its rather specialized qualifications in terms of available hours of work, mobility and experience, it is hardly surprising that the demand increase was insufficient. Moreover, it must be noted that there is no evidence that youth were squeezed out of their traditional jobs. Quite the contrary, they apparently took over jobs that had not previously been open to them.

One must conclude, then, that although the demand for youth labor has not expanded as rapidly as would have been necessary to prevent youth unemployment from rising, the increase in youth employment has been extraordinarily rapid, despite the exceptionally rapid growth of the youth labor force after 1962. Finally, the pattern of increased occupational and industrial penetration by youth does not reveal any sectors of particular difficulty for young workers. This tends to refute the assertions of increased "structural unemployment" arising out of differential growth of demand among industries and occupation. Given the fact that youth are concentrated in slowly growing or shrinking occupations and industries, it is still doubtful that this would have led to rising unemployment without the enormous influx of youth into the labor force.

The principal cause of rising youth unemployment during the 1960s has been the increase in labor supply. The larger groups of young job seekers crowding into the depressed labor market in the late 1950s competed for a smaller number of jobs. Unemployment rose rapidly, and the proportion of long-term unemployment also increased. The abortive recovery from the 1958 recession had little effect on the youth unemployment rate and the 1961 recession raised rates even more. The even larger labor-force increments of 1962 and after made the problem still worse. Under these supply impacts, youth employment expanded rapidly in the 1960s, but youth unemployment rates stayed at depression levels.

The problem was complicated by the fact that most of the growth in the labor force occurred in part-time workers. The increases in unemployment during the period 1957 to 1964 were about the same for the part-time and full-time labor forces. These changes were the result primarily of growing school enrollment.

During the post-World War II period the seasonal increase in the labor force from January to June has grown, once again reflecting growing school enrollment. The seasonal increase did not exceed 50 percent before 1955 and did not fall below 50 percent thereafter. There was no trend in the seasonal increase of youth employment, rather it reached a peak in 1961 and thereafter decreased.

But in the middle 1960s, increase in youth unemployment was still quite high.

Increased seasonality of the labor force certainly accounts for some of the growth in youth unemployment in recent years. Seasonality and part-time job seeking together impose significant constraints on the availability of young workers. In effect, the job market must provide one kind of job during the school year and another in the summer.

Another result of increasing school enrollment is higher labor-force turnover, with larger proportions of workers moving back and forth between "not in labor force" and "labor-force" statuses. Because of this movement, unemployment associated with job search after reentry has probably increased, although the amount of this increase has not yet been measured.

The total result of these changes has been an increase in frictional unemployment associated with job changing and labor-force mobility. The proportion of short-term unemployment as a percentage of total youth unemployment has grown during the period when the youth unemployment rate was rising relative to the unemployment rates of other groups. This is conclusive evidence that the mismatch between jobs and workers has not worsened. If, as is the case, the structure of unemployment among youth has changed, with increasing proportions being composed of the younger, the nonwhite and the female youth, this is not evidence of an increase in structural unemployment by any of the usual definitions. Rather, the changing structure of youth unemployment, and the changing rates of the various groups of youth, can be explained quite directly as a result of the "glut" of younger workers and of employer selectivity (or discrimination) among job seekers. Consequently, the proportions of jobs going to youth do not equal the proportions that the groups make up of the total youth labor force. The jobs that are available are disproportionately filled by preferred groups of younger workers.

This article is analytical in intent but it has obvious implications for policy. If the analysis is correct, no single explanation of high or of rising youth unemployment is sufficient to explain the growth of youth unemployment in recent years. Some of the popular explanations, such as the slow growth of teen-age intensive industries and occupations, increasing structural unemployment, and effects of the minimum wage do not appear to be supported by the data. The two important causes of high and rising youth unemployment seem to be, first, the increasing frictional unemployment that is the result of the labor-force behavior of enrolled youth and, second, employer discrimination. Although it was not possible to establish the magnitudes of these causes, they do seem to be consistent with the unemployment rates that have been observed in recent years. The increased frictional unemployment of youth is also a direct result of the rapid increases in the youth labor force. The glut of youth has increased unemployment rates because it is a glut of students who show high labor-force turnover and, consequently, high frictional unemployment. The increase in the youth labor force has meant that at any point of time there are more youth competing for a given number of youth jobs. As a result, employers discriminate within the youth group and only gradually substitute youth for older workers. The process does not work rapidly enough to prevent the unemployment rates of the least preferred young workers from rising relative to the unemployment rates of more preferred groups of youth.

According to the Bureau of Labor Statistics the rate of growth of the youth labor force is forecast as decreasing in successive five-year periods. This suggests that at no time will the surge of youth into the labor force be as overwhelming as it was during the period 1960-65. This is a good thing, too, because the oversupply was the underlying cause of rising youth unemployment during the period.

Nevertheless, the rate of growth during the coming years is uncomfortable enough. Even if employers have been reasonably successful in substituting youth for older workers in the past, there is no reason to expect that they can achieve the same success in the future. There are sound reasons to expect substitution to become harder, rather than easier in the future, and these include the increasing complexity of production processes, the continued shrinkage or relatively slow growth of teen-age intensive industries and occupations, and the growth of large firms with rigid, formal hiring systems, many of which almost automatically exclude youth under age 18 from employment.

The labor-force growth will consist largely of part-time and summer workers, and a continuation of the trend toward increasing seasonality in the labor force can probably be expected. The extraordinarily large unemployment rates of the least preferred groups of workers in the last few years and the distinct trends in these rates create grave doubts about the capacity of the competitive labor market to provide jobs in anything like sufficient numbers for these groups. During a period when adult unemployment rates have been as low as any in peacetime, the least preferred youth groups have experienced unemployment that probably is somewhat higher than that of the Great Depression. While much of their unemployment is short-term and intermittent, it is no less a serious problem for that.

September 1969

FURTHER READING:

Manpower Policies for Youth edited by Eli Cohen and Louise Kapp (New York: Columbia University Press, 1966).

Work, Youth and Unemployment edited by Melvin Herman, Stanley Sadofsky and Bernard Rosenberg (New York: Thomas Y. Crowell Co., 1968).

The Youth Labor Market by Edward Kalachek (Ann Arbor and Detroit: Institute of Labor and Industrial Relations, University of Michigan and Wayne State University, 1969).

White Gangs

WALTER B. MILLER

If one thinks about street corner gangs at all these days, it is probably in the roseate glow of *West Side Story*, itself the last flowering of a literary and journalistic concern that goes back at least to the late 1940s. Those were the days when it seemed that the streets of every city in the country had become dark battlefields where small armies of young men engaged their honor in terrible trials of combat, clashing fiercely and suddenly, then retiring to the warm succor of their girl cohorts. The forward to a 1958 collection of short stories, *The Young Punks*, captures a bit of the flavor:

These are the stories behind today's terrifying headlines—about a strange new frightening cult that has grown up in our midst. Every writer whose work is included in this book tells the truth. These kids are tough. Here are knife-carrying killers, and thirteen-year-old street walkers who could give the most hardened call-girl lessons. These kids pride themselves on their "ethics": never go chicken, even if it means knifing your own friend in the back. Never rat on a guy who wears your gang colors, unless he rats on you first. Old men on crutches are fair game. If a chick plays you for a sucker, blacken her eyes and walk away fast.

Today, the one-time devotee of this sort of stuff might be excused for wondering where they went, the Amboy Dukes and all those other adolescent warriors and lovers who so excited his fancy a decade ago. The answer, as we shall see, is quite simple—nowhere. The street gangs are still there, out on the corner where they always were.

The fact is that the urban adolescent street gang is as old as the American city. Henry Adams, in his *Education*, describes in vivid detail the gang fights between the North-siders and Southsiders on Boston Common in the 1840s. An observer in 1856 Brooklyn writes: ". . . at any and all hours there are multitudes of boys . . . congregated on the corners of the streets, idle in their habits, dissolute in their conduct, profane and obscene in their conversation, gross and vulgar in their manners. If a female passes one of the groups she is shocked by what she sees and hears. . . ." The Red Raiders of Boston have hung out on the same corner at least since the 1930s; similarly, gang fighting between the Tops and Bottoms in West Philadelphia, which started in the thirties is still continuing in 1969.

Despite this historical continuity, each new generation tends to perceive the street gang as a new phenomenon generated by particular contemporary conditions and destined to vanish as these conditions vanish. Gangs in the 1910s and 1920s were attributed to the cultural dislocations and community disorganization accompanying the mass immigration of foreigners; in the thirties to the enforced idleness and economic pressures produced by the Great Depression; in the fifties to the emotional disturbance of parents and children caused by the increased stresses and tensions of modern life. At present, the existence of gangs is widely attributed to a range of social injustices: racial discrimination, unequal educational and work opportunities, resentment over inequalities in the distribution of wealth and privilege in an affluent society, and the ineffective or oppressive policies of service agencies such as the police and the schools.

There is also a fairly substantial school of thought that holds that the street gangs are disappearing or have already disappeared. In New York City, the stage of so many real and fictional gang dramas of the fifties and early sixties, the *Times* sounded their death-knell as long ago as 1966. Very often, the passing of the gang is explained by the notion that young people in the slums have converted their gang-forming propensities into various substitute activities. They have been knocked out by narcotics, or they have been "politicized" in ways that consume their energies in radical or reform movements, or their members have become involved in "constructive" commercial activities, or enrolled in publicly financed education and/or work-training programs.

As has often been the case, these explanations are usually based on very shaky factual grounds and derived from rather parochial, not to say self-serving, perspectives. For street gangs are not only still widespread in United States cities, but some of them appear to have again taken up "gang warfare" on a scale that is equal to or greater than the phenomenon that received so much attention from the media in the 1950s.

In Chicago, street gangs operating in the classic formations of that city—War Lords, High Supremes, Cobra Stones—accounted for 33 killings and 252 injuries during the first six months of 1969. Philadelphia has experienced a wave of gang violence that has probably resulted in more murders in a shorter period of time than during any equivalent phase of the "fighting gang" era in New York. Police estimate that about 80 gangs comprising about 5,000 members are "active" in the city, and that about 20 are engaged in combat. Social agencies put the total estimated number of gangs at 200, with about 80 in the "most hostile" category. Between October 1962 and December 1968, gang members were reportedly involved in 257 shootings, 250 stabbings and 205 "rumbles." In the period between January 1968 and June 1969, 54 homicides and over 520 injuries were attributed to armed battles between gangs. Of the murder victims, all but eight were known to be affiliated with street gangs. The assailants ranged in age from 13 to 20, with 70 percent of them between 16 and 18 years old. Most of these gangs are designated by the name of the major corner where they hang out, the 12th and Poplar Streeters, or the 21 W's (for 21st and Westmoreland). Others bear traditional names such as the Centaurs, Morroccos and Pagans.

Gangs also continue to be active in Boston. In a single 90-minute period on May 10, 1969, one of the two channels of the Boston Police radio reported 38 incidents involving gangs, or one every 2 1/2 minutes. This included two gang fights. Simultaneous field observation in several white lower-class neighborhoods turned up evidence that gangs were congregating at numerous street corners throughout the area.

Although most of these gangs are similar to the classic types to be described in what follows, as of this summer the national press had virtually ignored the revival of gang violence. *Time* magazine did include a brief mention of "casual mayhem" in its June 27 issue, but none of the 38 incidents in Boston on May 10 was reported even in the local papers. It seems most likely, however, that if all this had been going on in New York City, where most of the media have their headquarters, a spate of newspaper features, magazine articles and television "specials" would have created the impression that the country was being engulfed by a "new" wave of gang warfare. Instead, most people seem to persist in the belief that the gangs have disappeared or that they have been radically transformed.

This anomalous situation is partly a consequence of the problem of defining what a gang is (and we will offer a definition at the end of our discussion of two specific gangs), but it is also testimony to the fact that this enduring aspect of the lives of urban slum youth remains complex and poorly understood. It is hoped that the following examination of the Bandits and the Outlaws—both of Midcity—will clarify at least some of the many open questions about street corner gangs in American cities.

Midcity, which was the location of our 10-year gang study project (1954-64), is not really a city at all, but a portion of a large one, here called Port City. Midcity is a predominantly lower-class community with a relatively high rate of crime, in which both criminal behavior and a characteristic set of conditions—low-skill occupations, little education, low-rent dwellings, and many others—appeared as relatively stable and persisting features of a developed way of life. How did street gangs fit into this picture?

In common with most major cities during this period, there were many gangs in Midcity, but they varied widely in size, sex composition, stability and range of activities. There were about 50 Midcity street corners that served as hangouts for local adolescents. Fifteen of these were "major" corners, in that they were rallying points for the full range of a gang's membership, while the remaining 35 were "minor," meaning that in general fewer groups of smaller size habitually hung out there.

In all, for Midcity in this period, 3,650 out of 5,740, or 64 percent, of Midcity boys habitually hung out at a particular corner and could therefore be considered members of a particular gang. For girls, the figure is 1,125 out of 6,250, or 18 percent. These estimates also suggest that something like 35 percent of Midcity's boys, and 80 percent of its girls, did *not* hang out. What can be said about them? What made them different from the approximately 65 percent of the boys and 20 percent of the girls who did hang out?

Indirect evidence appears to show that the practice of hanging out with a gang was more prevalent among lower-status adolescents, and that many of those who were not known to hang out lived in middle-class or lower-class I (the higher range of the lower-class) areas. At the same time, however, it is evident that a fair proportion of higher-status youngsters also hung out. The question of status, and its relation to gang membership and gang behavior is very complex, but it should be borne in mind as we now take a closer look at the gangs we studied.

The Bandit Neighborhood

Between the Civil War and World War II, the Bandit neighborhood was well-known throughout the city as a colorful and close-knit community of Irish laborers. Moving to a flat in one of its ubiquitous three-decker frame tenements represented an important step up for the impoverished potato-famine immigrants who had initially settled in the crowded slums of central Port City. By the 1810s the second generation of Irish settlers had produced a spirited and energetic group of athletes and politicos, some of whom achieved national prominence.

Those residents of the Bandit neighborhood who shared in some degree the drive, vitality and capability of these famous men assumed steady and fairly remunerative positions in the political, legal and civil service world of Port City, and left the neighborhood for residential areas whose green lawns and single houses represented for them what Midcity had represented for their fathers and grandfathers. Those who lacked these qualities remained in the Bandit neighborhood, and at the outset of World War II made up a stable and relatively homogeneous community of low-skilled Irish laborers.

The Bandit neighborhood was directly adjacent to Midcity's major shopping district, and was spotted with bars, poolrooms and dance halls that served as meeting places for an active neighborhood social life. Within two blocks of the Bandits' hanging-out corner were the Old Erin and New Hibernia dance halls, and numerous drinking establishments bearing names such as the Shamrock, Murphy and Donoghue's and the Emerald Bar and Grill.

A number of developments following World War II disrupted the physical and social shape of the Bandit community. A mammoth federally-financed housing project sliced through and blocked off the existing network of streets and razed the regular rows of wooden tenements. The neighborhood's small manufacturing plants were progressively diminished by the growth of a few large establishments, and by the 1950s the physical face of the neighborhood was dominated by three large and growing plants. As these plants expanded they bought off many of the properties which had not been taken by the housing project, demolished buildings, and converted them into acres of black-topped parking lots for their employees.

During this period, the parents of the Bandit corner gang members stubbornly held on to the decreasing number of low-rent, deteriorating, private dwelling units. Although the Bandits' major hanging corner was almost surrounded by the housing project, virtually none of the gang members lived there. For these families, residence in the housing project would have entailed a degree of financial stability and restrained behavior that they were unable or unwilling to assume, for the corner gang members of the Bandit neighborhood were the scions of men and women who occupied the lowest social level in Midcity. For them low rent was a passion, freedom to drink and to behave drunkenly a sacred privilege, sporadic employment a fact of life, and the social welfare and law-enforcement agencies of the state, partners of one's existence.

The Bandit corner was subject to field observation for about three years—from June 1954 to May 1957. Hanging out on the corner during this period were six distinct but related gang subdivisions. There were four male groups: The Brigands, aged approximately 18 to 21 at the start of the study period; the Senior Bandits, aged 16 to 18; the Junior Bandits, 14 to 16, and the Midget Bandits, 12 to 14. There were also two distinct female subdivisions: The Bandettes, 14 to 16, and the Little Bandettes, 12 to 14.

The physical and psychic center of the Bandit corner was Sam's Variety Store, the owner and sole employee of which was not Sam but Ben, his son. Ben's father had founded the store in the 1920s, the heyday of the Irish laboring class in the Bandit neighborhood. When his father died, Ben took over the store, but did not change its name. Ben was a stocky, round-faced Jew in his middle fifties, who looked upon the whole of the Bandit neighborhood as his personal fief and bounden responsibility—a sacred legacy from his father. He knew everybody and was concerned with everybody; through his store passed a constant stream of customers and noncustomers of all ages and both sexes. In a space not much larger than that of a fair-sized bedroom Ben managed to crowd a phone booth, a juke box, a pinball machine, a space heater, counters, shelves and stock, and an assorted variety of patrons. During one 15-minute period on an average day Ben would supply $1.37 worth of groceries to 11-year-old Carol Donovan and enter the sum on her mother's page in the "tab" book, agree to extend Mrs. Thebodeau's already extended credit until her ADC check arrived, bandage and solace the three-year-old Negro girl who came crying to him with a cut forefinger, and shoo into the street a covey of Junior Bandits whose altercation over a pinball score was impeding customer traffic and augmenting an already substantial level of din.

Ben was a bachelor, and while he had adopted the whole of the Bandit neighborhood as his extended family, he had taken on the 200 adolescents who hung out on the Bandit corner as his most immediate sons and daughters. Ben knew the background and present circumstances of every Bandit, and followed their lives with intense interest and concern. Ben's corner-gang progeny were a fast-moving and mercurial lot, and he watched over their adventures and misadventures with a curious mixture of indignation, solicitude, disgust and sympathy. Ben's outlook on the affairs of the world was never bland; he held and freely voiced strong opinions on a wide variety of issues, prominent among which was the behavior and misbehavior of the younger generation.

This particular concern was given ample scope for attention by the young Bandits who congregated in and around his store. Of all the gangs studied, the Bandits were the most consistently and determinedly criminal, and central to Ben's concerns was how each one stood with regard to "trouble." In this respect, developments were seldom meager. By the time they reached the age of 18, every one of the 32 active members of the Senior Bandits had appeared in court at least once, and some many times; 28 of the 32 boys had been committed to a correctional institution and 16 had spent at least one term in confinement.

Ben's stout arm swept the expanse of pavement which fronted his store. "I'll tell ya, I give up on these kids. In all the years I been here, I never seen a worse bunch. You know what they should do? They should put up a big platform with one of them stocks right out there, and as soon as a kid gets in trouble, into the stocks with 'im. Then they'd straighten out. The way it is now, the kid tells a sob story to some soft-hearted cop or social worker, and pretty soon he's back at the same old thing. See that guy just comin' over here? That's what I mean. He's hopless. Mark my word, he's gonna end up in the electric chair."

The Senior Bandit who entered the store came directly to Ben. "Hey, Ben, I just quit my job at the shoe factory. They don't pay ya nothin', and they got some wise guy nephew of the owner who thinks he can kick everyone around. I just got fed up. I ain't gonna tell Ma for awhile, she'll be mad." Ben's concern was evident. "Digger, ya just gotta learn you can't keep actin' smart to every boss ya have. And $1.30 an hour ain't bad pay at all for a 17-year-old boy. Look, I'll lend ya 10 bucks so ya can give 5 to ya Ma, and she won't know."

In their dealings with Ben, the Bandits, for their part, were in turn hostile and affectionate, cordial and sullen, open and reserved. They clearly regarded Ben's as "their" store. This meant, among other things, exclusive possession of the right to make trouble within its confines. At least three times during the observation period corner boys from outside neighborhoods entered the store obviously bent on stealing or creating a disturbance. On each occasion these outsiders were efficiently and forcefully removed by nearby Bandits, who then waxed indignant at the temerity of "outside" kids daring to consider Ben's as a target of illegal activity. One consequence, then, of Ben's seigneurial relationship to the Bandits was that his store was unusually well protected against theft, armed and otherwise, which presented a constant hazard to the small-store owner in Midcity.

On the other hand, the Bandits guarded jealously their

own right to raise hell in Ben's. On one occasion, several Senior Bandits came into the store with a cache of pistol bullets and proceeded to empty the powder from one of the bullets onto the pinball machine and to ignite the powder. When Ben ordered them out they continued operations on the front sidewalk by wrapping gunpowder in newspaper and igniting it. Finally they set fire to a wad of paper containing two live bullets which exploded and narrowly missed local residents sitting on nearby doorsteps.

Such behavior, while calculated to bedevil Ben and perhaps to retaliate for a recent scolding or ejection, posed no real threat to him or his store; the same boys during this period were actively engaged in serious thefts from similar stores in other neighborhoods. For the most part, the behavior of the Bandits in and around the store involved the characteristic activities of hanging out. In warm weather the Bandits sat outside the store on the sidewalk or doorstoops playing cards, gambling, drinking, talking to one another and to the Bandettes. In cooler weather they moved into the store as the hour and space permitted, and there played the pinball machine for such cash payoffs as Ben saw fit to render, danced with the Bandettes to juke box records, and engaged in general horseplay.

While Ben's was the Bandits' favorite hangout, they did frequent other hanging locales, mostly within a few blocks of the corner. Among these was a park directly adjacent to the housing project where the boys played football and baseball in season. At night the park provided a favored locale for activities such as beer drinking and lovemaking, neither of which particularly endeared them to the adult residents of the project, who not infrequently summoned the police to clear the park of late-night revellers. Other areas of congregation in the local neighborhood were a nearby delicatessen ("the Delly"), a pool hall, and the apartments of those Bandettes whose parents happened to be away. The Bandits also ran their own dances at the Old Erin and New Hibernia, but they had to conceal their identity as Bandits when renting these dance halls, since the proprietors had learned that the rental fees were scarcely sufficient to compensate for the chaos inevitably attending the conduct of a Bandit dance.

The Bandits were able to find other sources of entertainment in the central business district of Port City. While most of the Bandits and Bandettes were too young to gain admission to the numerous downtown cafes with their rock'n' roll bands, they were able to find amusement in going to the movies (sneaking in whenever possible), playing the coin machines in the penny arcades and shoplifting from the downtown department stores. Sometimes, as a kind of diversion, small groups of Bandits spent the day in town job-hunting, with little serious intention of finding work.

One especially favored form of downtown entertainment was the court trial. Members of the Junior and Senior Bandits performed as on-stage participants in some 250 court trials during a four-year period. Most trials involving juveniles were conducted in nearby Midcity Court as private proceedings, but the older Bandits had adopted as routine procedure the practice of appealing their local court sentences to the Superior Court located in downtown Port City. When the appeal was successful, it was the occasion for as large a turnout of gang members as could be mustered, and the Bandits were a rapt and vitally interested audience. Afterwards, the gang held long and animated discussions about the severity or leniency of the sentence and other, finer points of legal procedure. The hearings provided not only an absorbing form of free entertainment, but also invaluable knowledge about court functioning, appropriate defendant behavior, and the predilections of particular judges—knowledge that would serve the spectators well when their own turn to star inevitably arrived.

The Senior Bandits

The Senior Bandits, the second oldest of the four male gang subdivisions hanging out on the Bandit corner, were under intensive observation for a period of 20 months. At the start of this period the boys ranged in age from 15 to 17 (average age 16.3) and at the end, 17 to 19 (average age 18.1). The core group of the Senior Bandits numbered 32 boys.

Most of the gang members were Catholic, the majority of Irish background; several were Italian or French Canadian, and a few were English or Scotch Protestants. The gang contained two sets of brothers and several cousins, and about one third of the boys had relatives in other subdivisions. These included a brother in the Midgets, six brothers in the Juniors, and three in the Marauders.

The educational and occupational circumstances of the Senior Bandits were remarkably like those of their parents. Some seven years after the end of the intensive study period, when the average age of the Bandits was 25, 23 out of the 27 gang members whose occupations were known held jobs ordinarily classified in the bottom two occupational categories of the United States census. Twenty-one were classified as "laborer," holding jobs such as roofer, stock boy and trucker's helper. Of 24 fathers whose occupations were known, 18, or 83 percent, held jobs in the same bottom two occupational categories as their sons; 17 were described as "laborer," holding jobs of similar kinds and in similar proportions to those of their sons, e.g., construction laborers: sons 30 percent, fathers 25 percent; factory laborers: sons 15 percent, fathers 21 percent. Clearly the Senior Bandits were not rising above their fathers' status. In fact, there were indications of a slight decline, even taking account of the younger age of the sons. Two of the boys' fathers held jobs in "public safety" services—one policeman and one fireman; another had worked for a time in the "white collar" position of a salesclerk at Sears; a fourth had risen to the rank of Chief Petty Officer in the Merchant Marine. Four of the fathers, in other words, had attained relatively elevated positions, while the sons produced only one policeman.

The education of the Senior Bandits was consistent with their occupational status. Of 29 boys whose educational experience was known, 27 dropped out of school in the eighth, ninth, or tenth grades, having reached the age of 16. Two did complete high school, and one of these was reputed to have taken some post-high-school training in a local technical school. None entered college. It should be remarked that this record occurred not in a backward rural community of the 1800s, nor in a black community, but in the 1950s in a predominantly white neighborhood of a metropolis that took pride in being one of the major educational centers of the world.

Since only two of the Senior Bandits were still in school during the study, almost all of the boys held full-time jobs at some time during the contact period. But despite financial needs, pressure from parents and parole officers and other incentives to get work, the Senior Bandits found jobs slowly, accepted them reluctantly, and quit them with little provocation.

The Senior Bandits were clearly the most criminal of the seven gangs we studied most closely. For example, by the time he had reached the age of 18 the average Senior Bandit had been charged with offenses in court an average of 7.6 times; this compared with an average rate of 2.7 for all five male gangs, and added up to a total of almost 250 separate charges for the gang as a whole. A year after our intensive contact with the group, 100 percent of the

Senior Bandits had been arrested at least once, compared with an average arrest figure of 45 percent for all groups. During the 20-month contact period, just about half of the Senior Bandits were on probation or parole for some period of time.

To a greater degree than in any of the other gangs we studied, crime as an occupation and preoccupation played a central role in the lives of the Senior Bandits. Prominent among recurrent topics of discussion were thefts successfully executed, fights recently engaged in, and the current status of gang members who were in the process of passing through the successive states of arrest, appearing in court, being sentenced, appealing, re-appealing and so on. Although none of the crimes of the Senior Bandits merited front-page headlines when we were close to them, a number of their more colorful exploits did receive newspaper attention, and the stories were carefully clipped and left in Ben's store for circulation among the gang members. Newspaper citations functioned for the Senior Bandits somewhat as do press notices for actors; gang members who made the papers were elated and granted prestige; those who did not were often disappointed; participants and non-participants who failed to see the stories felt cheated.

The majority of their crimes were thefts. The Senior Bandits were thieves par excellence, and their thievery was imaginative, colorful and varied. Most thefts were from stores. Included among these was a department store theft of watches, jewelry and clothing for use as family Christmas presents; a daylight raid on a supermarket for food and refreshments needed for a beach outing; a daytime burglary of an antique store, in which eight gang members, in the presence of the owner, stole a Samurai sword and French duelling pistols. The gang also engaged in car theft. One summer several Bandits stole a car to visit girl friends who were working at a summer resort. Sixty miles north of Port City, hailed by police for exceeding speed limits, they raced away at speeds of up to 100 miles an hour, overturned the car, and were hospitalized for injuries. In another instance, Bandits stole a car in an effort to return a drunken companion to his home and avoid the police; when this car stalled they stole a second one parked in front of its owner's house; the owner ran out and fired several shots at the thieves, which, however, failed to forestall the theft.

The frequency of Senior Bandit crimes, along with the relative seriousness of their offenses, resulted in a high rate of arrest and confinement. During the contact period somewhat over 40 percent of the gang members were confined in correctional institutions, with terms averaging 11 months per boy. The average Senior Bandit spent approximately one month out of four in a correctional facility. This circumstance prompted one of the Bandettes to remark, "Ya know, them guys got a new place to hang—the reformatory. That bunch is never together—one halfa them don't even know the other half. . . ."

This appraisal, while based on fact, failed to recognize an important feature of gang relationships. With institutional confinement a frequent and predictable event, the Senior Bandits employed a set of devices to maintain a high degree of group solidarity. Lines of communication between corner and institution were kept open by frequent visits by those on the outside, during which inmates were brought food, money and cigarettes as well as news of the neighborhood and other correctional facilities. One Midcity social worker claimed that the institutionalized boys knew what was going on in the neighborhood before most neighborhood residents. The Bandits also developed well-established methods for arranging and carrying out institutional escape by those gang members who were so inclined. Details of escapes were arranged in the course of visits and inter-inmate contacts; escapees were provided by fellow gang members with equipment such as ropes to scale prison walls and getaway cars. The homes of one's gang fellows were also made available as hideouts. Given this set of arrangements, the Bandits carried out several highly successful escapes, and one succeeded in executing the first escape in the history of a maximum security installation.

The means by which the Senior Bandits achieved group cohesion in spite of recurrent incarcerations of key members merit further consideration—both because they are of interest in their own right, and because they throw light on important relationships between leadership, group structure, and the motivation of criminal behavior. Despite the assertion that "one halfa them guys don't know the other half," the Senior Bandits were a solidaristic associational unit, with clear group boundaries and definite criteria for differentiating those who were "one of us" from those who were not. It was still said of an accepted group member that "he hangs with us"—even when the boy had been away from the corner in an institution for a year or more. Incarcerated leaders, in particular, were referred to frequently and in terms of admiration and respect.

The system used by the Senior Bandits to maintain solidarity and reliable leadership arrangements incorporated three major devices: the diffusion of authority, anticipation of contingencies and interchangeability of roles. The recurring absence from the corner of varying numbers of gang members inhibited the formation of a set of relatively stable cliques of the kind found in the other gangs we studied intensively. What was fairly stable, instead, was a set of "classes" of members, each of which could include different individuals at different times. The relative size of these classes was fairly constant, and a member of one class could move to another to take the place of a member who had been removed by institutionalization.

The four major classes of gang members could be called key leaders, standby leaders, primary followers and secondary followers. During the intensive contact period the gang contained five key leaders—boys whose accomplishments had earned them the right to command; six standby leaders—boys prepared to step into leadership positions when key leaders were institutionalized; eight primary followers—boys who hung out regularly and who were the most dependable followers of current leaders; and 13 secondary followers—boys who hung out less regularly and who tended to adapt their allegiances to particular leadership situations.

Predictably, given the dominant role of criminal activity among the Senior Bandits, leadership and followership were significantly related to criminal involvement. Each of the five key leaders had demonstrated unusual ability in criminal activity; in this respect the Senior Bandits differed from the other gangs, each of which included at least one leader whose position was based in whole or in part on a commitment to a law-abiding course of action. One of the Senior Bandits' key leaders was especially respected for his daring and adeptness in theft; another, who stole infrequently relative to other leaders, for his courage, stamina and resourcefulness as a fighter. The other three leaders had proven themselves in both theft and fighting, with theft the more important basis of eminence.

Confinement statistics show that gang members who were closet to leadership positions were also the most active in crime. They also suggest, however, that maintaining a system of leadership on this basis poses special problems. The more criminally active a gang member, the greater the likelihood that he would be apprehended and removed from the neighborhood, thus substantially diminishing his opportunities to convert earning prestige into operative leadership. How was it possible, then, for the Senior Bandits to maintain effective leadership arrangements? They utilized a remarkably efficient system whose several features were ingenious and deftly contrived.

First, the recognition by the Bandits of five key leaders—a relatively large number for a gang of 32 members—served as a form of insurance against being left without leadership. It was most unlikely that all five would be incarcerated at the same time, particularly since collective crimes were generally executed by one or possibly two leaders along with several of their followers. During one relatively brief part of the contact period, four of the key leaders were confined simultaneously, but over the full period the average number confined at any one time was two. One Bandit key leader expressed his conviction that exclusive reliance on a single leader was unwise: ". . . since we been hangin' out [at Ben's corner] we ain't had no leader. Other kids got a leader of the gang. Like up in Cornerville, they always got one kid who's the big boss . . . so far we ain't did that, and I don't think we ever will. We talk about 'Smiley and his boys,' or 'Digger and his clique,' and like that. . . ."

It is clear that for this Bandit the term "leader" carried the connotation of a single and all-powerful gang lord, which was not applicable to the diffuse and decentralized leadership arrangements of the Bandits. It is also significant that the gangs of Cornerville which he used as an example were Italian gangs whose rate of criminal involvement was relatively low. The "one big boss" type of leadership found in these gangs derives from the "Caesar" or "Il Duce" pattern so well established in Italian culture, and it was workable for Cornerville gangs because the gangs and their leaders were sufficiently law-abiding and /or sufficiently capable of evading arrest as to make the removal of the leader an improbable event.

A second feature of Bandit leadership, the use of "standby" leaders, made possible a relatively stable balance among the several cliques. When the key leader of his clique was present in the area, the standby leader assumed a subordinate role and did not initiate action; if and when the key leader was committed to an institution, the standby was ready to assume leadership. He knew, however, that he was expected to relinquish this position on the return of the key leader. By this device each of the five major cliques was assured some form of leadership even when key leaders were absent, and could maintain its form, identity and influence vis-a-vis other cliques.

A third device that enabled the gang to maintain a relatively stable leadership and clique structure involved the phenomenon of "optimal" criminal involvement. Since excellence in crime was the major basis of gang leadership, it might be expected that some of those who aspired to leadership would assume that there was a simple and direct relationship between crime and leadership: the more crime, the more prestige; the more prestige, the stronger the basis of authority. The flaw in this simple formula was in fact recognized by the actual key leaders: in striving for maximal criminal involvement, one also incurred the maximum risk of incarceration. But leadership involved more than gaining prestige through crime; one had to be personally involved with other gang members for sufficiently extended periods to exploit won prestige through wooing followers, initiating noncriminal as well as criminal activities, and effecting working relationships with other leaders. Newly-returned key leaders as well as the less criminally-active class of standby leaders tended to step up their involvement in criminal activity on assuming or reassuming leadership positions in order to solidify their positions, but they also tended to diminish such involvement once this was achieved.

One fairly evident weakness in so flexible and fluid a system of cliques and leadership was the danger that violent and possibly disruptive internal conflict might erupt among key leaders who were competing for followers, or standby leaders who were reluctant to relinquish their positions. There was, in fact, surprisingly little overt conflict of any kind among Bandit leaders. On their release from confinement, leaders were welcomed with enthusiasm and appropriate observances both by their followers and by other leaders. They took the center of the stage as they recounted to rapt listeners their institutional experiences, the circumstances of those still confined, and new developments in policies, personnel and politics at the correctional school.

When they were together Bandit leaders dealt with one another gingerly, warily and with evident respect. On one occasion a standby leader, who was less criminally active than the returning key leader, offered little resistance to being displaced, but did serve his replacement with the warning that a resumption of his former high rate of crime would soon result in commitment both of himself and his clique. On another occasion one of the toughest of the Senior Bandits (later sentenced to an extended term in an adult institution for ringleading a major prison riot), returned to the corner to find that another leader had taken over not only some of his key followers but his steady girl friend as well. Instead of taking on his rival in an angry and perhaps violent confrontation, he reacted quite mildly, venting his hostility in the form of sarcastic teasing, calculated to needle but not to incite. In the place of a direct challenge, the newly returned key leader set about to regain his followers and his girl by actively throwing himself back into criminal activity. This course of action—competing for followers by successful performance in prestigious activities rather than by brute-force confrontation—was standard practice among the Senior Bandits.

The Junior Bandits

The leadership system of the Junior Bandits was, if anything, even farther removed from the "one big boss" pattern than was the "multi-leader power-balance" system of the Seniors. An intricate arrangement of cliques and leadership enabled this subdivision of the gang to contain within it a variety of individuals and cliques with different and often conflicting orientations.

Leadership for particular activities was provided as the occasion arose by boys whose competence in that activity had been established. Leadership was thus flexible, shifting and adaptable to changing group circumstances. Insofar as there was a measure of relatively concentrated authority, it was invested in a collectivity rather than an individual. The several "situational" leaders of the dominant clique constituted what was in effect a kind of ruling council, which arrived at its decisions through a process of extended collective discussion generally involving all concerned. Those who were to execute a plan of action thereby took part in the process by which it was developed.

A final feature of this system concerns the boy who was recognized as "the leader" of the Junior Bandits. When the gang formed a club to expedite involvement in athletic activities, he was chosen its president. Although he was an accepted member of the dominant clique, he did not, on the surface, seem to possess any particular qualifications for this position. He was mild-mannered, unassertive, and consistently refused to take a definite stand on outstanding issues, let alone taking the initiative in implementing policy. He appeared to follow rather than to lead. One night when the leaders of the two subordinate factions became infuriated with one another in the course of a dispute, he trailed both boys around for several hours, begging them to calm down and reconcile their differences. On another occasion the gang was on the verge of splitting into irreconcilable factions over a financial issue. One group accused another of stealing club funds; the accusation was hotly denied; angry recriminations arose that swept in a variety of dissatisfactions with the club and its conduct. In the course of this melee, the leader of one faction, the "bad boys," complained bitterly about the refusal of the president to take sides or assume any initiative in resolving the dispute, and called for a new election. This was agreed to and the election was held—with the result that the "weak" president was re-elected by a decisive majority, and was reinstated in office amidst emotional outbursts of acclaim and reaffirmation of the unity of the gang.

It was thus evident that the majority of gang members, despite temporary periods of anger over particular issues, recognized on some level the true function performed by a "weak" leader. Given the fact that the gang included a set of cliques with differing orientations and conflicting notions, and a set of leaders whose authority was limited to specific areas, the maintenance of gang cohesion required some special mechanisms. One was the device of the "weak" leader. It is most unlikely that a forceful or dominant person could have controlled the sanctions that would enable him to coerce the strong-willed factions into compliance. The very fact that the "weak" leader refused to take sides and was noncommittal on key issues made him acceptable to the conflicting interests represented in the gang. Further, along with the boy's nonassertive demeanor went a real talent for mediation.

The Outlaw Neighborhood

The Outlaw street corner was less than a mile from that of the Bandits, and like the Bandits, the Outlaws were white, Catholic, and predominantly Irish, with a few Italians and Irish-Italians. But their social status, in the middle range of the lower class, was sufficiently higher than that of the Bandits to be reflected in significant differences in both their gang and family life. The neighborhood environment also was quite different.

Still, the Outlaws hung out on a classic corner—complete with drug store, variety store, a neighborhood bar (Callahan's Bar and Grill), a pool hall and several other small businesses such as a laundromat. The corner was within one block of a large park, a convenient locale for card games, lovemaking and athletic practice. Most residents of the Outlaw neighborhood were oblivious to the deafening roar of the elevated train that periodically rattled the houses and stores of Midcity Avenue, which formed one street of the Outlaw corner. There was no housing project in the Outlaw neighborhood, and none of the Outlaws were project residents. Most of their families rented one level of one of the three-decker wooden tenements which were common in the area; a few owned their own homes.

In the mid-1950s, however, the Outlaw neighborhood underwent significant changes as Negroes began moving in. Most of the white residents, gradually and with reluctance, left their homes and moved out to the first fringe of Port City's residential suburbs, abandoning the area to the Negroes.

Prior to this time the Outlaw corner had been a hanging locale for many years. The Outlaw name and corner dated from at least the late 1920s, and perhaps earlier. One local boy who was not an Outlaw observed disgruntledly that anyone who started a fight with an Outlaw would end up fighting son, father and grandfather, since all were or had been members of the gang. A somewhat drunken and sentimental Outlaw, speaking at a farewell banquet for their field worker, declared impassionedly that any infant born into an Outlaw family was destined from birth to wear the Outlaw jacket.

One consequence of the fact that Outlaws had hung out on the same corner for many years was that the group that congregated there during the 30-month observation period included a full complement of age-graded subdivisions. Another consequence was that the subdivisions were closely connected by kinship. There were six clearly differentiated subdivisions on the corner: the Marauders, boys in their late teens and early twenties; the Senior Outlaws, boys between 16 and 18; the Junior Outlaws, 14 to 16; and the Midget Outlaws, 11 to 13. There were also two girls groups, the Outlawettes and the Little Outlawettes. The number of Outlaws in all subdivisions totalled slightly over 200 persons, ranging in age, approximately, from 10 to 25 years.

The cohesiveness of the Outlaws, during the 1950s, was enhanced in no small measure by an adult who, like Ben for the Bandits, played a central role in the Outlaws' lives. This was Rosa—the owner of the variety store which was their principal hangout—a stout, unmarried woman of about 40 who was, in effect, the street-corner mother of all 200 Outlaws.

The Junior Outlaws

The Junior Outlaws, numbering 24 active members, were the third oldest of the four male subdivisions on the Outlaw Corner, ranging in age from 14 to 16. Consistent with their middle-range lower-class status, the boys' fathers were employed in such jobs as bricklayer, mechanic, chauffeur, milk deliveryman; but a small minority of these men had attained somewhat higher positions, one being the owner of a small electroplating shop and the other rising to the position of plant superintendent. The educational status of the Junior Outlaws was higher than that of the Bandit gangs, but lower than that of their older brother gang, the Senior Outlaws.

With regard to law violations, the Junior Outlaws, as one might expect from their status and age, were considerably less criminal than the lower-status Bandits, but considerably more so than the Senior Outlaws. They ranked third among the five male gangs in illegal involvement during the observation period (25 involvements per 10 boys per 10 months), which was well below the second-ranking Senior Bandits (54.2) and well above the fourth-ranking Negro Kings (13.9). Nevertheless, the two-and-a-half-year period during which we observed the Juniors was for them, as for other boys of their status and age group, a time of substantial increase in the frequency and seriousness of illegal behavior. An account of the events of this time provides some insight into the process by which age-related influences engender criminality. It also provides another variation on the issue, already discussed in the case of the Bandits, of the relation of leadership to criminality.

It is clear from the case of the Bandits that gang affairs were ordered not by autocratic ganglords, but rather through a subtle and intricate interplay between leadership and a set of elements such as personal competency, intra-gang divisions and law violation. The case of the Junior Outlaws is particularly dramatic in this regard, since the observation period found them at the critical age when boys of this social-status level are faced with a serious decision—the amount of weight to be granted to law-violating behavior as a basis of prestige. Because there were in the Junior Outlaws two cliques, each of which was committed quite clearly to opposing alternatives, the interplay of the various elements over time emerges with some vividness, and echoes the classic morality play wherein forces of good and evil are locked in mortal combat over the souls of the uncommitted.

At the start of the observation period, the Juniors, 13-,

14-and 15-year-olds, looked and acted for the most part like "nice young kids." By the end of the period both their voices and general demeanor had undergone a striking change. Their appearance, as they hung out in front of Rosa's store, was that of rough corner boys, and the series of thefts, fights and drinking bouts which had occurred during the intervening two-and-one-half years was the substance behind that appearance. When we first contacted them, the Juniors comprised three main cliques; seven boys associated primarily with a "good boy" who was quite explicitly oriented to law-abiding behavior; a second clique of seven boys associated with a "bad boy" who was just starting to pursue prestige through drinking and auto theft; and a third, less-frequently congregating group, who took a relatively neutral position with respect to the issue of violative behavior.

The leader of the "good boy" clique played an active part in the law-abiding activities of the gang, and was elected president of the formal club organized by the Juniors. This club at first included members of all three cliques; however, one of the first acts of the club members, dominated by the "good boy" leader and his supporters, was to vote out of membership the leader of the "bad boy" clique. Nevertheless, the "bad boy" leader and his followers continued to hang out on the corner with the other Juniors, and from this vantage point attempted to gain influence over the uncommitted boys as well as members of the "good boy" clique. His efforts proved unsuccessful, however, since during this period athletic prowess served for the majority of the Juniors as a basis of greater prestige than criminal behavior. Disgruntled by this failure, the "bad boy" leader took his followers and moved to a new hanging corner, about two blocks away from the traditional one.

From there, a tangible symbol of the ideological split

within the Juniors, the "bad boy" leader continued his campaign to wean away the followers of the "good boy" leader, trying to persuade them to leave the old corner for the new. At the same time, behavior at the "bad boy" corner became increasingly delinquent, with, among other things, much noisy drinking and thefts of nearby cars. These incidents produced complaints by local residents that resulted in several police raids on the corner, and served to increase the antagonism between what now had become hostile factions. Determined to assert their separateness, the "bad boy" faction began to drink and create disturbances in Rosa's store, became hostile to her when she censured them, and finally stayed away from the store altogether.

The antagonism between the two factions finally became sufficiently intense to bring about a most unusual circumstance—plans for an actual gang fight, a "jam" of the type characteristic of rival gangs. The time and place for the battle were agreed on. But no one from either side showed up. A second battle site was selected. Again the combatants failed to appear. From the point of view of intragang relations, both the plan for the gang fight and its failure to materialize were significant. The fact that a physical fight between members of the same subdivision was actually projected showed that factional hostility over the issue of law violation had reached an unusual degree of bitterness; the fact that the planned encounters did not in fact occur indicated a realization that actual physical combat might well lead to an irreversible split.

A reunification of the hostile factions did not take place for almost a year, however. During this time changes occurred in both factions which had the net effect of blunting the sharpness of the ideological issues dividing them. Discouraged by his failure to win over the majority of the Outlaws to the cause of law-violation as a major badge of prestige, the leader of the "bad boy" clique began to hang out less frequently. At the same time, the eight "uncommitted" members of the Junior Outlaws, now moving toward their middle teens, began to gravitate toward the "bad boy" corner—attracted by the excitement and risk of its activities. More of the Juniors than ever before became involved in illegal drinking and petty theft. This trend became sufficiently pronounced to draw in members of the "good boy" clique, and the influence of the "good boy" leader diminished to the point where he could count on the loyalty only of his own brother and two other boys. In desperation, sensing the all-but-irresistible appeal of illegality for his erstwhile followers, he increased the tempo of his own delinquent behavior in a last-ditch effort to win them back. All in vain. Even his own brother deserted the regular Outlaw corner, although he did not go so far as to join the "bad boys" on theirs.

Disillusioned, the "good boy" leader took a night job that sharply curtailed the time he was able to devote to gang activities. Members of the "bad boy" clique now began a series of maneuvers aimed at gaining control of the formal club. Finally, about two months before the close of the 30-month contact period, a core member of the "bad boy" clique was elected to the club presidency. In effect, the proponents of illegality as a major basis of prestige had won the long struggle for dominance of the Junior Outlaws. But this achievement, while on the surface a clear victory for the "bad boy" faction, was in fact a far more subtle process of mutual accommodation.

The actions of each of the opposing sides accorded quite directly with their expressed convictions; each member of the "bad boy" faction averaged about 17 known illegal acts during the observation period, compared to a figure of about two per boy for the "good boy" faction. However, in the face of these sharp differences in both actions and sentiments respecting illegality, the two factions shared important common orientations. Most importantly, they shared the conviction that the issue of violative behavior as a basis of prestige was a paramount one, and one that required a choice. Moreover, both sides remained uncertain as to whether the choice they made was the correct one.

The behavior of both factions provides evidence of a fundamental ambivalence with respect to the "demanded" nature of delinquent behavior. The gradual withdrawal of support by followers of the "good boy" leader and the movement toward violative behavior of the previously "neutral" clique attest to a compelling conviction that prestige gained through law-abiding endeavor alone could not, at this age, suffice. Even more significant was the criminal experience of the "good boy" leader. As the prime exponent of law-abiding behavior, he might have been expected to serve as an exemplar in this respect. In fact, the opposite was true; his rate of illegal involvement was the highest of all the boys in his clique, and had been so even before his abortive attempt to regain his followers by a final burst of delinquency. This circumstance probably derived from his realization that a leader acceptable to both factions (which he wanted to be) would have to show proficiency in activities recognized by both as conferring prestige.

It is equally clear, by the same token, that members of the "bad boy" faction were less than serenely confident in their commitment to law-violation as an ideal. Once they had won power in the club they did not keep as their leader the boy who had been the dominant figure on the "bad boy" corner, and who was without question the most criminally active of the Junior Outlaws, but instead elected as president another boy who was also criminally active, but considerably less so. Moreover, in the presence of older gang members, Seniors and Marauders, the "bad boy" clique was far more subdued, less obstreperous, and far less ardent in their advocacy of crime as an ideal. There was little question that they were sensitive to and responsive to negative reactions by others to their behavior.

It is noteworthy that members of both factions adhered more firmly to the "law-violation" and "law-abiding" positions on the level of abstract ideology than on the level of actual practice. This would suggest that the existence of the opposing ideologies and their corresponding factions served important functions both for individual gang members and for the group as a whole. Being in the same orbit as the "bad boys" made it possible for the "good boys" to reap some of the rewards of violative behavior without undergoing its risks; the presence of the "good boys" imposed restraints on the "bad" that they themselves desired, and helped protect them from dangerous excesses. The behavior and ideals of the "good boys" satisfied for both factions that component of their basic orientation that said "violation of the law is wrong and should be punished;" the behavior and ideals of the "bad boys" that component that said "one cannot earn manhood without some involvement in criminal activity."

It is instructive to compare the stress and turmoil attending the struggle for dominance of the Junior Outlaws with the leadership circumstances of the Senior Bandits. In this gang, older and of lower social status (lower-class III), competition for leadership had little to do with a choice between law-abiding and law-violating philosophies, but rather with the issue of which of a number of competing leaders was *best* able to demonstrate prowess in illegal activity. This virtual absence of effective pressures against delinquency contrasts sharply with the situation of the Junior Outlaws. During the year-long struggle between its "good" and "bad" factions, the Juniors were exposed to constant pressures, both internal and external to the gang, to refrain from illegality. External sources included Rosa, whom the boys loved and respected; a local youth worker whom they held in high esteem; their older brother gangs, whose frequent admonitions to the "little kids" to "straighten out" and "keep clean" were attended with utmost seriousness. Within the gang itself the "good boy" leader served as a consistent and persuasive advocate of a lawabiding course of action. In addition, most of the boys' parents deplored their misbehavior and urged them to keep out of trouble.

In the face of all these pressures from persons of no small importance in the lives of the Juniors, the final triumph of the proponents of illegality, however tempered, assumes added significance. What was it that impelled the "bad boy" faction? There was a quality of defiance about much of their delinquency, as if they were saying—"We know perfectly well that what we are doing is regarded as wrong, legally and morally; we also know that it violates the wishes and standards of many whose good opinion we value; yet, if we are to sustain our self-respect and our honor as males we *must*, at this stage of our lives, engage in criminal behavior." In light of the experience of the Junior Outlaws, one can scarcely argue that their delinquency sprang from any inability to distinguish right from wrong, or out of any simple conformity to a set of parochial standards that just happened to differ from those of the legal code or the adult middle class. Their delinquent behavior was engendered by a highly complex interplay of forces, including, among other elements, the fact that they were males, were in the middle range of the lower class and of critical importance in the present instance, were moving through the age period when the attainment of manhood was of the utmost concern.

In the younger gang just discussed, the Junior Outlaws, leadership and clique structure reflected an intense struggle between advocates and opponents of law-violation as a prime basis of prestige.

The Senior Outlaws

Leadership in the older Senior Outlaws reflected a resolution of the law-conformity versus law-violation conflict, but with different results. Although the gang was not under direct observation during their earlier adolescence, what we know of the Juniors, along with evidence that the Senior Outlaws themselves had been more criminal when younger, would suggest that the gang had in fact undergone a similar struggle and that the proponents of conformity to the law had won.

In any case, the events of the observation period made it clear that the Senior Outlaws sought "rep" as a gang primarily through effective execution of legitimate enterprises such as athletics, dances, and other non-violative activities. In line with this objective, they maintained a consistent concern with the "good name" of the gang and with "keeping out of trouble" in the face of constant and ubiquitous temptations. For example, they attempted (without much success) to establish friendly relations with the senior priest of their parish—in contrast with the Junior Outlaws, who were on very bad terms with the local church. At one point during the contact period when belligerent Bandits, claiming that the Outlaws had attacked one of the Midget Bandits, vowed to "wipe out every Outlaw jacket in Midcity," the Senior Outlaws were concerned not only with the threat of attack but also with the threat to their reputation. "That does it," said one boy, "I knew we'd get into something. There goes the good name of the Outlaws."

Leadership and clique arrangements in the Senior Outlaws reflected three conditions, each related in some way to the relatively low stress on criminal activity: the stability of gang membership (members were rarely removed from the area by institutional confinement), the absence of significant conflict over the prestige and criminality issue, and the importance placed on legitimate collective activities. The Senior Bandits were the most unified of the gangs we observed directly; there were no important cleavages or factions; even the distinction between more-active and less-active members was less pronounced than in the other gangs.

But as in the other gangs, leadership among the Senior Outlaws was collective and situational. There were four key leaders, each of whom assumed authority in his own sphere of competence. As in the case of the Bandit gangs there was little overt competition among leaders; when differences arose between the leadership and the rank and file, the several leaders tended to support one another. In one significant respect, however, Outlaw leadership differed from that of the other gangs; authority was exercised more firmly and accepted more readily. Those in charge of collective enterprises generally issued commands after the manner of a tough army sergeant or work-gang boss. Although obedience to such commands was frequently less than flawless, the leadership style of Outlaw leaders approximated the "snap-to-it" approach of organizations that control firmer sanctions than do most corner gangs. Compared to the near-chaotic behavior of their younger brother gang, the organizational practices of the Senior appeared as a model of efficiency. The "authoritarian" mode of leadership was particularly characteristic of one boy, whose perogatives were somewhat more generalized than those of the other leaders. While he was far from an undisputed "boss," holding instead a kind of *primus inter pares* position, he was as close to a "boss" as anything found among the direct-observation gangs.

His special position derived from the fact that he showed superior capability in an unusually wide range of activities, and this permitted him wider authority than the other leaders. One might have expected, in a gang oriented predominantly to law-abiding activity, that this leader would serve as an exemplar of legitimacy and rank among the most law-abiding. This was not the case. He was, in fact, one of the most criminal of the Senior Outlaws, being among the relatively few who had "done time." He was a hard drinker, an able street-fighter, a skilled football strategist and team leader, an accomplished dancer and smooth ladies' man. His leadership position was based not on his capacity to best exemplify the law-abiding orientation of the gang, but on his capabilities in a variety of activities, violative and non-violative. Thus, even in the gang most concerned with "keeping clean," excellence in crime still constituted one important basis of prestige. Competence as such rather than the legitimacy of one's activities provided the major basis of authority.

We still have to ask, however, why leadership among the Senior Outlaws was more forceful than in the other gangs. One reason emerges by comparison with the "weak leader" situation of the Junior Bandits. Younger and of lower social status, their factional conflict over the law-violation-and-prestige issue was sufficiently intense so that only a leader without an explicit commitment to either side could be acceptable to both. The Seniors, older and of higher status, had developed a good degree of intragang consensus on this issue, and showed little factionalism. They could thus accept a relatively strong leader without jeopardizing gang unity.

A second reason also involves differences in age and social status, but as these relate to the world of work. In contrast to the younger gangs, whose perspectives more directly revolved around the subculture of adolescence and its specific concerns, the Senior Outlaws at age 19 were on the threshold of adult work, and some in fact were actively engaged in it. In contrast to the lower-status gangs whose orientation to gainful employment was not and never would be as "responsible" as that of the Outlaws, the activities of the Seniors as gang members more directly reflected and anticipated the requirements and conditions of the adult occupational roles they would soon assume.

Of considerable importance in the prospective occupational world of the Outlaws was, and is, the capacity to give and take orders in the execution of collective enterprises. Unlike the Bandits, few of whom would ever occupy other than subordinate positions, the Outlaws belonged to that sector of society which provides the men who exercise direct authority over groups of laborers or blue collar workers. The self-executed collective activities of the gang—organized athletics, recreational projects, fund-raising activities—provided a training ground for the practice of organizational skills—planning organized enterprises, working together in their conduct, executing the directives of legitimate superiors. It also provided a training ground wherein those boys with the requisite talents could learn and practice the difficult art of exercising authority effectively over lower-class men. By the time they had reached the age of twenty, the leaders of the Outlaws had experienced in the gang many of the problems and responsibilities confronting the army sergeant, the police lieutenant and the factory foreman.

The nature and techniques of leadership in the Senior Outlaws had relevance not only to their own gang but to the Junior Outlaws as well. Relations between the Junior and Senior Outlaws were the closest of all the intensive-contact gang subdivisions. The Seniors kept a close watch on their younger fellows, and served them in a variety of ways, as athletic coaches, advisers, mediators and arbiters. The older gang followed the factional conflicts of the Juniors with close attention, and were not above intervening when conflict reached sufficient intensity or threatened their own interests. The dominant leader of the Seniors was particularly concerned with the behavior of the Juniors; at one point, lecturing them about their disorderly conduct in Rosa's store, he remarked. "I don't hang with you guys, but I know what you do. . . ." The Seniors did not, however, succeed in either preventing the near-break-up of the Junior Outlaws or slowing their move toward law-breaking activities.

The Prevalence of Gangs

The subtle and intricately contrived relations among cliques, leadership and crime in the four subdivisions of the Bandits and Outlaws reveal the gang as an ordered and adaptive form of association, and its members as able and rational human beings. The fascinating pattern of inter-gang variation within a basic framework illustrates vividly the compelling influences of differences in age and social status on crime, leadership and other forms of behavior—even when these differences are surprisingly small. The experiences of Midcity gang members show that the gang serves the lower-class adolescent as a flexible and adaptable training instrument for imparting vital knowledge concerning the value of individual competence, the appropriate limits of law-violating behavior, the uses and abuses of authority, and the skills of interpersonal relations. From this perspective, the street gang appears not as a casual or transient manifestation that emerges intermittently in response to unique and passing social conditions, but rather as a stable associational form, coordinate with and complementary to the family, and as an intrinsic part of the way of life of the urban low-status community.

How then can one account for the widespread conception of gangs as somehow popping up and then disappearing again? One critical reason concerns the way one defines what a gang is. Many observers, both scholars and non-scholars, often use a *sine qua non* to sort out "real" gangs from near-gangs, pseudo-gangs, and non-gangs. Among the more common of these single criteria are: autocratic one-man leadership, some "absolute" degree of solidarity or stable membership, a predominant involvement in violent conflict with other gangs, claim to a rigidly defined turf, or participation in activities thought to pose a threat to other sectors of the community. Reaction to groups lacking the *sine qua non* is often expressed with a dismissive "Oh, them. That's not a *gang*. That's just a bunch of kids out on the corner."

For many people there are no gangs if there is no gang warfare. It's that simple. For them, as for all those who concentrate on the "threatening" nature of the gang, the phenomenon is defined in terms of the degree of "problem" it poses: A group whose "problematic" behavior is hard to ignore is a gang; one less problematic is not. But what some people see as a problem may not appear so to others. In Philadelphia, for example, the police reckoned there were 80 gangs, of which 20 were at war; while social workers estimated there were 200 gangs, of which 80 were "most hostile." Obviously, the social workers' 80 "most hostile" gangs were the same as the 80 "gangs" of the police. The additional 120 groups defined as gangs by the social workers were seen as such because they were thought to be appropriate objects of social work; but to the police they were not sufficiently troublesome to require consistent police attention, and were not therefore defined as gangs.

In view of this sort of confusion, let me state our definition of what a gang is. A gang is a group of urban adolescents who congregate recurrently at one or more nonresidential locales, with continued affiliation based on self-defined criteria of inclusion and exclusion. Recruitment, customary places of assembly and ranging areas are based in a specific territory, over some portion of which limited use and occupancy rights are claimed. Membership both in the gang as a whole and in its subgroups is determined on the basis of age. The group maintains a versatile repertoire of activities, with hanging out, mating, recreational and illegal activity being of central importance; and it is internally differentiated on the basis of authority, prestige, personality and clique-formation.

The main reason that people have consistently mistaken the prevalence of gangs is the widespread tendency to define them as gangs on the basis of the presence or absence of one or two characteristics that are thought to be essential to the "true" gang. Changes in the forms or frequencies or particular characteristics, such as leadership, involvement in fighting, or modes of organization, are seen not as normal variations over time and space, but rather as signs of the emergence or disappearance of the gangs themselves. Our work does not support this view; instead, our evidence indicates that the core characteristics of the gang vary continuously from place to place and from time to time without negating the existence of the gang. Gangs may be larger or smaller, named or nameless, modestly or extensively differentiated, more or less active in gang fighting, stronger or weaker in leadership, black, white, yellow or brown, without affecting their identity as gangs. So long as groups of adolescents gather periodically outside the home, frequent a particular territory, restrict membership by age and other criteria, pursue a variety of activities, and maintain differences in authority and prestige—so long will the gang continue to exist as a basic associational form.

September 1969

FURTHER READING:

The Gang: A Study of 1313 Gangs in Chicago by Frederic M. Thrasher (Chicago: University of Chicago Press, 1927) is the classic work on American youth gangs. Although published in the 1920s, it remains the most detailed and comprehensive treatise on gangs and gang life ever written.

Delinquent Boys: The Culture of the Gang by Albert K. Cohen (Glencoe, Ill.: Free Press, 1955) is the first-major attempt to explain the behavior of gang members using modern sociological theory.

Delinquency and Opportunity: A Theory of Delinquent Gangs by Richard A. Cloward and Lloyd E. Ohlin (Glencoe, Ill.: Free Press, 1960) explains the existence, both of gangs, and major types of gangs. It has had a profound impact on American domestic policy.

Group Process and Gang Delinquency by James F. Short Jr. and Fred L. Strodtbeck (Chicago: University of Chicago Press, 1965). An empirical "test" of divergent theories of gangs and delinquency, it includes the first extensive application of statistical techniques and the first systematic application of the social-psychological conceptual framework to the study of gangs.

Vietnam:
Why Men Fight

CHARLES C. MOSKOS, JR.

This study is based on my observations of American soldiers in combat made during two separate stays in South Vietnam. During the first field trip in 1965, I spent two weeks with a weapons squad in a rifle platoon of a paratrooper unit. The second field trip in 1967 included a six-day stay with an infantry rifle squad, and shorter periods with several other combat squads. Although identified as a university professor and sociologist, I had little difficulty gaining access to the troops because of my official status as an accredited correspondent. I entered combat units by simply requesting permission from the local headquarters to move into a squad. Once there, I experienced the same living conditions as the squad members. The novelty of my presence soon dissipated as I became a regular participant in the day-to-day activities of the squad.

The soldiers with whom I was staying were performing combat missions of a patrolling nature, the most typical type of combat operation in Vietnam. Patrols are normally small-unit operations involving squads (9-12 men) or platoons (30-40 men). Such small units made up patrols whose usual mission was to locate enemy forces which could then be subjected to ground, artillery or air attack. Patrols normally last one or several days and are manned by lower-ranking enlisted men, noncommissioned officers leading squads and lieutenants heading platoons.

In the vast majority of instances these patrols turn out to be a "walk in the sun," meeting only sporadic or no enemy resistance. Even when enemy contact is not made, however, patrols suffer casulties from land mines and booby traps. But it is primarily on those occasions when enemy forces are encountered that casualty rates are extremely high. Upon return to the permanent base camp, members of the patrol are able to enjoy a modicum of physical comfort. They live in large tents, eat hot food, get their mail more or less regularly, see movies, and can purchase beer, cigarettes and toilet articles at field Post Exchanges. They spend the bulk of their time in camp on guard duty and maintaining equipment.

In both the 1965 and 1967 field trips, I collected data through informal observations and personal interviewing of combat soldiers. During the second field trip I also conducted 34 standardized interviews with the men of the particular squads with whom I was staying. Some of the information contained in these 34 interviews is amenable to tabular ordering. Yet even when given in tabular form the data are not to be conceived as self-contained, but rather as supportive of more broadly based observations. The attitudes expressed by the formally interviewed soldiers constantly reappeared in conversations I had with numerous other combat soldiers in both 1965 and 1967. Again and again, I was struck by the common reactions of soldiers to the combat experience and their participation in the war. By myself being in the combat situation, I could conduct lengthy interviews on an intimate basis. I assert with some confidence that the findings reflect a set of beliefs widely shared by American combat soldiers throughout Vietnam during the period of the field work.

A prefatory comment is needed on the social origins of the men I interviewed. The 34 soldiers had the following civilian backgrounds prior to entering the service: ten were high-school dropouts, only two of whom were ever regularly employed; 21 were high-school graduates, six directly entering the service after finishing school; and three were college dropouts. None were college graduates. Eighteen of the 34 men had full-time employment before entering the service, 12 in blue-collar jobs and six in white-collar employment. About two-thirds of the soldiers were from working-class backgrounds with the remainder being from the lower-middle class.

As for other social background characteristics: eight were black; one was a Navajo; another was from Guam; the other 20 men were white including three Mexican-Americans and one Puerto Rican. Only seven of the squad members were married (three after entering the service). All the men, except two sergeants, were in their late teens and early twenties, the average age being 20 years. Again excepting the sergeants, all were on their initial enlistments. Twenty of the men were draftees and 14 were Regular Army volunteers. Importantly, except for occasional sardonic comments directed toward the regulars by the draftees, the behavior and attitudes of the soldiers toward the war were very similar regardless of how they entered the service.

Few stories to come out of the Vietnam War are so poignant as the story of Company A of the 196th Light Infantry Brigade, Third Battalion. As told by Associated Press reporters Horst Fass and Peter Arnett in a cable dated August 26, 1969, Company A had been pushing for five days through enemy-held territory in an effort to recover the bodies of eight Americans killed in a helicopter crash 31 miles south of Da Nang. Now, its strength halved to 60 men, its platoon leaders dead or wounded, Company A was ordered to move down a jungle rocky slope of

Nuilon Mountain. They refused. Most of the men were 19 to 20 years old, draftees, and many of them had only a short time to go before being rotated back to the States. They were ordered to move out and they refused.

The rest of the story is unimportant; as far as the military command is concerned the whole story is unimportant. But for many Americans, Company A's refusal to fight that day must have raised terrible questions—perhaps above all questions about one's own personal courage, but questions too about how and why American soldiers continue to expose themselves to death and pain in a war that few civilians any longer believe in.

The most popular notion of how men are brought to kill and be killed in combat has to do with the presumed national character of the soldiers. Different national armies perform better or worse according to the putative martial spirit of their respective citizenries. Italians make "poor" soldiers, Germans "good" ones. Another view has it that combat performance is basically a consequence of the operation of the formal military organization—the strict discipline, military training, unit esprit de corps and so forth. This viewpoint is, naturally enough, found in traditional military thought; but the importance of military socialization is similarly emphasized—albeit from different premises —by antimilitarists concerned with the perversions that military life allegedly inflicts on men's minds. Another interpretation—often the hallmark of political rhetoric— holds that combat performance depends on the soldier's conscious allegiance to the stated purposes of the war. Whether motivated by patriotism or a belief that he is fighting for a just cause, the effective soldier is ultimately an ideologically inspired soldier.

Yet another explanation of combat motivation developed out of the social science studies of World War II. This interpretation deemphasizes cultural, formal socialization and ideological factors and focuses attention instead on the crucial role of face-to-face or "primary" groups. The motivation of the individual combat soldier rests on his solidarity and social intimacy with fellow soldiers at small-group levels. This viewpoint was characteristic of the studies that Samuel Stouffer and his associates reported in *The American Soldier*, as well as of the analysis of the *Wehrmacht* by Edward Shils and Morris Janowitz. The rediscovery of the importance of primary groups by social scientists was paralleled in the accounts given by novelists and other writers about combat behavior such as Norman Mailer, James Jones, J. Glenn Gray and S. L. A. Marshall. In a few of the more extreme elaborations of this theory, primary relations among men in combat were viewed as so intense that they overrode not only preexisting civilian values and formal military goals, but even the individual's own sense of self-preservation.

My own research among American soldiers in Vietnam has led me to question the dominant influence of the primary group in combat motivation on at least two counts. First, the self-serving aspects of primary relations in combat units must be more fully appreciated. War is a Hobbesian world and, in combat, life is truly short, nasty and brutish. But, to carry Hobbes a step farther, primary group processes in combat are a kind of rudimentary social contract, a contract that is entered into because of its advantages to oneself. Second, although the American soldier has a deep aversion to overt political symbols and patriotic appeals, this fact should not obscure his even deeper commitments to other values that serve to maintain the soldier under dangerous conditions. These values—misguided or not—must be taken into account in explaining the generally creditable combat performance American soldiers have given. Put most formally, I would argue that combat motivation arises out of the linkages between individual self-concern and the shared beliefs of soldiers as these are shaped by the immediate combat situation.

To convey the immediacy of the combat situation is hard enough for the novelist, not to say the sociologist. But to understand the fighting soldier's attitudes and behavior, it is vital to comprehend the extreme physical conditions under which he must try to live. It is only in the immediate context of battle that one can grasp the nature of the group processes developed in combat squads. For within the network of his relations with fellow squad members, the combat soldier is also fighting a very private war, a war he desperately hopes to leave alive and unscathed.

The concept of relative deprivation—interpreting an individual's evaluation of his situation by knowing the group he compares himself with—has been one of the most fruitful in social inquiry. We should not, however, forget that there are some conditions of life in which deprivation is absolute. In combat, a man's social horizon is narrowly determined by his immediate life chances in the most literal sense. The fighting solider, as an absolutely deprived person, responds pragmatically to maximize any and all short-run opportunities to improve his chances of survival. For the soldier the decisions of state that brought him into combat are irrelevant, meaningless.

Under fire, the soldier not only faces an imminent danger of his own death and wounding; he also witnesses the killing and suffering of his buddies. And always there are the routine physical stresses of combat life—the weight of the pack, tasteless food, diarrhea, lack of water, leeches, mosquitos, rain, torrid heat, mud and loss of sleep. In an actual firefight with the enemy, the scene is generally one of terrible chaos and confusion. Deadening fear intermingles with acts of bravery and, strangely enough, even moments of exhilaration and comedy. If prisoners are taken, they may be subjected to atrocities in the rage of battle or its immediate aftermath. The soldier's distaste for endangering civilians is overcome by his fear that any Vietnamese, of any age or sex, could very well want him dead. Where the opportunity arises, he will often loot. War souvenirs are frequently collected, either to be kept or later sold to rear-echelon servicemen.

As Stendahl and Tolstoy noted long ago, once the fight is over, the soldier still has little idea of what has been accomplished in a strategic sense. His view of the war is limited to his own observations and subsequent talks with others in the same platoon or company. The often-noted reluctance of soldiers to discuss their war experiences when back home doesn't hold true in the field. They talk constantly, repetitiously, of the battles and skirmishes they have been through. They talk about them not just to talk, but more importantly to nail down tactics that may save their lives in future encounters with the enemy.

For the individual soldier, the paramount factor affecting combat motivation is the operation of the rotation system. Under current assignment policies Army personnel serve a 12-month tour of duty in Vietnam. Barring his being killed or severely wounded, then, every soldier knows exactly when he will leave Vietnam. His whole being centers on reaching his personal "DEROS" (Date Expected Return Overseas). It is impossible to overstate the soldier's constant concern with how much more time—down to the day—he must remain in Vietnam.

Within the combat unit, the rotation system has many consequences for social cohesion and individual motivation. The rapid turnover of personnel hinders the development of primary group ties, even as it rotates out of the unit men who have attained fighting experience. It also, however, mitigates those strains (noted in World War II in *The American Soldier*) that occur when new replacements are confronted by seasoned combat veterans. Yet because of the tactical nature of patrols and the somewhat random likelihood of encountering the enemy, a new arrival may soon experience more actual combat than some of the men in the same company who are nearing the end of their tour in Vietnam. Whatever its effects on the long-term combat effectiveness of the American forces as a whole however, the rotation system does largely account for the generally high morale of the combat soldier.

During his one-year stint in Vietnam, the fighting soldier finds his attitude undergoing definite changes. Although attitudes depend a good deal on individual personality and combat exposure, they usually follow a set course. Upon arrival at his unit and for several weeks thereafter, the soldier is excited to be in the war zone and looks forward to engaging the enemy. After the first serious encounter, however, he loses his enthusiasm for combat. He becomes highly respectful of the enemy's fighting abilities and begins to fear and scorn the South Vietnamese. He grows skeptical of victory statements from headquarters and of the official reports of enemy casualties. From about the third to the eighth month of his tour, the soldier operates on a kind of plateau of moderate commitment to his combat role.

Toward the ninth and tenth months, the soldier begins to regard himself as an "old soldier," and it is usually at this point that he is generally most effective in combat. As he approaches the end of his tour in Vietnam, however, he begins noticeably to withdraw his efficiency. He now becomes reluctant to engage in offensive combat operations; and increasingly, he hears and repeats stories of men killed the day they were to rotate back home.

It is significant, though, that "short-timer's fever" is implicitly recognized by the others, and demands on short-timers are informally reduced. The final disengagement period of the combat soldier is considered a kind of earned prerogative which those earlier in the rotation cycle hope eventually to enjoy.

Overall, the rotation system reinforces a perspective which is essentially private and self-concerned. Somewhat remarkably, for example, I found little difference in the attitudes of combat soldiers in Vietnam over a two-year interval. The consistency was largely due, I believe, to the fact that each soldier goes through a similar rotation experience. The end of the war is marked by the date a man leaves Vietnam, and not by its eventual outcome—whether victory, defeat or stalemate. Even discussion of broader military strategy and the progress of the war—except when directly impinging on one's unit—appears irrelevant to the combat soldier: "*My* war is over when I go home."

When the soldier feels concern over the fate of others, it is for those he personally knows in his own outfit. His concern does not extend to those who have preceded him or will eventually replacd him. Rather, the attitude is typically, "I've done my time; let the others do theirs," Or, as put in the soldier's vernacular, he is waiting to make the final entry on his "FIGMO" chart—"Fuck it, got my order [to return to the United States]." Whatever incipient identification there might be with abstract comrades-in-arms is flooded out by the private view of the war fostered by the rotation system.

Conventionally, the primary group is described as a network of interpersonal relationships in which the group's maintenance is valued for its own sake rather than as a mechanism that serves one's own interests. And, as has been noted, social science descriptions of combat motivation in World War II placed particular emphasis on the importance of groupings governed by intimate face-to-face relations. Roger Little's observations of a rifle company during the Korean War differed somewhat by pointing to the two-man or "buddy system" as the basic unit of cohesion rather than the squad or platoon.

My observations in Vietnam, however, indicate that the concept of primary groups has limitations in explaining combat motivation even beyond that suggested by Little. The fact is that if the individual soldier is realistically to improve his survival chances, he must *necessarily* develop and take part in primary relationships. Under the grim conditions of ground warfare, an individual's survival is directly dependent upon the support—moral, physical and technical—he can expect from his fellow soldiers. He gets such support to the degree that he reciprocates to the others in his unit. In other words, primary relations are at their core mutually pragmatic efforts to minimize personal risk.

Interpreting the solidarity of combat squads as an outcome of individual self-interest can be corroborated by two illustrations. The first deals with the behavior of the man on "point" in a patrolling operation. The point man is usually placed well in front of the main body, in the most exposed position. Soldiers naturally dread this dangerous assignment, but a good point man is a safeguard for the entire patrol. What happens, as often as not, is that men on point behave in a noticeably careless manner in order to avoid being regularly assigned to the job. At the same time, of course, the point man tries not to be so incautious as to put himself completely at the mercy of an encountered enemy force. In plain language, soldiers do not typically perform at their best when on point; personal safety overrides group interest.

The paramountcy of individual self-interest in combat units is also indicated by the letters soldiers write. Squad members who have returned to the United States seldom write to those remaining behind. In most cases, nothing more is heard from a soldier after he leaves the unit. Perhaps even more revealing, those still in the combat area seldom write their former buddies. Despite protestations of life-long friendship during the shared combat period, the rupture of communication is entirely mutual, once a soldier is out of danger. The soldier writes almost exclusively to those he expects to see when he leaves the service: his family and relatives, girl friends, and civilian male friends.

Do these contrasting interpretations of the network of social relations in combat units—the primary groups of World War II, the two-man relationships of the Korean War, and the essentially individualistic soldier in Vietnam described here—result from conceptual differences on the part of the commentators, or do they reflect substantive differences in the social cohesion of the American soldiers being described? If substantive differences do obtain, particularly between World War II and the wars in Korea and Vietnam, much of this variation could be accounted for by the disruptive effects on unit solidarity caused by the introduction of the rotation system in the latter two wars.

Even if we could decide whether combat primary groups are essentially entities *sui generis* or outcomes of pragmatic self-interest, there remain other difficulties in understanding the part they play in maintaining organizational effectiveness. For it has been amply demonstrated in many contexts that primary groups can hinder as well as serve to attain the formal goals of the larger organization. Thus, to describe effective combat motivation principally in terms of primary group ties leaves unanswered the question of why various armies—independent of training and equipment—perform differently in time of war. Indeed, because of the very ubiquity of primary groups in military organizations, we must look for supplementary factors to explain variations in combat motivation.

I propose that primary groups maintain the soldier in his combat role only when he has an underlying commitment to the worth of the larger social system for which he is fighting. This commitment need not be formally articulated, nor even perhaps consciously recognized. But the soldier must at some level accept, if not the specific purposes of the war, then at least the broader rectitude of the society of which he is a member. Although American combat soldiers do not espouse overtly ideological sentiments and are extremely reluctant to voice patriotic rhetoric, this should not obscure the existence of more latent beliefs in the legitimacy, and even superiority, of the American way of life. I have used the term "latent ideology" to describe the social and cultural sources of those beliefs about the war held by American soldiers. Latent ideology, in this context, refers to those widely shared sentiments of soldiers which, though not overtly political, nor even necessarily substantively political, nevertheless have concrete consequences for combat motivation.

Students of political behavior have too often been uninterested in answers that do not measure up to their own standards of expressiveness. When a person responds in a way that seems either ideologically confused or apathetic, he is considered to have no political ideology. But since any individual's involvement in any polity is usually peripheral, it is quite likely that his political attitudes will be organized quite differently from those of ideologists or political theorists. Yet when one focuses on underlying value orientations, we find a set of attitudes having a definite coherence —especially within the context of that individual's life situation.

Quite consistently, the American combat soldier displays a profound skepticism of political and ideological appeals. Somewhat paradoxically, then, anti-ideology itself is a recurrent and integral part of the soldier's belief system. They dismiss patriotic slogans or exhortations to defend democracy with "What a crock," "Be serious, man," or

"Who's kidding who?" In particular, they have little belief that they are protecting an outpost of democracy in South Vietnam. United States Command Information pronouncements stressing defense of South Vietnam as an outpost of the "Free World" are almost as dubiously received as those of Radio Hanoi which accuse Americans of imperialist aggression. As one soldier put it, "Maybe we're supposed to be here and maybe not. But you don't have time to think about things like that. You worry about getting zapped and dry socks tomorrow. The other stuff is a joke."

In this same vein, when the soldier responds to the question of why he is in Vietnam, his answers are couched in a quite individualistic frame of reference. He sees little connection between his presence in Vietnam and the national policies that brought him there. Twenty-seven of the 34 combat soldiers I interviewed defined their presence in the war in terms of personal misfortune. Typical responses were: "My outfit was sent over here and me with it," "My tough luck in getting drafted," "I happened to be at the wrong place at the wrong time," "I was fool enough to join this man's army," and "My own stupidity for listening to the recruiting sergeant." Only five soldiers mentioned broader policy implications—to stop Communist aggression. Two soldiers stated they requested assignment to Vietnam because they wanted to be "where the action is."

Because of the combat soldier's overwhelming propensity to see the war in private and personal terms, I had to ask them specifically what they thought the United States was doing in Vietnam. When the question was phrased in this manner, the soldiers most often said they were in Vietnam "to stop Communism." This was about the only ideological slogan these American combat soldiers could be brought to utter; 19 of the 34 interviewed soldiers saw stopping Communism as the purpose of the war. But when they expressed this view it was almost always in terms of defending the United States, not the "Free World" in general and certainly not South Vietnam. They said: "The only way we'll keep them out of the States is to kill them here," "Let's get it over now, before they're too strong to stop," "They have to be stopped somewhere," "Better to zap this country than let them do the same to us."

Fifteen of the soldiers gave responses other than stopping Communism. Three gave frankly cynical explanations of the war by stating that domestic prosperity in the United States depended on a war ecomony. Two soldiers held that the American intervention was a serious mistake initially; but that it was now too late to back out because of America's reputation. One man even gave a Malthusian interpretation, arguing that war was needed to limit population growth. Nine of the soldiers could give no reason for the war even after extensive discussion. Within this group, one heard responses such as: "I only wish I knew" "Maybe Johnson knows, but I sure don't" and "I've been wondering about that ever since I got here."

I asked each of the 19 soldiers who mentioned stopping Communism as the purpose of the war what was so bad about Communism that it must be stopped at the risk of his own life. The first reaction to such a question was usually perplexity or rueful shrugging. After thinking about it, and with some prodding, 12 of the men expressed their distaste for communism by stressing its authoritarian aspects in social relations. They saw Communism as a system of excessive social regimentation which allows the individual no autonomy in the pursuit of his own happiness. Typical descriptions of Communism were: "That's when you can't do what you want to do," "Somebody's always telling you what to do," or "You're told where you work, what you eat, and when you shit." As one man wryly put it, "Communism is something like the army."

While the most frequently mentioned features of Communism concerned individual liberty, other descriptions were also given. Three soldiers mentioned the atheistic and antichurch aspects of Communism; two specifically talked of the absence of political parties and democratic political institutions; and one man said Communism was good in theory, but could never work in practice because human beings were "too selfish." Only one soldier mentioned the issues of public versus private property ownership.

I should stress once again that the soldiers managed to offer reasons for the war or descriptions of communism only after extended discussion and questioning. When left to themselves, they rarely discussed the goals of America's military intervention in Vietnam, the nature of Communist systems, or other political issues.

To say that the American soldier is not overtly ideological is not to deny the existence of salient values that do contribute to his motivation in combat. Despite the soldier's lack of ideological concern and his pronounced embarrassment in the face of patriotic rhetoric, he nevertheless displays an elemental American nationalism in the belief that the United States is the best country in the world. Even though he hates being in the war, the combat soldier typically believes—with a kind of joyless patriotism—that he is fighting for his American homeland. When the soldier does articulate the purposes of the war, the view is expressed that if Communist aggression is not stopped in Southeast Asia, it will be only a matter of time before the United States itself is in jeopardy. The so-called domino theory is just as persuasive among combat soldiers as it is among the general public back home.

The soldier definitely does *not* see himself fighting for South Vietnam. Quite the contrary, he thinks South Vietnam is a worthless country, and its people contemptible. The low regard in which the Vietnamese—"slopes" or "gooks"—are held is constantly present in the derogatory comments on the avarice of those who pander to GIs, the treachery of all Vietnamese, and the numbers of Vietnamese young men in the cities who are not in the armed forces. Anti-Vietnamese sentiment is most glaringly apparent in the hostility toward the ARVN (Army of the Republic of Vietnam, pronounced "Arvin") who are their supposed military allies. Disparaging remarks about "Arvin's" fighting qualities are endemic.

A variety of factors underlie the soldier's fundamental pro-Americanism, not the least of them being his immediate reliance on fellow Americans for mutual support in a country where virtually all indigenous people are seen as actual or potential threats to his physical safety. He also has deep concern for his family and loved ones back home. These considerations, however, are true of any army fighting in a foreign land. It is on another level, then, that I tried to uncover those aspects of American society that were most relevant and important to the combat soldier.

To obtain such a general picture of the soldier's conception of his homeland. I asked the following question, "Tell me in your own words, what makes America different from other countries?" The overriding feature in the soldier's perception of America is the creature comforts that American life can offer. Twenty-two of the soldiers described the United States by its high-paying jobs, automobiles, consumer goods and leisure activities. No other description of America came close to being mentioned as often as the high—and apparently uniquely American— material standard of living. Thus, only four of the soldiers emphasized America's democratic political institutions; three mentioned religious and spiritual values; two spoke of the general characteristics of the American people; and one said America was where the individual advanced on his own worth; another talked of America's natural and physical beauties; and one black soldier described America as racist. Put in another way, it is the materialistic—and I do not use the word pejoratively—aspects of life in America that are most salient to combat soldiers.

The soldier's belief in the superiority of the American way of life is further reinforced by the contrast with the Vietnamese standard of living. The combat soldier cannot help making invidious comparisons between the life he led in the United States—even if he is working class— and what he sees in Vietnam. Although it is more pronounced in the Orient, it must be remembered that Americans abroad—whether military or civilian—usually find themselves in locales that compare unfavorably with the material affluence of the United States. Indeed, should American soldiers ever be stationed in a country with a markedly higher standard of living than that of the United States, I believe they would be severely shaken in their belief in the merits of American society.

Moreover, the fighting soldier, by the very fact of being in combat, leads an existence that is not only more dangerous than civilian life, but more primitive and physically harsh. The soldier's somewhat romanticized view of life back home is buttressed by his direct observation of the Vietnamese scene, but also by his own immediate lower standard of living. It has often been noted that front-line soldiers bitterly contrast their plight with the physical amenities enjoyed by their fellow countrymen, both rear-echelon soldiers as well as civilians back home. While this is superficially true, the attitudes of American combat soldiers toward their compatriots are actually somewhat more ambivalent. For at the same time the soldier is begrudging the civilian his physical comforts, it is these very comforts for which he fights. Similarly, they envy rather than disapprove of those rear-echelon personnel who engage in sub rosa profiteering.

The materialistic ethic is reflected in another characteristic of American servicemen. Even among front-line combat soldiers, one sees an extraordinary amount of valuable paraphernalia. Transistor radios are practically *de rigueur*. Cameras and other photographic accessories are widely evident and used. Even the traditional letter-writing home is becoming displaced by tape recordings. It seems more than coincidental that American soldiers commonly refer to the United States as "The Land of the Big PX."

Another factor that plays a part in combat motivation is the notion of masculinity and physical toughness that pervades the soldier's outlook toward warfare. Being a combat soldier is a man's job. Front-line soldiers often cast aspersions on the virility of rear-echelon personnel ("titless WAC's"). A soldier who has not experienced combat is called a "cherry" (i.e. virgin). Likewise, paratroopers express disdain for "legs," as nonairborne soldiers are called. This he-man attitude is also found in the countless joking references to the movie roles of John Wayne and Lee Marvin. These definitions of masculinity are, of course, general in America and the military organization seeks to capitalize on them with such perennial recruiting slogans as "The Marine Corps Builds Men" and "Join the Army and Be a Man."

Needless to say, however, the exaggerated masculine ethic is much less evident among soldiers after their units have been bloodied. As the realities of combat are faced, more prosaic definitions of manly honor emerge. (Also, there is more frequent expression of the male role in manifestly sexual rather than combative terms, for example, the repeatedly heard "I'm a lover not a fighter.") That is, notions of masculinity serve to create initial motivation to enter combat, but recede once the life-and-death facts of warfare are confronted. Moreover, once the unit is tempered by combat, definitions of manly honor are not seen to encompass individual heroics. Quite the opposite, the very word "hero" is used to describe negatively any soldier who recklessly jeopardizes the unit's welfare. Men try to avoid going out on patrols with individuals who are overly anxious to make contact with the enemy. Much like the slacker at the other end of the spectrum, the "hero" is also seen as one who endangers the safety of others. As is the case with virtually all combat behavior, the ultimate standard rests on keeping alive.

On both of my trips to Vietnam I repeatedly heard combat soldiers—almost to a man—vehemently denounce peace demonstrators back in the United States. At first glance such an attitude might be surprising. After all, peaceniks and soldiers both fervently want the troops brought home. In fact, however, the troops I interviewed expressed overt political sentiments only when the antiwar demonstrations came up in the talk. Significantly, the soldier perceived the peace demonstrations as being directed against himself personally and not against the war. "Did I vote to come here? Why blame the GI?" There was also a widespread feeling that if peace demonstrators were in Vietnam they would change their minds. As one man stated: "How can they know what's happening if they're sitting on their asses in the States. Bring them here and we'd shape them up quick enough." Or as one of the more philosophically inclined put it, 'I'd feel the same way if I were back home. But once you're here and your buddies are getting zapped, you have to see things different."

Much of the soldier's dislike of peace demonstrators is an outcome of class hostility. To many combat soldiers—themselves largely working class—peace demonstrators are socially privileged college students. I heard many remarks such as the following: "I'm fighting for those candy-asses just because I don't have an old man to support me." "I'm stuck here and those rich draft dodgers are having a ball raising hell." "You'd think they'd have more sense with all that smart education."

The peace demonstrators, moreover, were seen as undercutting and demeaning the losses and hardships already suffered by American soldiers. Something of this sort undoubtedly contributed to the noticeable hawklike sentiments of combat soldiers. "If we get out now, then every GI died for nothing. Is this why I've been putting my ass on the line?" Here we seem to have an illustration of a more general social phenomenon: the tendency in human beings to justify to themselves sacrifices they have already made. Sacrifice itself can create legitimacy for an organization over a short period of time. It is only after some point when sacrifices suddenly seem too much, that the whole enterprise comes under critical reevaluation. But sharp questioning of past and future sacrifices does not generally occur among combat soldiers in Vietnam. I believe this is because the 12-month rotation system removes the soldier from the combat theater while his personal stake remains high and before he might begin to question the whole operation. The rotation system, in other words, not only maintains individual morale but also fosters a collective commitment to justify American sacrifices.

The soldier's hostility toward peace demonstrators is reinforced by his negative reactions to the substance of certain antiwar arguments. For while the combat soldier is constantly concerned with his own and his fellow American's safety, as well as being a fundamental believer in the American way of life and profoundly apolitical to boot, the radical element of the peace movement mourns the suffering of the Vietnamese, is vehement in its anti-Americanism, and is self-consciously ideological. At almost every point, the militant peace movement articulates sentiments in direct opposition to the basic values of the American soldier. Statements bemoaning civilian Vietnamese casualties are interpreted as wishes for greater American losses. Assertions of the United States' immorality for its interventionism run contrary to the soldier's elemental belief in the rectitude of the American nation. Arguments demonstrating that the Viet Cong are legitimate revolutionaries have no credence both because of the soldier's ignorance of Vietnamese history and—more importantly—because the Viet Cong are out to kill him. As one man summed it up: "I don't know who are the good guys or the bad guys, us or the V.C. But anybody who shoots at me ain't my friend. Those college punks are going to answer to a lot of us when we get back."

It must be stressed, however, that the soldier's dislike of peace demonstrators is reactive and does not imply any preexisting support for the war. Paradoxically, then, the more militant peace demonstrations have probably created a level of support for the war among combat soldiers that would otherwise be absent. This is not to say that the soldier is immune to antiwar arguments. But the kind of arguments that would be persuasive among soldiers (e.g. Vietnam is not worth American blood, South Vietnam is manipulating the United States, the corruptness of the Saigon regime and ineptitude of the ARVN make for needless U.S. casualties) are not the ones usually voiced by radical peace groups. *The combat soldier is against peace-demonstrators rather than for the war.* For it should also be known that he has scant affection for "support-the-boys" campaigns in the United States. Again, the attitude that "they don't know what it's all about" applies. As one soldier succinctly put it—and his words spoke for most: "The only support I want is out."

November 1969

FURTHER READING

The American Soldier: Combat and Its Aftermath by Samuel A. Stouffer (Princeton, N.J.: Princeton University Press, 1949) is a sociological classic of the analyses of empirical data drawn from massive surveys conducted among servicemen during World War II by the Research Branch, Information and Education Division, War Department.

Up Front by Bill Mauldin (New York: Holt, Rinehart and Winston, 1945) contains the tragicomical cartoons of World War II's "Willie and Joe" along with a perceptive discussion of combat from the viewpoint of the average GI.

The Warriors by J. Glenn Gray (New York: Harcourt, Brace, 1959) is a philosopher's recollections of the experiences of warfare.

Men Against Fire by S.L.A. Marshall (New York: William Morrow, 1947) contains after-battle interviewing to assess combat tactics.

ROTC Retreat

JOSEPH W. SCOTT

Students across the country, in growing numbers, have been picketing, protesting and demonstrating against the presence of Reserve Officer Training Corps units (ROTC) on their college campuses. Acceding in part to student demands, about 55 colleges and universities have eliminated compulsory ROTC enrollment where it existed, and have taken steps to "demilitarize" the ROTC curriculum. Most recently, notably at the Ivy League institutions, undergraduates have been putting pressure upon educational administrators to withdraw academic credit for ROTC courses. Following the student seizure of University Hall this past spring, Harvard officials agreed to discontinue course credit for ROTC and even promised to consider abandoning ROTC altogether.

Actually, undergraduate dissatisfaction with military training began to crystallize and make itself heard in the 1950s, and since then the content and administration of ROTC programs have been progressively altered. Now, the students are challenging ROTC's very existence. A brief look at ROTC's objectives, its history and its performance record will provide some insight into the reasons for student antagonism and how persistent opposition has forced the military into accommodating itself to the will of the civilian sector.

America's participation in three major wars has resulted in a military policy of "preparedness," a policy that depends a great deal upon the successful recruitment and retention of young lower-ranking officers. With the Vietnam war, the expansion of the present standing military forces and the rapid turnover of the junior officers have made officer recruitment an acute and continuing problem. To meet the need for an average of 13,000 new second lieutenants each year, the Army has contracted with colleges and universities throughout the country to have professors of military science and tactics along with ROTC units. By September, 277 campuses will offer Army ROTC programs that are expected to produce most of the 13,000-15,000 officers needed this year.

ROTC, since the Korean conflict, has been the Army's major source of officers. "Without ROTC," proclaims *Where the Leaders Are*, an Army ROTC recruitment brochure, "the rapid expansion of the American Army during the two World Wars, the Korean conflict and other periods of national crisis would have been difficult if not impossible." This academic-military collaboration is the chief concern of many of today's student demonstrators; they argue that if the universities were to withdraw their support, the Army would be forced to reduce the number of American troops in Vietnam. The protesters feel that the hypocrisy of industry in supplying napalm in the name of peace-seeking is exceeded only by that of the universities in their willingness to provide military manpower to carry on the war.

ROTC dates back to Civil War days. The Army's need for a steady supply of trained officers was one of the rationales behind the passage of the Morrill Act in 1862. This bill, sometimes known as the Land Grant Act, provided that tracts of federal land be given to the states for the support and maintenance of at least one college where the main teaching emphasis would be on agriculture, military tactics and mechanical arts. The act clearly required the offering of courses in military tactics; student enrollment procedures were to be left to the discretion of individual schools. Most participating schools chose to make attendance mandatory.

ROTC as it is known today began during World War I with the National Defense Act of 1916. Under its provisions the federal government provided, as it still does, staff and materials to qualified colleges and universities applying to it for a four-year military curriculum. The curriculum comprised two years of basic training and two years of advanced training, which includes six weeks of summer camp instruction. Contracts are renewed each year and can be terminated by either side after one year's advance notice. The legislation also outlined the areas to be covered in the curriculum, the qualifications for a full commission, and the rate of pay for officer candidates. The reason for the act, of course, was to provide officers for the Great War, but because the ROTC provisions were not fully implemented until after the Armistice, most World War I officers were provided by officer candidate Schools on military posts rather than by ROTC.

Nevertheless, swept along in the tide of patriotism that surged through the country from 1916 to 1920, college officials rushed to the government with applications requesting ROTC units on their campuses. By 1919, Army ROTC units had been established on 191 campuses. Once the fever had abated, however, the number fell to 124.

During World War II, more than 100,000 ROTC graduates served as commissioned officers in the Army. But again, when the need was immediate the four-year ROTC training period was found too long a time to wait; Officer Candidate Schools on military reservations were activated, as in World War I, to assure the rapid training of urgently needed officers.

Since the Korean War, however, the officer recruitment picture has changed. The number of officers produced by ROTC has consistently exceeded the output of Officer Candidate Schools. In 1952, OCS produced 12,541 officers as compared with 13,825 commissioned by the Army ROTC (12,857 reservists and 968 regular army). Since 1952, ROTC has produced 12,000 or more officers annually. About 85 percent of the Army second lieutenants and about 65 percent of first lieutenants now serving on the combat-arms units (Infantry, Armor, Artillery) were commissioned through ROTC. As the major supplier of young officers entering the Army each year, the ROTC program commissions nearly 20 times as many new officers as the United States Military Academy at West Point, which graduates about 800 men annually; and ROTC turns out about 10 times as many second lieutenants as Officer Candidate Schools. Even so, by 1964, lagging recruitment into ROTC had reached a crisis point and the military realized that something had to be done.

With the passage of the ROTC Vitalization Act of 1964, the program has been modified to incorporate a number of additional inducements to prospective enrollees. It authorizes a pay increase for all students enrolled in the advanced course of the traditional four-year program and it creates a new two-year program for transfer students from junior colleges and for students in four-year colleges who have not participated in ROTC during their first two years. A six-week stint at summer training camp after the sophomore year takes the place of the basic course required of students in the full four-year program.

In addition to reducing the on-campus training period, the Act provides for scholarship aid to qualified students enrolled in the four-year program. Such scholarships cover all college expenses with the exception of room and board.

The military establishment and most educational institutions are separated by vast differences in values, structure, style and function. Anathema to the university, with its long-standing tradition of humanism, are all the trappings of the military life—the wearing of uniform clothing, the lock-step discipline, the saluting, the parading, the "yes-sirring" and the general authoritarian structure of military discipline. The gulf fills with hostility when the two are forced to work in a close, symbiotic relationship.

One of the sources of conflict is the dual allegiance of the ROTC unit on each campus. Functioning as a detachment of its parent service, the unit must at the same time, as a paying guest, conform with all the practices and regulations of its host institution. The officers assigned as instructors are subject to military discipline and control; their appointment must be approved by the university and they are expected as well to assume all of the duties and responsibilities required of the rest of the faculty. Their course content and teaching performance are subject to the same review accorded to all other curricula. Gene M. Lyons and John W. Masland, in their book published in 1957, *Education and Military Leadership: A Study of the ROTC,* compare the ROTC staff's dilemma to that of foreign embassies within otherwise soverign territories.

Still, the inherent danger of the university-federal government liaison is the opportunity it creates for government control over the actual educational process. Unlike other federally-funded programs, ROTC's curriculum, its instructors and its textbooks are determined by the federal government.

In *The College Student and the ROTC: A Study of Eight Colleges*, Raymond Fink interviewed several hundred students involved in the compulsory program in 1958. His findings showed that most would not have participated had they been allowed a free choice. Fink reported that even though the last two years of ROTC programs are voluntary, the majority of students who enroll in the advanced courses after being forced into the first two years, do so largely for reasons other than patriotism or the serious pursuit of a military career. A great many reportedly continue in ROTC solely to avoid the draft, others to qualify for ROTC scholarships; some are motivated by the desire to spend their obligatory two years of duty in the more comfortable life-style of the officer, and still others continue through default—they have nothing better planned and ROTC permits them to pursue two careers at once.

Fink's conclusions are supported by the findings of a study conducted in 1956 by the Operations Evaluation Unit of the Adjutant General's office. This evaluation of ROTC officers while they were on active duty shows, in rounded figures, that at the end of their two-year stint only 6 percent would choose to remain in service, 19 percent planned to continue their education, 59 percent planned to take a civilian job and 15 percent were undecided.

Motivating college students toward a career in the armed forces continues to be one of the military's most difficult problems and one of its most conspicuous failures. Yet the demands upon career officers call for the talents of college-trained men. Masland's and Lawrence I. Radway's 1959 study, *Soldiers and Scholars: Military Education and National Policy*, illustrates conclusively that young men simply do not come to college to enter upon a military career. The armed forces' difficulties in attracting college graduates as career officers will persist, the study points out, until a military career is made more attractive in a highly competitive economy and until American society places a higher value upon the military profession. As Morris Janowitz puts it in *The Professional Soldier* (1960): "In contrast to the public acclaim accorded individual military heroes, officership remains a relatively low-status profession."

But recruitment efforts suffer not only because of the low status of the military career, but also because students generally dislike most features of the campus-based compulsory military training program. At schools where military training is mandatory for freshmen and sophomores, *Newsweek* reports, "they tend to regard classes in Military Logistics the same way their fathers regarded KP." ROTC field manuals, say the students, are written "by and for cretins." Pragmatic rather than pacifist considerations would appear to be the root cause of anti-ROTC sentiment on campus; most students resent the interference of military courses and service with their training for and pursuit of a civilian career. The long hours required by ROTC have become "an intolerable burden" in the face of increasing academic demands on students.

From his interviews with approximately 1,000 cadets enrolled in basic ROTC at the University of Illinois, David Young reported in the February 1962 *Military Review* that a majority said that ROTC was academically inferior to other courses. Many viewed the military science program as "a waste of time."

Among the list of specific grievances garnered from a number of student surveys are enforced attendance at publicly conspicuous close-order drill, (euphemistically referred to as "leadership laboratory"), adherence to military customs and rituals, wearing of the uniform, and instruction in weaponry and methods of professional killing.

More schematically, the military science curriculum has been the target of the following criticisms:

☐ The military insistence upon regimentation and utilitarian knowledge is diametrically opposed to stated academic goals of individual development and the pursuit of theoretical, abstract knowledge.

☐ The military emphasis on duty, tradition, obedience and rote learning conflict with the declared academic values of free inquity, skepticism, criticism and innovation.

☐ The Army's objective is to produce narrow specialists, ritually proficient in a particular skill; the university is supposed to educate the whole man so that he can use his intellect in acquiring knowledge in a variety of fields.

We have the students' appraisal of their ROTC experiences. But how does ROTC measure up under the eye of a professional social scientist? Gene Lyons wrote in the October 1959, *Nation* a summary of his study of the complete ROTC program—its curricula, staff and materials. He dismisses the curriculum as fragmented and nonintellectual. Courses in military and naval history provide the only relief from technical instruction. Instruction in social science courses is generally substandard and the service-prepared texts in those courses are both biased and dull.

Professors interviewed by David Young attacked the ROTC staff as being overburdened with noncommissioned officers who lack college educations themselves, and with officers who are apathetic about teaching in ROTC.

Carrying more weight than these unofficial detractors are the university administrators whose disaffection for ROTC courses has often resulted in further diminishing ROTC's status. As evidence of their negative attitude, Young cites the fact that some schools allow students only partial credit for the hours spent in basic ROTC class. And a few refuse to give any credit at all.

But perhaps the chief complaint, and the one that militates most dramatically against rapport between the university and the military, is in those institutions where enrollment is compulsory. Conpulsory ROTC is unpopular at all university levels—among faculty, students adminstrators; it requires a large number of students, who have no intention of becoming officers, to participate in an objectionable program for two years. To these unwilling recruits ROTC seems especially unfair because the Army has at its disposal a number of volunteer sources for officers—the United States Military Academy, Officer Candidate Schools, the National Guard and direct commissions. Many students and faculty members, Young reports, feel that compulsory programs infringe upon the university's academic freedom. Its use of compulsion in an atmosphere of voluntary education severely hampers the Army's efforts to sell students on the comparative advantages of a military career.

That most students in these schools take ROTC only because they have to, and that they therefore resist it silently, is borne out by reports in *ArNavAF Journal and Register* (April 21, 1962) and *ArNavAF Register* (December 1960) that show fewer enrollments in ROTC when colleges and universities change from compulsory to voluntary enrollment. The University of Wisconsin in Madison, for example, reported a 66.1 percent drop in the enrollment of first year ROTC students and a 63.6 percent drop in second year participation. In the face of rising total campus enrollments, Cornell University recorded a 57 percent drop in first year strength and a 66.8 percent loss in the second year. The University of Puerto Rico recorded a 50.2 percent drop in first year enrollments and a 65.2 percent casualty rate in the second year. Without compulsory enrollments, the Army was in recruitment trouble; changes in ROTC were imminent.

Mounting dissatisfaction with ROTC has spawned the following modifications in the organization, funding and curriculum of ROTC.

□ *Eliminating compulsory enrollment.* As of the 1959-60 school year, only three of the 68 land-grant schools had a voluntary program. During the Land Grant Centennial celebration in 1961-62, it was disclosed that a total of 14 institutions had abandoned compulsory ROTC as of the academic year 1962-63. Several others subsequently announced plans to abandon the compulsory programs in the fall of 1963. Since 1953 there has been an increase of 103 schools with elective programs, a decrease of 64 compulsory programs. As the number of voluntary programs increase, undergraduate enrollments have fallen off markedly: 166,000 in 1953, 155,000 in 1959 and 151,000 in 1968.

The trend toward optional ROTC is a direct response to the active student protest against ROTC programs on many college campuses. The opposition gained momentum in 1960 when the National Student Association, representing student governments of 397 colleges, passed a resolution urging the elimination of compulsory ROTC.

Another accommodation to this pressure was the 1964 ROTC Vitalization Act, designed to help the military establishment through the crisis of a steadily diminishing officer supply. It broadened the recruitment base by permitting more ROTC programs to be instituted at more colleges and by offering financial inducements.

Maj. Gen. Frederick M. Warren, Chief of the U.S. Army Reserves and ROTC Affairs, writing in *Army Information Digest* of January 1961, explains the Army's willingness to accommodate students: "The latest modifications in the ROTC program are only part of the Army's constant search for ways and means to improve both its attractiveness to the students and the caliber of the graduate entering the leadership level of the national security effort."

□ *Increasing the Financial Inducements.* Advanced ROTC students formerly received $27 per month; they are now paid a minimum of $40 and a maximum of $50 per month. The regular summer camp pay has been raised from $78 to $120.60 per month. And as of the Fall semester of 1970-71, the Department of the Army reports that 5,500 ROTC students will be attending college under the scholarships created by the 1964 Vitalization Act.

□ *"Demilitarizing" the curriculum.* During the expansion of Army ROTC in the wake of the Korean conflict, there was a general switch from branch-affiliated training (preparing candidates for reserve commissions in a specific Army corps) to the "General Military Science" curriculum. Since 1953-54 no less than 213 educational institutions have converted from technical-specialist or branch-specific programs to the broader, more flexible GMS program. The Ivy League schools, such as Harvard, Yale and Princeton, were pushing for approval of an even more civilian-type curriculum. In proposing a broader education for officers, they suggested that regular academic courses be substituted for some military science courses. Even as far back as the early 1950s, the controversial Princeton plan had experimented with university-produced texts based on great military writers and the use of its own professors for courses in military history and political geography. Princeton's arguments resounded across many campuses, lending new impetus to the attacks of anti-ROTC factions. Military "training" versus broad liberal "education" emerged as the key issue, resting on opposition to compulsory enrollment and regimented learning. But early 1960, over 90 percent of all Army ROTC units had a ROTC General Military Science curriculum. It was, however, subject to widespread criticism because of its failure to include information useful beyond the initial period of active duty, and serious questions were being raised even about that.

The Army has most recently responded to criticism of the ROTC staff's calibre by requiring at least a master's degree of all its professors of military science beginning in 1970. According to *U.S. News and World Report* (May 19,1969), one Pentagon official says: "We are working on important changes in ROTC curricula—more elective courses, greater local control of the programs, more university-level training, and much less military drill." This curriculum, known as "curriculum C," is the result of a proposal drawn up in 1964 by the Mershon Committee at Ohio State University, and the Defense Department is experimenting with it at 11 volunteer campuses across the country.

Frequent incursions into the instructional territory have aggravated the training dilemma confronting the military establishment. The civilian justification for the curricular changes is that the present-day Army needs more men of technical competence, broad outlook and sound judgment.

But as ROTC has evolved toward an increasingly "demilitarized" curriculum, the young officers it produces are more poorly prepared for military occupational specialities than ever before. According to an Army review board, the "General Military Science" ROTC graduate is the least prepared when compared to graduates of OCS, USMA and college programs geared to training men for service in specific branches of the Army (Signal, Transportation, Engineering). ROTC graduates entering active duty in combat-branch line units are unable to handle their initial assignments without considerable additional training.

The reduction of military subjects in the General Military Science curriculum has broadened the gap between the preservice training and actual military job requirements.

One company commander has commented: "The ROTC graduate is not a well-trained soldier, and was never meant to be. He receives criticism because he is expected to perform with men who have a better background."

The dilution of its preservice training means that the Army must now assume responsibility for still further preparation of ROTC officers in the form of on-the-job training after they have entered active duty and are on their initial assignment. A newly commissioned ROTC officer must spend from eight weeks to three months learning the skills he will need as a member of a particular Army branch.

A break between the universities and the military would seriously impair the conduct of the war in Vietnam and, for that matter, of any major war. By attacking the armed forces' major source of leadership potential, antiwar activists have discovered the most effective method to date for curbing the military establishment's ability to wage war.

□ *Removing academic credit from ROTC courses.* One of the best ways of threatening ROTC's survival, short of abolishing it outright, is to strip it of academic credit. Harvard is in the process of dropping course credit and withdrawing faculty status from officers assigned to the ROTC staff. The faculty at Brown has voted to abolish ROTC. Faculties at Yale, Dartmouth, Bowdoin, Stanford, Princeton, Notre Dame, Washington University and the University of Pennsylvania have voted to deny academic credit to military-science courses. The report of Cornell's Presidential Commission on Military Training recommends the wider use of civilian instructors, the refusal of credit for exclusively military courses and a change of name from "military science department" to "military science program." Unless there are substantial changes in ROTC within three years, the Commission recommends that Cornell seek other means of meeting the Morrill Act provisions.

The decision of a number of schools to strip ROTC of academic standings poses a serious threat to the military. Since such actions are in violation of military-university contracts, the Army is legally required to withdraw its units from those campuses that deviate from the contractual arrangement. To counteract the prospect of widespread withdrawals, the military will have to press for a further liberalization of ROTC legislation; to avoid the predominance of noncredit courses in its curriculum, we can expect the military to move drill, map reading, weaponry and tactics off the campus and into the summer camps.

In yielding to the series of accommodations forced upon it by campus dissidents, the ROTC has been reduced to a position of tenuous control over its most sought-after resource. Hoping to stem the swelling tide of opposition, the ROTC establishment has resorted to "inducement manipulation" in the form of scholarships and various forms of career advantages; it has reduced course-hour requirements and liberalized the curriculum in an effort to make ROTC more attractive.

The military will clearly have to accommodate, as it has had to do in the past, to the will of the university community. It may be forced to restrict its recruiting efforts to those institutions with a demonstrated pro-military bias. Or it may have to abandon preservice training by pulling its units from the campuses altogether and concentrating exclusively on in-service training through an expanded network of Officer Candidate Schools. Unless additional legislation provides more autonomy to participating institutions, the removal of ROTC units from the campuses of high-quality schools is a distinct and real possibility.

September 1969

"Hell, No, We Won't Go!"

JOHN COONEY/DANA SPITZER

*Rather than have war, I would give up
everything. I would give up my country.*
                    Hynmahtu Yalat-keht (Chief Joseph)

What kinds of young men are defying their country by
refusing to enter the military service or refusing to stay in
once they have joined? Are they so disenchanted with their
country that they don't care about not being able ever to
return home without punishment? Why do they choose not
to fight in a war that demands the presence of 500,000
American troops in Vietnam, where 40,000 have already
died? Are they heroes or cowards, or simply acting the way
sane people should act when confronted with a government which says it wants to end the war but doesn't know
how to do it?

Bruce Bell is 19 years old and for most of his life he has
been everything his parents ever wanted in a son. A fair
athlete, an active member of his Unitarian Church in
Schenectady, New York, where his father is an engineer
for General Electric, he was always among the top in his
high school class. In matters of dress and manners his
clothes followed the styles advertised in *Sports Illustrated*

and his hair grew only to his ears. Unlike some students who received good grades, he never embarrassed his parents by taking to radical politics or other forms of controversy. The rules Bell broke were of the sort that kids all over the country disregarded in the latter half of the sixties; boozing, balling and smoking pot were things his parents were unlikely to find out about. When Stanford accepted him as a member of its freshman class in 1967 his parents were elated. When his name appeared on the Dean's list after a semester their pride grew. Then things began to change.

Bell found classroom lessons to be rather dull when compared to events outside. He developed interests in the war in Vietnam and in student politics. When students revolted at Stanford he sat in the administration building with hundreds of others. To Bell the sit-in was "beautiful" and the speeches by faculty and students more "relevant" than anything he had yet encountered at college.

Doubts set in about whether he needed the education one of America's most distinguished universities was offering him. When he returned to school in the fall of 1968 it was with the attitude that he would give it a try. He would try to make a go of it for his parents who were proud of him. But by Thanksgiving he realized it was no good. He dropped out of school and went home to think about what he was going to do with his life.

America in the late sixties does not allow its young men to leave college and ponder their futures. A few weeks after Bell went home he received a notice from his draft board that his student deferment had been suspended and that he was reclassified 1-A, meaning he had been placed in the prime category from which draftees are drawn. He appealed the ruling, asking to be reclassified as a conscientious objector. At Stanford he felt he had learned about the war in Vietnam. It was not the kind of war he wanted anything to do with.

Bell's hearing before Local Board 31 in Schenectady was very cordial but very short. He spoke for a few minutes, explaining why he should be allowed conscientious-objector status.

"I began by reminding them of Christ's teaching on nonviolence," he recalls. "I explained that the basis of all great religions was love, that war violated that spirit. I reminded them of Nuremberg—that it can be somebody's moral obligation to disobey orders from the state."

The eight men and one woman, whom Bell guessed to be anywhere from 50 to 70 years old, listened politely. When he finished, a man on the draft board spoke. "So you don't base your conscientious objection on any particular religious grounds," he said, part observation, part question.

"I knew then that I really hadn't gotten across. For me, I knew it would have to be jail or Canada."

As he told the story one evening last June in Toronto, Bell, a fuzzy-cheeked blond with hair now below his ears, spoke with a soft, eager voice.

"I couldn't have taken jail," he said. "I came to Canada a month after my hearing. It took me about a month to get landed and now I'm just living here. I suppose I'll get a job eventually, or maybe go to school. My parents don't agree with my decision to come up here. But they have been very understanding. They send me money, not much, but enough to get by."

Thousands of miles away, on the island-city of Stockholm, the thread of antiwar protest that is weaving through America's youth unites Bell with a young man who lacked Bell's bourgeois background and who, without Vietnam, probably would never have had anything in common with the thoughtful college boy.

John Woods is a 19-year-old high-school dropout whom the Pentagon would describe as someone who "could not adjust to Army life, and was a disciplinary problem." Chunky, dark-haired with deep-set, dark eyes, Woods bummed around the country working at odd jobs. His most significant possession was a Harley-Davidson motorcycle, "a big American machine," he says, grasping imaginary handlebars and revving up the engine.

With his job prospects at rock-bottom until he got his military service out of the way, Woods looked at some brochures that told him he could learn a trade in the Army and joined up in December 1967. He soon realized the only trade he was learning was how to shoot a rifle. "You know," he muses now, "there isn't really too big a market for civilian killers in the States."

Almost a year elapsed and Woods still didn't have a trade. So he set out to get one. Woods became a journalist, helping to found *F.T.A.*, an antimilitary undergound newspaper at Fort Jackson, South Carolina. "It could mean Fun, Travel, Adventure," he says, referring to the Army enlistment slogan. "Or . . . it could mean Fuck The Army." But because of his new career, Woods found himself one day before his superiors who told him that he was being sent to Germany. "They got me orders in a couple of hours that normally take weeks," he says, still marveling at the efficiency the Army can show when it meets threats.

So Woods, who hails from Steubenville, Ohio, was shipped to Frankfurt, Germany. From his new station, he continued to distribute *F.T.A.* Then he was busted for distributing "subversive literature." Although this charge influenced his decision to desert, Woods made up his mind to go after talking with servicemen who had returned from Vietnam. "Some of them were broken up about what they had done. Some bragged about how many they killed. I'm not a pacifist, but I have to know who I'm shooting at and why."

In January of this year, Woods went to the Cologne chapter of Students for a Democratic Society and asked the members to help him escape to Sweden. From Cologne, SDS sent him back to Frankfurt and two weeks later put him on a train for Hamburg.

"By then I was really shaking," he remembers. "It had been weeks that I was hiding out. They told me to go into a bar and sit two tables down on the left and be reading an American magazine. I had a copy of *Ramparts* with me and I was shaking and holding the magazine right below my eyes and looking over the top of it at everybody in the place. I was trying to let them know it was me: *I'm the guy you're helping out of here.*"

"Then this guy and girl who were sitting near me came over and asked me if I was the soldier, and I said yes. They took me to the Denmark border. They told me I was the 100th GI they helped this way. There was a border crossing about 800 yards wide that I had to run across. By now I'm shaking like a leaf and I'm all sweaty. It's night and the moon isn't very bright. I'm running across the field and a wire catches me waist high. I didn't know what it was at first and it really knocked me in the air. But I got up in a second and kept on running until I got to the other side. Another guy met me when I got there."

Traveling through Denmark wasn't difficult, Woods recalls. When he was on a boat from Copenhagen to southern Sweden, however, his nervousness caused a memory blackout concerning what he was to say when landing in Sweden. "I couldn't remember the words 'political asylum.' This guy was with me and I kept asking him what it was and he would tell me and then I'd forget. Things like 'insane asylum' and words like that were going through my mind and I thought 'My God to get all the way there and not to be able to get in because I can't remember the right words.' And then I'd turn to this guy again and ask him what the words were. But when I finally got there and needed to say them I remembered 'political asylum.' "

More and more young Americans are sharing Bell's and Woods' antipathy towards their government's involvement in Vietnam and are following their footsteps to foreign countries rather than fighting in an unpopular war. To the embarrassment of the United States, these young men are being granted refuge in Canada, Sweden and to a limited degree in other countries as well.

There is in both Canada and Sweden a strong anti-Americanism that makes it easier for the war resisters to cope once they arrive. Generally, those Canadians who resent the economic and cultural domination of their country by the United States are the ones most friendly to American exiles, often giving moral support and financial assistance. Most Canadians, however, including the government, have adopted a disinterested "live and let live" attitude. The only criterion for landed-immigrant status is that one pass a test based on age, job skills, education and other qualifications the Canadian government desires in immigrants. Once landed, an immigrant from the States must wait five years before applying for citizenship, but in the meantime he has most of the rights and obligations of citizenship, except voting.

The Swedish case is somewhat different. The anti-Americanism running through Swedish society is based on a widespread fear of the tremendous world power wielded by the United States. Such is the extent of this mistrust and hostility that often last year one heard Swedes bitterly joke that many other countries should participate in the election of the president of the United States, because he clearly controls the destinies of everyone, not just Americans. Moreover, the Swedish government, following public opinion, has opposed the United States in Vietnam, and this too gives support to American refugees' feelings that they made the right choice. Indeed, the title "deserter" often adds prestige to a youth in the eyes of the community.

The number of draft dodgers and deserters in Canada cannot be known exactly because the Canadian government has no way of finding out whether a young man entering the country is a dodger or an evader. There are no questions concerning such matters on the application to obtain landed-immigrant status.

Nevertheless, in 1967, the Royal Canadian Mounted Police, piecing together information from the Canadian Immigration Bureau, the United States Defense Department and the Federal Bureau of Investigation, estimated that there were 1,500 dodgers and deserters in Canada, a figure considerably higher than official U.S. estimates. If the RCMP estimate was reasonably accurate two years ago, then there are probably at least twice as many in Canada today. In a normal week, the Toronto Anti-Draft Programme, for example, helps about 20 dodgers or deserters find housing, jobs or other assistance. Since January, a spokesman says, the figure has doubled. *The Toronto Daily Telegram,* one of three daily newspapers in the city, claimed that 2,800 dodgers arrived in Canada in 1968, but the source of the figure was not given. The best estimate that can be made is that evaders number from 3,000 to 5,000, while deserters probably total less than 500.

In Sweden, accurate figures on the number of deserters living there are not available either. Representatives of the government, groups working with the deserters, and deserters themselves, however, estimate the number of American GIs who have sought refuge there at about 300. As of May 14, 1969, residence permits had been granted to 218 deserters, while another 39 had applied for them. But with the constant influx of servicemen and the occasional laxity in immediately applying for a permit, the actual number of deserters is higher.

Desertion Rates per 1000	
World War II 1944	
Army	63.00
Navy	3.00
Marines	6.90
Korea 1953	
Army	19.50
Navy	8.70
Marines	29.60
Vietnam 1968	
Army	29.10
Navy	8.50
Marines	22.40
Air Force	.44

There are fewer than 25 draft dodgers in Sweden and many of them work with the highly organized deserter movement there. They are reluctant to present their story, saying the deserters in Sweden are more important. For this reason there will be no details about the war resisters who fled to Sweden to avoid the draft. There are relatively few evaders in Sweden because most draftees, of course, receive their induction notices in the United States and it is much easier to get to Canada than to Sweden. Canada is also much better known as a haven for draft resisters than is Sweden. The large number of deserters in Sweden is due to the country's having spoken out against United States presence in Vietnam and its having granted soldiers humanitarian asylum during other wars.

The age of deserters living in Sweden ranges between 18 and 37, with most in their early twenties. They rank from private to captain; they came from Vietnam, Japan, Germany and the United States; and most of them had enlisted. The deserters estimate that 10 percent had served in Vietnam and that 50 percent were under immediate orders to report there. They represent all branches of the service, but the vast majority deserted from the Army. Although no racial data are available, government officials estimate that 10 percent of the deserters are black, which is below the percentage of blacks serving in the U.S. armed forces.

Since July 1966, according to the Defense Department, there have been more than 53,000 desertions from all branches of the service, of which only 1,068 are thought to be in foreign countries. The comparatively small number of deserters living in Canada and Sweden, the Defense Department says, is because most deserters "go home or hide out someplace."

Draft dodgers and deserters in Canada, for the most part, are found in Toronto, Montreal and Vancouver, where there are well-established organizations to help them. In Sweden, the core of the deserter movement is in Stockholm, where more than half the refugees are settled. The rest are spread throughout the country.

Politically and organizationally, there is a major distinction between the draft dodgers and deserters in Canada and those in Sweden. In Canada, the draft dodgers are the center of radicalism among the exiles, while deserters tend not to see their act in a political context and, in fact, resent the radical war resisters' attempts to define their political view of the world. In Sweden, there is no division between dodgers and deserters. While there are many nonradical deserters, the most prominent deserter organization in the country holds radical viewpoints and many of its members consider themselves revolutionaries in the New Left mold.

In Toronto, two major organizations are available to help American war resisters. Both are staffed by evaders and deserters and are financially supported by sympathizers in Canada and the United States. The Toronto Anti-Draft Programme, headquartered in two sparsely furnished rooms in an office building at 2279 Younge Street, is primarily a counseling service. It will help an exile through the maze of Canadian law affecting immigrants, and once an émigré has attained landed status, it will refer him to employment agencies or a sympathetic business where he might find a job.

Although a few exiles live on money sent to them from home, most expect to find jobs once in Canada. But getting the job they expected when they left the states is sometimes difficult. Richard Kapp, a draft dodger who had just graduated from the University of Illinois with a masters degree in history, illustrated the dilemma of many college educated exiles.

Kapp, 27, well-groomed and wearing a brown business suit, discussed his job problems one day at the Anti-Draft Programme office:

"With a masters degree in history I've got no special skills," he explained. "On the other hand, when I tell these guys about my education, many of them feel I'm too educated for the jobs they have open." Because of a Canadian requirement that teachers complete a special one-year curriculum, his graduate degree was no help in getting him a teaching job which he had counted on when he left. After a week of interviewing through employment agencies, he had one solid prospect, a manager traineeship at $85 a week.

Kapp, who grew up in New Brunswick, New Jersey, the son, in his words, of a "lower middle-class racist," says he refused his draft call because "If I got killed in Vietnam, it wouldn't make any difference. So what's in it for me? I don't want to die. I've got a money hang-up and a lot of living to do."

The Toronto Anti-Draft Programme, in addition to job counseling, publishes a "Manual for Draft-Age Immigrants to Canada" that is a rich encyclopedia of information. Written by professors, lawyers, clergymen and businessmen, it is edited by Mark Satin, a Texas radical who founded the antidraft organization. The manual answers almost any question a young man might have about Canada. Since it was first published last year, more than 25,000 copies have been mailed out.

The Union of American Exiles at 44 St. George Street functions primarily as a housing service, but it also provides other sorts of "social action" for dodgers and deserters. Located on the campus of the University of Toronto, it is more attuned to the student movement and New Left ideology than is the Toronto Anti-Draft Programme, which concerns itself with the nuts and bolts of getting exiles settled. Charles Novogrodsky, press secretary of UAE, described the reasoning behind its political involvement. "The need for expanded services alone would never have been enough to generate the movement toward an organization of American exiles. Union members recognize the identity of social and political factors that have shaped and continue to shape their personal lives. For this reason, the Union is a place where talk, information, and action can be found that relates one's life in Canada to the broader, repressive aspects of North American society and politics in general." Yet both Toronto organizations work closely together, with a minimum of friction, despite the resistance of a large number of refugees to what they think of as "radicalization" efforts on the part of the leftist ideologues.

In contrast to the Toronto groups, the American Deserters Committee in Montreal is less cooperative with political radicals. Although founded by two politically active civilians, the ADC is now completely in the hands of apolitical deserters. Located in a run-down French section along the St. Lawrence River, the ADC office is bare and filthy. Two shabby couches face each other across a room. A fireplace mantel along one wall serves as a library. Vietnam and adventure stories are popular. Beside *Che Guevara Speaks* lies a copy of *The World's Greatest Dog Stories*.

That was the scene last June when about 30 deserters and a few wives and girlfriends gathered at the ADC office. The meeting was a climax to several weeks of agitation among deserters who thought that the civilians who started the committee more than a year before and had been running it autocratically ever since, should step aside and allow the deserters to run the committee. The founders, Bill Hertzog and Jerry Bornstein, were not present, but the deserters were trying to be as kind to them as possible while firmly insisting that they must go.

Grant Fox, a 22-year-old deserter from Holbrook, Massachusetts, was more or less in charge. While he was explaining the issue, several young men were slugging each other playfully and wrestling. "God damn it, you guys, quit fucking around will you?" Fox yelled.

"Fuckin' around? Who's fuckin' around," giggled the errants, faces as scarlet as school boys caught by a teacher. Things settled down and Fox explained that most deserters were appreciative of everything Hertzog and Bornstein had done, but some resented their efforts to align the committee with radical politics.

"I mean it's whatever you guys want," Fox says. "Some of the guys don't think we should be messin' around with this politics shit. So whatever you guys decide, we should take a vote on it and stick to our decision." The vote ended formal ties with Bornstein and Hertzog, but there is a provision to consult with them periodically.

If the severance seems crude and thankless, that is not how Bornstein, a young sociologist from New York City, takes it. To him, a former CORE organizer and fund raiser, the rebellion was expected and natural. "They should run their own group now. There are enough of them to do it; and it will be better all the way around if they assume the responsibility for each other."

Fox, the ad hoc leader of the deserters, was sympathetic

to Bornstein. "Jerry was around when we needed him. Without him a lot of guys up here would never have made it. He had the contacts we needed, for money, housing, the works. He was just too radical for most guys." But Fox did sense that the move by the deserters may have been a mistake.

"I don't know, frankly, whether we can keep the committee going without him, but the guys decided they wanted to go it alone. So here we are." Fox, who entered the Army in 1966 shortly after graduating from high school, seems well suited for the new task, which consists primarily of coordinating the wishes of the deserters with their sympathizers in Canada and the U.S. who provide both moral and economic support. Supporters, however, like Bornstein, tend to be "political," and their values often conflict with the deserters who are uninterested in getting "radicalized." Fox feels that differences in the educational backgrounds of many deserters and their supporters is a reason for the friction.

"Only a few of the deserters who come in have college educations," he says. "Sometimes the guys without much schooling get pissed off at the college boys for trying to take over. But shit, most of the time it's only the college guys or the guys who haven't gone to college but who are a little older who want to do anything for the committee."

The split that was formalized at the June Montreal meeting of the American Deserters Committee had already taken place in the Stockholm ADC. Two political factions had emerged, differing basically in their degree of radicalism. Far from backing off from politics as the deserter committee in Montreal has done, the ADC in Stockholm is highly political and many members are self-proclaimed revolutionaries. The second faction, which called itself the Underground Railway after breaking with the ADC, is also composed of very political people, but the UR's members do not always agree with the often dogmatic stands of the ADC Deserters who do not wish to become politically involved at all can bypass either organization.

John Toler is one of the key UR people. A founder of the ADC when it was set up in 1968, Toler was instrumental in organizing a limited walkout of ADC members a year later. A philosophy student at Stockholm University, he is one of three deserters in the city taking the most advanced language training available. "Initially, my decision to desert was moral. I now know it was political," he says, summing up the metamorphosis of the deserters who become political. The thin, blond, 23-year-old has "no regrets whatsoever" about his desertion. "I felt it was the only thing I could do."

Toler said the first six months are the hardest in terms of adjustment. "You have to watch the death of much of your culture right down to your music and thoughts of mom. You've got to go on or stay in limbo." Toler said many deserters are living with girl friends. "And that makes it a lot easier." Toler lives with an attractive, politically active brunette, though whether it was her good looks or her politics that made it "easier," he didn't say.

Because of the difficulty Toler mentioned concerning the first six months after desertion, the ADC helps new deserters learn the bureaucratic maze and also provides friendship. Just as important as these functions, however, is the attempt by radical members of the ADC to orient new deserters towards their political philosophy. Of the estimated 180 deserters living in the Stockholm area, the ADC claims the majority belong to the committee and this was supported by several deserter-connected groups. Many deserters devote their time and effort to the ADC on a daily basis; others volunteer spare time to committee activities. The ADC is the deserters' prime political forum and has steadily evolved into a revolutionary organization.

Like radicals in the United States and elsewhere, many ADC members see war, racism, poverty and American imperialism as springing from a corrupt system. As its radical horizons broadened, so did the ADC's affiliations. Last fall, it became an SDS chapter.

The political activity of the radical deserters led to their breaking relations with the Swedish Vietnam Committee, one of 40 organizations in the country that are against the war in Vietnam and actively support the act of desertion. Composed of liberals supporting the Hanoi government and the aims of the National Liberation Front, the Swedish Vietnam Committee is the target of criticism from more leftist Swedish groups as well as radical deserters. Its opponents say it is afraid to let the deserters speak out because there might be economic boycotts by America against Swedish products.

Bertil Svahnstrom, executive secretary of the Swedish Vietnam Committee, while acknowledging a fear of boycotting denies that this is an influence on his group. He feels that the deserters should say anything they want. "The only thing we are against is deserters being pressured to become political when they do not want to be."

While most gave a moral reason as to why they deserted, those who became radicals felt that political activism gave more substance to the justification of desertion. For them, morality is secondary to the political reasons for opposing the war and United States domestic and foreign policy in general. They see themselves as true witnesses to the fact that there is a viable alternative to passive acceptance of what they call United States tyranny.

"If we were to become silent Swedes and not be involved in politics, then everything would be fine with Svahnstrom," says Bill Jones, a former co-chairman and founder of the ADC before it became a leaderless SDS chapter. Now a theoretician of the ADC's more revolutionary attitudes, Jones believes the radical movement in the United States will reach an ultimate violent confrontation, with "the people" seizing control of the power structure from "those who oppress them." Paraphrasing Che Guevera, Jones hopes the revolution in America will be accomplished with a "minimum of bloodshed."

Jones views the deserters' position as "the most moral of all . . . and at least the most sane" when compared to those who fight a war they know nothing about and compared to people who profit from war. The war, he says, is the result of a "mass neurosis on the part of the American people." And he feels that working for change in the United States, albeit 3,000 miles away in Sweden, is a logical follow-through of the act of desertion.

"Ideally, if you want to effect change in the United States, you have to be there. But since we obviously are not in a position to do that, we have to do what we can from where we can . . . and that means here."

Jones bluntly says that the deserters' complete assimilation into Swedish society would destroy the ADC's effectiveness. If they lose their identity as deserters, they will no longer be symbols of American resistance to the war. "We can still retain out own culture . . . we are a community apart from the Swedish. It is important that we do this to keep external pressure on the Army and the war effort."

A thin, bearded ex-seminarian, Jones joined the Army because his student deferment was a "cop out." Assigned to Germany as a medic, the 22-year-old youth deserted because he felt any position in the Army was giving at least passive support to United States presence in Vietnam. Although he does not believe amnesty will ever be granted, Jones gave one reason for wanting to return to the States —"to work for the Movement." Many deserters expressed the same desire and gave it as their chief reason for wanting to go home.

The Stockholm headquarters of the ADC is at Upplandsgattan 18. There in the dank cellar of a massive gray apartment building, ADC members work to increase desertion from the service. A newspaper, *The Second Front,* which is published from the poster-padded offices, is aimed at the Army. Another publication, *The Second Front Review,* is circulated among deserters in France, Canada and Sweden to keep them abreast of the deserter movement. Besides these enterprises, the deserters make radio tapes encouraging desertion which are transmitted from North Vietnam, East Germany and Cuba.

Though ADC members have Swedish friends and many of them live with Swedish girls, their radicalism, focused on America, is a shield against being absorbed into the Swedish lifescape, and losing their identities as Americans. Even those who are fluent in the language and know Swedish customs, exist along with the others as an American colony working to "save America." As part of the radicalizing process, the ADC holds closed-door meetings where theory and experiences are analyzed. Many of their ideas stem from the New Left literature that fills their bookshelves and is greedily read, often by people who said they previously had no desire to read. Underground newspapers and the radical weekly, *The Guardian,* supplement their literary diet. They feel they are treated more fairly by *The Guardian* than by established news media. Committee members are vitally interested in the most recent phases of the movement in the United States and elsewhere, but particularly the United States. The effectiveness of the orientation can be seen in the fact that only two men interviewed in Sweden had been involved in peace, civil rights or radical movements prior to their military careers. Now many of them are aware of the most subtle nuances of leftist thought.

Yet, oddly, there is still much of the military about the ADC members. Many still wear parts of their uniforms and their speech is salted with military references. This atmosphere and the holdover of military paraphernalia turn off some deserters. Herb Rains is one of these. A 25-year-old photographer from Kaneohe, Hawaii, Rains differs from most deserters in that he was involved in peace and civil rights issues before his desertion. A reservist activated after the Pueblo affair, Rains deserted because many reservists were being sent to Vietnam.

With his thick, curly beard and long, dark-brown hair, dungarees and blue work shirt, Rains looks the part of the young radical. But he doesn't want to channel his energies into the ADC because its "barracks atmosphere is part of what I was trying to get away from." Instead of working with the Americans, Rains wants to help the National Liberation Front Support Group, which is composed of Swedish radicals working for the aims of the NLF.

Like many deserters in Sweden, Rains is in a government-sponsored language school and living off the $20 a week paid unemployed deserters by the Swedish government. Besides this money, the deserters' rent is paid by the Social Bureau and they receive a small clothing allowance as well.

Again like many other deserters, Rains would consider going back to the United States, but not if a dishonorable discharge were the only way he could get there. Not one deserter interviewed said he would accept anything less than an honorable discharge, and few expressed regrets about the possibilities of never being able to return home. One deserter summed up the prevailing sentiment concerning amnesty: "I'll go home if they admit that we were right and they were wrong . . . and I don't think that is going to happen."

While deserters in the Stockholm area have ample opportunity to express their opposition to the war, those living in the heavily wooded, rural areas do not. Ron Crow lives about 150 miles north of the city, on a farm that was donated to the deserters by a Swedish philanthropist. Tall, wiry and heavily bearded, Crow considers himself a radical but he also knows he is a farmer. His childhood was spent dirt-farming around Fort Worth, Texas, and his family was always on the brink of poverty. After dropping out of school in the ninth grade, Crow said he eventually joined the Army hoping to learn a trade so he could "get somewhere in the world."

Now 22, Crow first thought of opposing the war when he talked with returning Vietnam veterans. Their descriptions of what they had been through ("a lot of them just didn't think we had any business being over there") planted the seeds of desertion in his mind. He started listening more closely to talk about the war and reading about it. He concluded, "I just wouldn't go fight over there." So he deserted from Germany, but it took him two tries to make it.

"I was in a medical outfit and one day I got into one of our trucks and just started driving north. Wouldn't you know that I ran out of gas right in the middle of an intersection in a city. All I could do was sit there and wait for them to take me away." Besides desertion, he was charged with theft and because of the medical supplies in the truck, narcotics and abortion charges were added to his crimes. After a stretch in the stockade, however, he was ready to try again.

"I was smarter the second time. I went down to the reenlistment station and signed up for another six years. I needed the $700 bonus pay to desert. This time I went to the train station and jumped on a train and they never caught me. There are a lot of people deserting on their bonus pay."

Crow is going to language school and is getting married shortly. After language training, he plans on working the farm full time and not returning to his job in a nearby steel mill. He was one of five deserters interviewed in Sweden who would not return to the United States under any conditions. "My life is here where I have everything I ever wanted," he says, "and it's away from the war and racism and a few rich people living off a lot of poor people. Why would I ever want to go back?"

Very few deserters or draft dodgers in either Canada or Sweden felt remorse at the prospect of not being able to return home. Most accepted their decision to leave the United States as final, although they would return if granted amnesty. But while amnesty is being spoken of in some liberal governmental circles in the United States, few deserters or dodgers believe it will become a reality. As one deserter in Sweden put it, "How can they dare to give us amnesty? If they did, nobody would fight in their next war. Everybody would just move to another country and wait for amnesty to be given again."

The deserters and evaders who are radicalized still believe the United States can be changed, either by violent revolution or less drastic internal and external pressures. Those who do not take an aggressive stance against their homeland's policies are more inclined to be less educated and more willing to lose their American identities. The radicals have ambivalent feelings about the United States. They believe it "must" be saved; at the same time, they loath what America is doing domestically and in foreign affairs. Those not radicalized put their act on either a moral plane or a more pragmatic, "Why should I get my ass shot off for nothing?"

As well as being an outlet for their thoughts and emotions, radicalism for many young exiles helps to make them feel still a part of what is happening in the United States.

Though physically isolated, most are deeply committed to America and still want to play a part in whatever changes do take place here. They maintain their American identity in the hope of remolding America. It does not matter what country they are living in as long as they remain free to continue their efforts.

Graduate students and high school dropouts, Christians and nonbelievers, track stars and acid heads, radicals and hippies; they are all there, linked by a stubborn independence, a common revulsion against their country's war in Vietnam and by the 5-to-10-year prison sentences they face if they should ever return. Whether they come home is a question only the future can answer. Today, their ranks are swelling.

September 1969

NOTES ON CONTRIBUTORS

Bennett M. Berger   "Hippie Morality—More Old Than New"

Professor of sociology at the University of California at Davis. He is the author of *Working Class Suburb* and *Looking for America*. His major research interest is in youth, and he is presently directing a study of child rearing in communal families.

Michael E. Brown   "The Condemnation and Persecution of Hippies"

Assistant professor of sociology at Queens College of the City University of New York. He is on the staff of the Center for Movement Research there and is an active member of the New University Conference. With Amy Goldman he co-authored *Collective Behavior: Unauthorized Social Action* and now he is working on a book on the underground press.

John Cooney   "Hell, No, We Won't Go!"

Currently working as a reporter for a national publication. He formerly worked for the *Philadelphia Inquirer*; during a leave of absence he was a Russell Sage Fellow working with *trans*action.

Fred Davis   "Why All of Us May Be Hippies Someday"

Professor of sociology at the University of California, San Francisco. He is the author of *Passage Through Crisis, Polio Victims and Their Families* and the editor of *The Nursing Profession, Five Sociological Essays*. He is presently conducting research in the areas of youth culture and the spontaneous termination of deviant careers.

Hugh Folk   "The Oversupply of the Young"

Professor of economics and of labor and industrial relations at the University of Illinois, Urbana-Champaign, where he directs the University's Program on Social Implications of Science and Technology. He is author of a book on *The Shortage of Scientists and Engineers*. Currently he is doing research on central city labor markets and postwar economic adjustment policy and programs.

Edgar Z. Freidenberg

Professor of education at Dalhousie University, Nova Scotia, Canada (for more detail, see the back cover.)

Walter B. Miller   "White Gangs"

An anthropologist, he is a research associate at the Massachusetts Institute of Technology-Harvard University Joint Center for Urban Studies. He is a member of the Subcommittee on Research of the National Manpower Advisory Committee.

Charles C. Moskos, Jr.   "Why Men Fight"

Associate Professor of sociology at Northwestern University. In 1969-70 he observed peacekeeping operations in Cypress. He is the author of a recently published book, *The American Enlisted Man*.

David Riesman   "Universities on Collision Course"

Henry Ford professor of social sciences at Harvard University. He is author of many books including *The Lonely Crowd*, *Faces in the Crowd*, and is co-author (with Joseph Gusfield and Zelda Gamson) of *Academic Values and Mass Education: The Early Years of Oakland and Monteith*.

Joseph W. Scott   "ROTC Retreat"

Associate professor of sociology and director of black studies at the University of Notre Dame. His interests include deviant behavior, social conflict and race relations. Author of numerous articles, he is working on a book on sources of social change in community, family and fertility in a Puerto Rican town.

Geoffrey Simon   "Hippies in College—From Teeny-Boppers to Drug Freaks"

Graduate student in sociology at Michigan State University. His interest in youth cultures has been heightened by his past participation in and increasingly informed observation of the hippie subculture.

Jerome Skolnick   "The Generation Gap"

Professor of criminology at the University of California at Berkeley School of Criminology and a research sociologist at the Center for the Study of Law and Society there. He was the director of the Task Force on Violent Aspects of Protest and Confrontation of the National Commission on the Causes and Prevention of Violence. He has edited or authored several books including *The Politics of Protest* and *Justice Without Trial*.